D0474827

Born in Hertfordshire in 1959, Dougie Brimson joined the RAF directly from school where he trained as a mechanical engineer. After serving for over eighteen years, and attaining the rank of sergeant, he left the forces in 1994 to forge a career as a writer.

Following the co-authorship of four non-fiction books examining the culture of football hooliganism, Dougie struck out on his own and made the move into fiction with the Lynda La Plante-inspired thriller, *The Crew*.

The following year, he returned to the issue of hooliganism with another non-fiction work, *Barmy Army*, but followed this book with more fiction, *Billy's Log* and *Top Dog*.

He is currently involved with the film adaptation of *The Crew* and, aside from writing, has a burgeoning career as a television presenter and producer.

Dougie has been married to Tina since 1983 and they have three children.

Also by Dougie and Eddy Brimson

Everywhere We Go
England, My England
Capital Punishment
Derby Days

Also by Dougie Brimson

The Geezers Guide to Football
The Crew
Barmy Army
Billy's Log
Top Dog

Full details can be found at www.brimson.net

EUROTRASHED

The Rise and Rise
of Europe's Football Hooligans

Dougie Brimson

headline

Copyright © 2003 Dougie Brimson

The right of Dougie Brimson to be identified as the Author
of the Work has been asserted by him in accordance with
the Copyright, Designs and Patents Act 1988.

First published in 2003
by HEADLINE BOOK PUBLISHING

10 9 8 7 6 5 4

All rights reserved. No part of this publication may be
reproduced, stored in a retrieval system, or transmitted,
in any form or by any means without the prior written
permission of the publisher, nor be otherwise circulated
in any form of binding or cover other than that in which
it is published and without a similar condition being
imposed on the subsequent purchaser.

ISBN 0 7553 1110 8

Typeset in Sabon by Avon DataSet Ltd,
Bidford-on-Avon, Warwickshire

Printed and bound in Great Britain by
Mackays of Chatham plc, Chatham, Kent

HEADLINE BOOK PUBLISHING
A division of Hodder Headline
338 Euston Road
London NW1 3BH

www.headline.co.uk
www.hodderheadline.com

Dedication

To Tina.

Acknowledgements

With huge thanks to Lorella, Heather and all at Pollingers, Ian and Rebecca at Headline, Steve Banks, SIBV, Pat, Oaksy, Axel, Thomas Gravgaard, Lorenzo, Stan Thain and Yvonne Scott, Piotr, Oleg, the lads from CSKA Moscow, Zgro, Peter, Lovro, Brighton 90, Karen Warner, Mr Café, Joel, David, Barry Smit, Ruben, Erwin Walbeek, Rasit, Lion, Ziogiukas, Laxa, the lads from Dynamo Kyiv, the fantastic Nikola from Red Star Belgrade and all those who for various reasons wanted to remain anonymous.

And, of course, to Jacque Evans.

This book was written with the help of an LCD display supplied by GNR Corporation Ltd (www.gnrintl.com).

Good luck to Dave and John in their new venture.

CONTENTS

INTRODUCTION

On 5 April 2000, two Leeds United fans, Kevin Speight and Chris Loftus-were sitting in a bar in the middle of Istanbul. They were in the city to watch their side play the first leg of a UEFA Cup semi-final against Galatasaray the following day. However, as they walked back to their hotel later that evening, they were brutally attacked by a group of local men and died from the horrific stab wounds they suffered.

Although what happened on that fateful night is covered in depth elsewhere, I mention it here because those tragic murders were really the catalyst for this book. Or to be more specific, it was the media reaction to them.

For reasons that have never been fully explained, the attack on the Leeds fans took place in the full glare of the media spotlight and, within hours, the resulting pictures had been beamed around the world. Almost immediately, as someone who has written extensively on the subject of hooliganism, I was contacted by numerous organisations and asked to comment. As if there was anything I, or anyone else, could usefully say in such horrific circumstances.

As the calls continued to pour in to my office, it soon became apparent to me that despite what remains some of the most horrific and barbaric footage I have ever seen, certain sections of the press were intent on blaming

Kevin and Chris for what had happened to them. They were, after all, English football fans so, by association, must have been hooligans. What other possible reason could there have been to explain their presence in the city a day before the actual game?

Leaving aside the simple truth that almost a million Britons visit Turkey every year, the inference that 'they got what they deserved' made me sick to my stomach. Not simply because it was totally untrue and wholly unjust but because of what it suggested; the idea that English football has become so tainted, that being murdered is an almost acceptable consequence of travelling to support it. Follow that thinking and the next step is obvious: why bother to find the culprit? After all, if you live by the sword, sooner or later, you're going to get cut, right?

Now I am not suggesting for one second that the term 'The English Disease' isn't richly deserved, nor am I saying that we have completely cleaned up our act. We haven't. But what I am saying is that if we are at the stage where even decent law-abiding football fans are at risk of serious injury or worse when they set foot in another country, we must start to look seriously at the reasons why. And at the heart of the issue is the realisation that hooliganism has spread throughout the modern game far more than anyone thought it had. More worryingly, many hooligan groups, including a large number on mainland Europe, have taken the concept of football violence to new levels. And while the image of English supporters might continue to rank alongside that of Attila the Hun, on the continent things that even hardcore hooligans in the UK would consider 'unacceptable' are being witnessed on a regular basis.

For example, in the last 18 months alone, police in both Greece and Holland have been forced to fire live rounds into crowds to disperse them. In Turkey, a

Fenerbahçe supporter was kidnapped and had his ears sliced off by rival fans. In France, an amateur match was abandoned when 200 supporters stormed the pitch and attacked the players, putting nine of them in hospital; and in Italy, players held up kick-offs for 15 minutes to protest against the rising tide of crowd violence. The list, sadly, is almost endless and the catalogue of tragedies shows no signs of tailing off. In August 2002, Sweden suffered its first hooligan-related death when, during a pre-arranged fight between two rival mobs, a supporter was killed by someone repeatedly jumping on his head.

It would of course be easy to dismiss what is going on overseas as being nothing to do with us, but that would be a huge mistake because such incidents have a direct impact on the game in England. Not only do they reflect on a culture that started here and for which we continue to be blamed, but as various clubs, including Leeds, have discovered, whenever our fans go abroad, they are targeted as being 'the enemy'. It is a feature of the hooligan culture that groups will always seek to test their mettle against the so-called best and, for the vast majority, certainly across Europe, that means the English. Proof of which can be found in the number of Union Jacks and St George Crosses that adorn the fences of clubs from Stockholm to Sarajevo and the fact that the Casual culture, which has become an integral element of the British game, has been embraced with both hands by groups in almost every country where football is played.

In many instances, at least post-Italia 90, such thinking is why English supporters are often seen fighting in foreign lands. Without wishing to excuse such behaviour in any way, it is a fact that with a few notable exceptions the arrival of England's most notorious export no longer carries the fear it once did. Instead, it holds excitement and anticipation.

That is not to suggest by any means that English football has rid itself of the travelling hooligan element, because it patently has not. But it is a proven fact that the days of wanton destruction laid upon such places as Luxembourg, Malmö and Dublin are long gone and these days, in many, many cases, the English supporters will have been subjected to hours of provocation, abuse, missile-throwing or worse before finally responding. And when your backs are against the wall, the only option many see as being open to them is to fight. Sometimes, as recent history has shown, that fight can be for your very life.

It is worth noting, however, that hooliganism abroad is very often a totally different animal from the one we have here in the UK. While some follow the now traditional Casual path, others will not. They prefer instead to embrace a scene built on politics, passion, hate, extreme violence or even a mixture of all four. It is also fair to say that few, if any, domestic leagues in Europe have the level of travelling support that we see in this country, which in turn means that rivalries tend to remain more localised. Similarly, those same rivalries are too entrenched to be set aside for international games, which is why few countries have hooligan elements attached to them on their travels.

In a nutshell, that is what this book is about. For in the wake of the Istanbul murders and the realisation that many people still do not understand that hooliganism is now a global phenomenon, I decided that the time was right to try to provide some insight into what is happening in Europe and, hopefully, make people aware that while we still have a significant problem in England, it is nothing compared to what is going on elsewhere.

The key was how to do it and, quite early on, I took the decision that where possible I would get someone from each country to explain what was going on in their home nation in their own words. Not only do they have a far greater insight into their own particular situation than I could ever have, but they also have an obvious passion that, as you will see, brings a lot to the individual chapters. Thankfully, after years of writing I had a fairly lengthy contact book, which helped enormously because, with a project of this nature, trust is everything.

In terms of the actual process, each contribution was translated where required and then edited to deal with both the obvious language problems and to remove anything potentially libellous or worse! Once that had been done, the details were checked as far as is practical and the finished article then passed to a third party with knowledge of that specific country or region. Once everyone was happy with the finished item, then, and only then, would it have made the final cut.

However, it must be remembered that some contributions will inevitably focus on a particular club and, as such, in some instances will give a certain slant on events and rivalries. And, make no mistake, some of those rivalries run very deep, and impact on life way beyond football. As proof, what follows was sent to me by the Galatasaray supporter who supplied the bulk of the information for the chapter in Part Six on Turkey. The penultimate sentence is especially telling!

Speaking of F*nerbahçe: I don't know if you are in contact with any of them for your book, but I feel I must warn you about the nature of F*ner supporters. They are scum of the worst sort: ugly, devious, untrustworthy and extremely unintelligent. Don't believe a word they say!

Their nickname, The Canaries, is perfect for them. While Galatasaray's Lions have class and dignity, the little yellow bastards chirp chirp chirp all day, every day, about how great they are. Which they are not.

Their team is far wealthier than Gala. But when a non-Turk thinks of Turkish football, who comes to mind? Galatasaray, of course, the pride of Turkey. Not the scum from across the Bosphorus. Last season they were a national embarrassment when they crashed out of the Champions League with no points. Also, many of them are gays and paedophiles who enjoy raping men, children and animals. That's really all you need to know about them.

Where sourcing correspondents has not been possible, tried and trusted research methods have been employed using information gleaned from a variety of contacts and archives. Together, I hope that this book provides a snapshot of the scene across Europe and some of the reasoning behind why things are as they are.

It is not, however, a definitive work and should not be considered as such. Certain countries have been all but impossible to research properly and so information on them isn't as comprehensive as I would like it to be. Similarly, specific groups that I really wanted to feature failed to respond to my requests for either information or interview, while a couple turned me down flat. The only option therefore was to work around them and, where possible, utilise what information I already had or which was made available to me. Not perfect, but better than nothing.

Finally, I must also make it absolutely clear that this book is not an examination of why and how people become involved in hooliganism, nor is it any kind of investigation into why the problem exists. That ground has been covered in previous books by both myself and numerous others, and to go over it again would be needless. Suffice to say, the driving force behind everyone who becomes part of, or is involved in, hooliganism is the same no matter where in the world they watch their football. It is a love of a team and the desire to be a part of something that, to people on the outside, remains a complete and utter mystery.

Up the 'Orns!

Part One

CHAPTER ONE
The Beginnings

It may come as a surprise to discover that although the English game has been blighted with incidents of crowd disorder since as far back as the fourteenth century, hooliganism is a relatively recent phenomenon on mainland Europe. Indeed, in some countries, it is all but impossible to find anything significant that occurred prior to 1980.

That is not to say that there were none. In Italy, for example, one of the first recorded examples took place in 1920 at the end of a game between Viareggio and Lincques. Following a fight between the two teams at the end of the game, the police went pouring on to restore order but, during the subsequent skirmish, the referee was shot dead. The ensuing rioting spilled out of the stadium and resulted in widespread civil disorder and vandalism. And in what was the former Yugoslavia, the 1950s saw a wave of trouble sweep through the game. Labelled Zuism – a Serbo-Croat acronym for killing – the worst incidents involved large numbers of fans storming pitches to fight with knives, metal bars and chains.

Yet such incidents were extremely rare, and the fact remains that the stranglehold the hooligans began to exert on the English game from the early 1960s onwards was not replicated on the mainland until the mid to late 1970s if not even later. However, rather than examine why there was a delay, we should instead look at why it happened

at all. After all, hooliganism isn't an obligatory consequence of football, it is a product of the mood and
atmosphere created around it. And, as was proved only
too well during the 2002 World Cup, football without
hooliganism can be a positively breathtaking experience.
So why did the European game, having watched the
hooligans drag football to its knees in England, sit back
and do nothing as it too became infected? The answers to
that question can be found, inevitably, within the history
of English hooliganism.

Much of this history was documented in my previous
book *Barmy Army*. However, what that book did not
examine was the European dimension and, given its
relevance here, it is vital that people understand not just
why, but how, the problem first left these shores. Because
no one should be in any doubt that the English game was
– as was the growth of television – instrumental in the
eruption of violence within European football.

In the mid 1960s, when England's football terraces
were no place for the faint-hearted and certain town
centres would regularly become no-go areas on match
days, television provided the ideal alternative for the law-
abiding football fan. Watching games on the small screen
was not only easier and cheaper, it was also a great deal
safer. As a result, people began staying away from
grounds in their thousands. While this in itself was bad
enough for the game, the knock-on effect was that in
purely percentage terms, as the crowds fell, the number
of hooligans rose. Not surprisingly, so did the amount
of violence.

The situation was not helped when, alongside the
actual games, television began showing graphic footage
of fighting in the crowds. Not only did this provide
both entertainment and encouragement to the hooligans
but, more worryingly, it also provided a new avenue of
publicity. The tabloids had for years sensationalised

football violence to the extent that being seen in the papers had become almost a national pastime. Indeed, for many, the keeping of scrapbooks was almost an obsession. That now changed to being seen on the telly. And, increasingly, the cameras acted as a catalyst. Wherever they appeared, the fans would play up, sure in the knowledge that if they escaped arrest on the day, nothing would or could be done to try and bring them to justice.

Across the Channel, the European game was watching what was happening with unease. The terrace battles being seen with regular monotony on our shores were now being broadcast to a bewildered continental audience, and with English clubs enjoying success on the bigger stage and significant numbers of fans travelling to watch them, the big fear was that sooner or later something bad was going to happen. Inevitably, it did. And in 1974 Tottenham Hotspur supporters gained the dubious honour of being the first English hooligans to become involved in large-scale violence outside the UK.

The occasion was the UEFA Cup final; a two-legged affair against the Dutch side Feyenoord. Following a 2–2 draw at White Hart Lane, the Spurs fans crossed the Channel in their thousands determined to drive the team on in the hope of securing an unexpected victory. For many, it was to be their first trip abroad, and the cheap alcohol, coupled with the arrogance that had already become an inherent part of the English hooligan scene, made for an intimidating atmosphere on the streets of Rotterdam. The police, totally unprepared for what was going on, simply adopted a high-profile stance, but it was not enough. As the drinking continued, trouble erupted in numerous bars and, by the time the Spurs fans arrived in the ground, their mood was decidedly hostile. When the referee disallowed what looked to them to be a perfectly legitimate goal, they erupted, tearing down fences and attacking the home supporters. The team were shell-shocked and Bill Nicholson, the then Spurs manager, was forced to make a loudspeaker appeal at half time, but to no avail. Only when a squad of riot police arrived and began baton-charging the visiting support did things inside the ground calm down, but afterwards it started again and continued for most of the night. The resulting tally of 200 injured and 70 arrested heaped shame on the club and the country.

UEFA were furious and ordered Tottenham to play their next two home games 250 kilometres from White Hart Lane.

Despite UEFA's anger, English hooligans started to wreak havoc on their travels. Only a year later, Leeds United supporters left a trail of wounded locals and empty shops as they made their way to Paris for the European Cup final against Bayern Munich. Sadly, their conduct inside the ground was also less than exemplary and, following a riot that was beamed live into homes across the continent, UEFA banned the club from European competition for four years.

Yet if they were hoping it would act as a deterrent, they were wrong. And as the hooligan scene in England grew, seemingly by the week, it was becoming increasingly obvious that their actions were not only being closely watched by supporters across the continent, they were also starting to be copied.

The Dutch fans, having witnessed at first hand an entirely new method of supporting, began to look at how they could replicate the behaviour of the English fans and, within months, Dutch clubs such as Ajax, Feyenoord and Utrecht discovered that hooliganism had found them.

The football authorities in England realised that unless something was done to stop it, and quickly, the problem was going to spread. The trouble was, no one knew what to do and so nothing was done. This resulted in things suddenly getting dramatically worse. And then some.

The murder of a Millwall supporter at New Cross station in December 1976 was taken so seriously that the police in England even called for the game to be suspended. Yet even as football was still reeling from this disaster, it was dealt a further blow when television stepped back into the equation with the broadcast of the now infamous *Panorama* documentary about Millwall and its hooligan following.

It is impossible to overstate the impact this programme had on the hooligan scene not just in England, but also across Europe. Suddenly, Millwall were *the* hooligan club and The Den went from being simply a nightmare place to visit, to being home to a collection of identifiable individuals who belonged to gangs – gangs who, for the first time, had names: The Treatment, F-Troop and The Halfway Liners.

Within days, this phenomenon was repeated at clubs the length and breadth of Britain and, as both Liverpool and Manchester United carried the yobs' torch across Europe, fledgling hooligans on the continent lapped up reports of what was going on in what had already come to be regarded as the spiritual home of football violence: England.

Yet still it got worse. When England supporters caused mayhem in Luxembourg in October 1977, both the media and supporters across Europe suddenly realised that this was a new and potentially frightening dimension to the problem. For not only were the hooligans putting aside their club loyalties to travel with the national side but, with the right wing already making inroads into the game in England, the potential for a political dimension developing was immense.

More importantly, the envious eyes that had been cast in our direction from the mainland suddenly recognised that hooliganism went way beyond simple violence. It was about excitement, adventure, but above all, it was about power. That realisation signalled a sharp rise in incidents involving both Italian and German supporters. Many of which, according to a number of commentators, aped what was going on in England, albeit on a much smaller scale.

By 1980, local hooligans on the continent were even looking to have a go back at their less welcome visitors. The most famous example of this involved 50 Manchester United fans who had to be rescued by German riot police when they came under attack from FC Nuremberg supporters. Yet such incidents were few and far between, and with English football in the grip of the burgeoning Casual movement – a movement which ironically was fuelled by Liverpool supporters' exploits in Europe – things were only ever going to get worse before they got better.

It has been said many times before, but in the early 1980s, the Casual movement *was* football violence in England. Revolving as it did – and to a certain extent still does – around designer clothing and arrogance, it was tailor-made for the hooligans who suddenly found themselves with not just an identity, but a uniform. However, while the Europeans continued to regard the English scene as the ultimate manifestation of the hooligan culture, they never embraced the Casual scene to the same degree as supporters did in this country. Instead, hooliganism developed along different lines. In many instances, this involved far more overt displays of passion and support than were seen in England as well as, increasingly, the involvement of politics. This was particularly so in Italy where the Ultra groups, who had been around since the 1960s, now took on a new and added significance.

Unlike the English hooligan gangs who were largely disorganised and existed purely for their own devices, the Ultras were extremely well organised and motivated. They provided their predominantly youthful following with a focus which often went way beyond football, and so successful were they, that they quickly spawned similar movements in other countries such as Spain, France and Greece.

However, at the core of the Ultra movement was pride and it was inevitable that as incidents of trouble continued to increase around the European game, a clash of cultures was coming. The first signs of that came, somewhat predictably, in Italy during the 1980 European Championships.

Instrumental in what happened were the Italian media who, having covered the activities of the Ultra groups for a number of years previously, now whipped them into a frenzy about the forthcoming invasion of the English hooligans. As a result, the English support was baited and abused at every turn and by the time the travelling fans arrived in Turin for the Belgium game the mood was already ugly. When the Belgians scored a first half equaliser, the Italian fans in the stadium began taunting the English support who responded in time-honoured fashion. Immediately, the Italian riot police baton-charged the English and then fired tear gas at them – a tactic that resulted in the game being held up for five minutes as the gas drifted across the pitch. When an apparently perfectly legitimate England goal was disallowed later on in the second half, things erupted again and continued afterwards. In all, a total of 70 people were hospitalised and UEFA hit England with a huge fine. But, for the Italian fans, it had been a huge result, and the claim that they 'ran' the English is one still being made to this day. More importantly, it set the scene for two things: a sudden explosion of hooliganism across Europe and a period of violence involving English football fans the like of which the game had never experienced.

With UEFA's threats still ringing in their ears, both the British authorities and the English Football Association went on the offensive. They were determined to clean up the game no matter what it took. But to the mobs, this merely added to the challenge. By the time the new season kicked off, they had already started to become more organised and when, in September, a 17-year-old Middlesbrough fan was stabbed to death outside Ayresome Park, it was clear that English domestic football was in for a rough time.

Abroad, the pattern continued. English clubs caused mayhem whenever they crossed the Channel and the followers of England did likewise. But, increasingly, problems were being seen in the domestic leagues of our near neighbours and, with the local police usually ill prepared, incidents often became incredibly violent.

Worryingly, at least for the English, the locals were also starting to go on the offensive. When Spurs travelled to Amsterdam in 1981, they were expecting some degree of trouble, but what they got was something else. For almost the first time, an English club ran up against serious local opposition, as gangs of Ajax fans, in some cases 200 strong, went for them in the biggest possible way. At least three Spurs fans were stabbed and over 20 were arrested but, significantly, the Dutch police laid the blame squarely at the feet of the Ajax fans.

Just a year later, England, having seen its supporters cause trouble in Switzerland and Norway during the qualifying rounds, travelled to Spain for the 1982 World Cup. With the Falklands War still taking place even as the tournament got under way, tensions and xenophobia were running at an all time high. Inevitably, it all went badly wrong but, for once, the followers of the England side were on the receiving end as Spanish fans, fired up by anti-British rhetoric, attacked anything that moved. Even the British media were aghast and went to town on the Spanish authorities, accusing them of doing nothing to protect their English guests. Both UEFA and FIFA seemed strangely quiet. The inference was obvious.

Later that same year, English fans were again the victims when they came under attack from local gangs before a World Cup qualifier in Denmark. However, this time, convinced that the local police were happy to see assaults on English fans go unpunished, the hooligans decided to exact their own brand of justice. As the final whistle blew, trouble erupted which, according to some sources, was among the worst violence English football fans had ever been involved in.

Inevitably, neither UEFA nor the FA made any comment on the fact that the England fans hadn't started the trouble, but what UEFA did point out was that if things didn't improve soon, they would have no alternative but to ban England and English clubs from overseas competition.

However, while all eyes had been fixed on the English, of growing concern to UEFA was the burgeoning hooligan scene in the rest of Europe. Incidents were becoming increasingly frequent, particularly in Germany where violence between rival gangs was becoming extremely vicious. In one example, a 16-year-old boy was killed during a battle with stones and fireworks. Similarly, in Italy, a youth was killed when the train he was travelling on was set alight.

For the English hooligans, however, trouble and travel continued to go hand in hand and, in 1983, Tottenham Hotspur fans were involved in more violent scenes during a trip to Rotterdam. Significantly, the first leg in London had seen the appearance of a hooligan group from Feyenoord. Although their activities were well policed and nothing of note happened, the fact that they came at all sent a clear message to the Spurs fans who travelled for the second leg ready, and more than willing, for the inevitable violence. With a large group having purchased tickets in the home end of the Feyenoord Stadium, fighting broke out early on and continued after the game, resulting in over 30 serious injuries. As a result, Spurs were hauled up in front of UEFA again and fined nearly £8000. However, if that was meant to send a warning to other English clubs or to England fans, it failed dismally. Just a few months later, England travelled to Luxembourg and, despite a 4–0 victory, the team failed to qualify for the 1984 European Championships. The fans ran riot and once again UEFA stepped in with a warning that if anything happened again all English clubs would be banned from European competition.

Despite this, in February 1984, English hooligans were involved in more trouble – this time in Paris when local skinheads mobbed-up and attacked the visiting fans in the Porte de Saint Cloud area of the city prior to an international against France. After the game, there were more incidents that resulted in some 80 wounded, 40 arrests and a reported £700,000 worth of damage. Even more worryingly, later that year, a Tottenham supporter was shot dead in a Brussels bar prior to the first leg of the UEFA Cup final against Anderlecht; a game that also saw some 200 Spurs fans detained by the Belgian police.

Yet despite having issued numerous warnings, UEFA once again failed to act. Just a year later, that failure was to result in a tragedy of previously unimagined proportions.

There can be no doubt that 29 May 1985 saw one of the darkest but most significant events in the history of European football. The condemnation which poured on the English game in the aftermath of the death of 38 Juventus fans and one Belgian at Heysel was immense, well deserved and, to be fair, long overdue. What many people do not realise, however, is that it was the final link in a complex chain of events that had begun the previous season.

In the early 1980s, Liverpool, then possibly the greatest club side in world football, was one of the few major English clubs without a significant hooligan following. They had been involved in trouble for sure, but nothing compared to the big London clubs, Leeds or Manchester United. Instead, their reputation was for humour, noise, passion and, on occasions – particularly during their many European excursions – the 'liberation' of property.

In 1984, having made it to their fourth European Cup final, the team and its fans travelled to Italy looking to build on what was already a formidable reputation. However, unlike previous occasions, this time they went as underdogs. For the game was to be played in Rome and on the home pitch of their opponents, AS Roma.

Inevitably, with so much at stake for the local side and a support that outnumbered them by many, many thousands, the reception given to the Liverpool fans was less than welcoming. As they entered the stadium, stewards and policemen confiscated coins, bunches of keys, watches and even cameras, which, if anything, fuelled a degree of hostility among the Liverpool support especially when they soon came under attack from a hail of missiles.

Despite the obvious tension inside the ground, the English side went on to win the game in a penalty shoot-out, but even as the players celebrated on the pitch, things on the terraces began to take a very nasty turn.

Almost immediately, the police became openly hostile towards the Liverpool fans and it quickly became clear, especially to the seasoned travellers, that there would be trouble outside the ground. What no one expected was that it would be quite as bad as it was.

While some of the Liverpool support managed to make their way to the centre of the city to be pictured dancing in the famous Trevi Fountain, others headed for their hotels and supposed safety. However, they soon found themselves the target of local youths who seemed totally indifferent to the fact that many of the English supporters were family groups some of whom included quite young children. Worryingly, the police seemed unsympathetic to their plight and in many cases actually became a part of the problem, lashing out at the English fans as they pleaded for protection. Inevitably, the situation deteriorated. Scooter gangs began chasing the Liverpool fans along narrow streets and slashing out at them with knives as they rode past. In one horrific incident, a 13-year-old was almost hacked to death and required over 200 stitches to his wounds.

To make matters worse, coach drivers who had been due to take some of the Liverpool fans to Rome airport after the game simply went home leaving them stranded and at the mercy of the roving gangs. Equally, some hoteliers, whether in fear for their premises or resentment at the result, refused entry to their English guests, some of whom were forced to seek sanctuary in the British Embassy.

It was a shameful episode, and the fact that it received so little media attention in both Italy and England caused outrage among the Liverpool support as well as among the English hooligan community. Revenge was sworn and, only a year later, the opportunity to take it arrived when the team, having made it to the European Cup final yet again, discovered that they were heading for Belgium to face another Italian side, Juventus.

Even leaving aside the simmering tensions, quite how or why the Heysel stadium was chosen to host this fixture is something of a mystery. The ground failed to meet many basic safety standards, and a lack of investment meant that large sections of the terracing were crumbling and covered in knee-high weeds while security for even domestic games was regarded by the locals as something of a joke. For a fixture of this stature, it was simply laughable.

Ironically, the Liverpool fans arrived in Brussels in a subdued mood. Just 18 days previously, the game in England had suffered a horrific double tragedy when 56 fans had died in a fire during a game at Bradford and a young supporter had been crushed to death at Birmingham City when Leeds fans went on the rampage. Sadly, their mood didn't last.

Trouble erupted in Brussels early on as Liverpool fans, many of them veterans of the game in Rome, once again found themselves the target of an Italian Ultra group. This time, however, they were ready and fought back. More importantly, elements among the Liverpool support took the Italians' aggression as a sign that they had called it on. As a result, as far as they were concerned, the opportunity to avenge the events of the previous year had now been handed to them on a plate.

Despite this, the Liverpool fans did not immediately go on the offensive. Instead, they merely sat back and responded where necessary until the Belgian police, who seemed totally unprepared for what was happening, eventually decided that rather than arrest or detain people, the best tactic was to get the fans into the ground as quickly as possible. It was to prove to be a huge mistake for one simple reason: poor segregation.

The ticketing situation had been a shambles from the start. Many of those who had bothered to buy theirs from official sources found themselves separated from the Italians by a flimsy fence and a few uninterested stewards. Others, who had bought their tickets from touts or simply worked out that they could get into the ground by climbing under, over or even through the perimeter fencing, ended up spread around the terraces. As a result, segregation was almost non-existent and with over two hours to go, in a stadium full of some of the most embittered supporters the game has ever seen, small pockets of Liverpool fans soon began to gather together. It was payback time.

Ironically, it was the Italian fans who kick-started the trouble inside the ground when the bulk of the Liverpool fans, who were gathered together on one half of the large Western terrace, came under attack from a barrage of bottles, coins and flares. This quickly escalated into direct violence as Juventus supporters began attacking groups of Liverpool fans located in other areas of the ground. As the Scousers fought back, and with the police seemingly unable or unwilling to take control of the situation, these small skirmishes rapidly escalated into large terrace-battles.

At approximately 8.45 p.m. local time, a section of the Liverpool support on the Western terrace decided enough was enough and forced their way through a fence and charged at the mass of Juventus fans who had been hurling a steady stream of missiles at them. Immediately, panic set in among the Italians, who turned and fled. However, with the other three sides of the terrace surrounded by a concrete wall, they simply had nowhere to go.

The Liverpool fans, unaware of what was happening, continued to attack the Juventus supporters, who by now were desperately climbing over each other in an effort to escape. As the police were still trying to work out what to do, the inevitable happened and the crumbling wall at the eastern end of the terrace collapsed. The release of pressure sent the helpless Italians who had been crushed against it tumbling to the floor. Yet even as they lay there, the remainder of the Juventus support poured through the gap, crushing their fellow supporters underfoot.

As the rest of the ground witnessed the tragedy unfolding, all hell broke loose. Italian fans in other parts of the ground invaded the pitch in an effort to get at the Liverpool support and at one stage it even appeared that a Juventus supporter was firing a gun into the English section (it later turned out to be a starting pistol). With the situation now seemingly out of control, the Belgian police were finally spurred into action and when reinforcements arrived, supplemented by units from the Belgian army, order was quickly restored.

Incredibly, despite the death of 38 Italian fans and one Belgian, and with neither set of players wanting to take part, the decision was taken that the game had to go ahead. The reasoning being that if it didn't the fans would cause even more mayhem in the streets of Brussels. So, in one of the most controversial games in the history of football, Juventus won the 1985 European Cup final 1–0. But the result was meaningless.

With the game being broadcast live, pictures of the disaster were seen around the world and, inevitably, every ounce of blame fell on the Liverpool fans. The Belgian authorities, in a desperate but ultimately flawed damage-limitation exercise, accused the Englishmen of being 'fighting mad' and told of one who had to be injected with enough tranquilliser to knock out six horses before he would calm down. There was even talk that those held in custody would be charged with mass murder.

But, almost immediately, stories began circulating that among the Liverpool fans had been known hooligans from a variety of clubs including Chelsea, Newcastle, West Ham, Millwall and Leeds. Desperate for a new angle on the hooligan issue, the tabloid press jumped on these rumours and informed the world that Heysel had actually been a planned show of strength by the English hooligan élite as revenge for the events in Rome the previous year. It was also claimed that it had been a group of Chelsea fans that had kicked everything off.

However, in all the research I have ever done on this incident, no one has ever provided a shred of evidence that supports that claim. Where the rumours came from is still unclear, but given that Liverpool have always enjoyed a wealth of support across the whole of

England, it is possible that regional accents heard at the time have more to do with these theories than any ounce of reality. Indeed, many Liverpool fans I have spoken to who were at Heysel angrily refute the suggestion and make it plain that this was very much their fight and it was one they wanted.

Whatever the truth of the matter, what is clear is that National Front literature was found on the terraces afterwards but, at a time when the right wing were still heavily involved with English football, that was nothing unusual, especially considering what had gone on the previous year.

Official condemnation was instant. A stunned UEFA finally acted against the hooligans and all English teams were banned from European competition for five years with Liverpool having to serve a further two-year ban on top of that. Equally, the authorities in England went on the offensive like never before. A number of high-profile police operations took place that saw various hooligan groups torn apart. Others who had been actively involved in terrace violence simply gave up, too shocked at what they had seen on their television screens to take any further part.

Surprisingly, the ban didn't include the England side but, thankfully, largely due to the cost and distance involved in getting to Mexico, the 1986 World Cup was remarkably trouble-free. However, just a matter of weeks later, English football was once again dragged onto the front pages by its travelling fans. Although this time they never actually made it onto foreign soil.

Unbeknown to many, in the wake of the World Cup and a 50 per cent reduction in trouble at domestic league games, UEFA had relaxed the ban on English clubs travelling abroad to play pre-season friendlies. Two of the first to take advantage of this were Manchester United – who had arranged a fixture with Ajax – and West Ham, who had accepted an invitation to take part in a tournament in Groningen. To avoid any repeat of previous problems both clubs took the decision to keep news of the trips secret from their fans. However, it wasn't long before it leaked out and travel plans were soon being made.

On 7 August 1986, the ferry *Koningin Beatrix* sailed out of Harwich with a couple of hundred football supporters on board. A good proportion of those were simply fans of both teams intent on enjoying a trip to Holland to watch their respective sides play, but drinking heavily in the bars were a group of 150 Manchester United lads. More importantly, sitting in first class were 14 of the main faces from West Ham United's ICF – the notorious Inter City Firm who had hit the headlines in 1985 when the now infamous documentary *Hooligan* had been shown on British television.

With a trip of several hours ahead of them and an intense rivalry between the two sets of fans that dated back to 1967, a confrontation of some kind was inevitable and it took just over two hours before it exploded.

After the usual exchange of verbal abuse and a small but violent skirmish, the outnumbered ICF retreated to the sanctuary of first class and prepared for the inevitable attack. Using a variety of weapons including bottles, fire extinguishers and even a fire hose spraying at full blast, they stood firm at the top of the various stairs leading up from the lower decks and repeatedly drove back the United fans who tried desperately to get up at them.

As the fighting continued seemingly out of control, and with the stairs and decks awash with blood, the captain decided that the journey was simply too risky to continue and, having sent out a distress signal, turned the boat around and headed back to Harwich where it was met by hordes of policemen and a huge media circus.

Over 20 Manchester United fans were taken off the boat and rushed to hospital while 11 were arrested for their part in the fighting, which had been so fierce that a group of *Hell's Angels* who happened to be on the boat heading for a rally in Holland had refused to become involved, telling the West Ham lads that they were simply too violent.

In hooligan terms, it was a result that cemented the ICF's reputation as a legendary firm but, for the English game, it was nothing less than a disaster. Not only did it end any lingering hopes of an early end to the ban but UEFA actually increased it by an additional year as a punishment.

Clearly relieved that they had been handed a reason to postpone the return of English clubs to European competition, UEFA sat back and got on with the business of running football. What they failed to notice was that across Europe hooliganism wasn't just developing, it was actually catching up with the English game.

Proof of this came in 1987 when Feyenoord fans en route to Aberdeen for a UEFA Cup tie caused havoc on the ferries taking them to Scotland. Not only was this the first example of any club bringing trouble *to* the UK, it also sent a message to the English hooligans that the fast-approaching Euro 88 was going to provide a severe test of their reputation.

The British media immediately jumped on this and began whipping up both the fans and the public. The *Sun* newspaper even compiled a league table of the participating nations based on the performance of their hooligans and, much to the annoyance of the English, placed the Dutch firmly at the top.

In the event, despite the best efforts of the media to say otherwise, the warnings proved to be false. Trouble involving England fans in Germany was fairly limited with the only major incident taking place at the main railway station in Düsseldorf where England fans came under attack from German hooligans but ended up giving them a good hiding. Of more significance was the riot in Hamburg that resulted in a number of Irish and Dutch supporters being given serious beatings by German hooligans.

Despite the fact that out of 1200 fans arrested, only 381 were English (over 800 were German) and the majority of them had simply been rounded up and deported, the English FA withdrew a planned application to have the European ban lifted on the grounds that the fans were not to be trusted. As a result, the then Prime Minister Margaret Thatcher warned that the very future of the game in England was in serious doubt as a result of the continuing problems associated with the hooligans.

However, as the end of the decade approached, what no one realised was that hooliganism was already on the decline in England. Not because of the police or the media, but because of music and, more importantly, drugs.

The rave scene that exploded across the UK in the late 1980s took lads away from football at a quite amazing rate. To a certain extent, it was also successful in making hooliganism unfashionable. Yet the impact that the new dance culture had on the hooligans was nothing compared to the effect that the events of 15 April 1989 had upon the English game.

The death of 96 Liverpool fans at Hillsborough changed football in England forever. The subsequent report on the tragedy by Lord Justice Taylor saw the fences surrounding pitches torn down and the terracing of the top-flight clubs replaced with seats. More importantly, it forced the police to go on the offensive and the hooligans to go undercover or, in many cases, simply give up altogether. It also attracted an offer from UEFA who told the fans that if they behaved at the fast approaching Italia 90, English clubs would be readmitted to European competition.

What happened in Italy has been well documented elsewhere, but what is important is that not for the first time England supporters came under sustained attack from both local fans and the police, the majority of whom seemed intent on exacting revenge for past misdemeanours. In one incident, for example, 25 England fans were attacked by a group of approximately 500 Italians but, when they fought back, they were beaten by the police and arrested.

Incredibly, the English media saw what was happening and reported the provocation accurately and sensibly, with the result that when the fans came home they were perceived not as scum, but as victims. Even UEFA recognised what had happened and rewarded the fans by readmitting Cup-winners Manchester United and league runners-up Aston Villa back into European competition; champions Liverpool were still barred. Astonishingly, they also invited England to bid for the 1998 World Cup.

To all intents and purposes, the bad times surrounding English football on its European travels were apparently over.

CHAPTER TWO
The post-Hillsborough years

There is no doubt that the early 1990s saw a huge change in English football. For once, everything was positive and that mood seemed to be well placed as various foreign excursions including England's qualification for Euro 92 passed by relatively peacefully. Indeed, there were even concerns voiced that Swedish hooligans would be looking to take the fight to the English fans.

In the event, there were a few incidents of trouble at the tournament but, once again, the only real rivals to confront the English were the police. However, at the end of the tournament they announced that they were more than happy with the behaviour of the England fans. Even UEFA were satisfied although they still had hooliganism to contend with – this time from the Germans, who rioted in Gothenburg after England had been knocked out.

But just as things were beginning to look good for England, it all went horribly wrong. For what no one had realised was that Europe's hooligans had finally caught up with their English mentors and some of them were looking to prove it. This fact was rammed home in the biggest possible way in May 1993 when England headed for Katowice and a World Cup qualifying fixture against Poland.

It was here for almost the first time that England's hooligans found themselves face-to-face with a huge mob intent on taking them on. The subsequent fighting saw the English fans bombarded with missiles and baton-charged by police and, while their reputation for standing firm was enhanced considerably, the fact that the Poles had a serious go did not go unnoticed across Europe. Tellingly, it was a trip that many England supporters still remember as being one of the most terrifying experiences of their lives.

That same sentiment arose among Manchester United supporters that October when the team travelled to Istanbul to play Galatasaray. The now infamous 'Welcome to Hell' atmosphere of the Ali Sami Yen Stadium was witnessed by television viewers across Europe but, more importantly, the United fans came under sustained attack from both the home support and the local riot police who by the end of the night had arrested over 200 United supporters, the majority of whom hadn't actually done anything. To make matters worse, two Manchester United players, Eric Cantona and former England captain Bryan Robson, were also attacked as they left the pitch.

Less than six months later, it happened again, this time in Holland. Dutch football had hit a low point at the time with a game at PSV Eindhoven being called off as a result of two separate bomb threats. Dutch hooligans were also still smarting from accusations that they had bottled out after failing to come to Wembley in the April of that year. This time, they made no mistake, attacking England fans at every opportunity. However, what made the news were the allegations of police brutality made by English fans following their treatment at the hands of the local authorities. Over two days, in excess of 1100 fans were arrested and deported from Holland. That figure remains an all-time record.

Failure to qualify for USA 94 and the nation being awarded Euro 96 in exchange for dropping their 1998 World Cup bid meant that the England team didn't have a competitive fixture until the start of the tournament. However, if anyone thought that their absence would encourage the English fans to settle down, they were completely wrong.

Domestically, trouble in England was still a major problem and, with Euro 96 approaching, the police embarked on a major offensive. They were determined to smash the hooligans once and for all and, with the full backing of the government and the FA, began to target known individuals using not only traditional methods, but an incredible array of technology, in particular CCTV.

To counter this, the groups began to pick and choose when and where they kicked things off. Aided by the increasing use of the cell phone, avoiding the police became an integral part of the hooligan game, and it was one that in the majority of cases they won hands-down. Conversely, at a number of clubs things did begin to quieten down as groups sought to avoid any unwarranted attention during the lead up to the biggest tournament to be held in England since the 1966 World Cup.

But in February 1995, England headed for Dublin and a friendly against the Republic of Ireland at Lansdowne Road where, it is fair to say, the reputation of England and its supporters reached an all-time low. Not for the first time, at the heart of it all was the extreme right-wing.

Political groups such as the National Front, the British Movement and the League of St. George had been involved with English football for at least two decades prior to Dublin and it is easy to see why. After all, where else in the 1970s and 1980s did large numbers of mainly working-class males gather together?

However, in the late 1980s the scourge of racism was recognised for the folly that it is, and campaigns to drive it out of the game began to gain momentum with the result that the impact of the political groups declined rapidly, particularly at club level. The England side, however, continued to be affected by their albeit small presence and various groups were involved in some shameful episodes on their travels. During the trip to Poland in 1993, some had even been photographed laughing and smiling at the Auschwitz museum.

This was not unique to England, of course. Every country in Europe had similar problems, with Italy suffering more than most. What was unique to England, however, was that the groups had a specific and very real focus for their hatred.

The singing of 'No Surrender to the IRA' had become so ingrained among the English support that it had almost come to be regarded as their theme song. Yet while many ridiculed both it and the people who sang it, its continuing presence highlighted the simple truth that among the support existed a deep loathing of the Irish Republican Army and everything it stood for. As the continuing Anglo-Irish peace process was viewed by the right wing as conceding more and more ground to the IRA, the trip to Dublin handed them an ideal opportunity to show their support for the loyalist community and send a warning to the British government that there was a section of the community who were far from happy with what was going on.

Looking at it purely in those terms, there is no escaping the fact that however misguided the intentions, the rioting that forced the abandonment of the game after only 27 minutes was an incredible success. But even as the players were trooping off the pitch and the pictures were being beamed around the world, hysterical politicians both in England and across Europe began screaming for the cancellation of Euro 96 to combat an apparent upsurge in extreme right-wing activity.

This stance was also adopted by certain sections of the media who in the days following the riot blamed the whole thing on a seemingly new and sinister neo-Nazi group called Combat 18.

With a name based on the initials of Adolf Hitler (the first and eighth letters of the alphabet) and a history of violence dating back to its formation in the early 1990s, C18 were a tabloid editor's dream. However, just as they were getting their teeth into the story, they changed tack. Suddenly, it wasn't simply the far-right who were to blame for Dublin, it was England football fans. After all, as history showed, they were the lepers of European football.

Quite why this happened is unclear, but in the face of any evidence to the contrary, I remain convinced that pressure was brought to bear on various organisations to underplay the role of the far-right. Whether that was to ensure the smooth progression of the peace process or to make sure that Euro 96 went ahead to avoid embarrassing the British government, who can tell? The fact is that whatever happened, it worked.

As the media began delving into the backgrounds of the people arrested during the trouble, UEFA came out fighting and said that the tournament would go ahead as planned. They regarded the severity of the incident as being strictly a one-off and were confident that Euro 96 would be trouble-free.

The British government and the Football Association were obviously delighted, but there can be little doubt that UEFA's response was not so much supportive as calculated. They knew as well as anyone that the only nation whose supporters were involved in regular incidents of crowd trouble on their travels were the English. Similarly, while domestically countries such as Holland and Germany could boast plenty of hardcore hooligans of their own, the chances of them crossing the channel to confront the English on home soil was almost certainly zero. Ironically, England was probably the safest place to hold it.

Among the European hooligan community, the impact of the Dublin riot was immense. Not only did it reaffirm England's status at the top of the hooligan ladder, but it sent a clear message to any groups that had been planning to cross the Channel that they were in for a rough time if they showed.

However, before the nation could breathe a collective sigh of relief and begin preparations for the party, it was given more football-related trouble to worry about. Only this time, the circumstances were a lot different.

Since Italia 90, it had been a running joke among English supporters, including the vast majority who neither had nor wanted anything to do with the hooligans, that whenever they left the country, they left their civil and human rights behind. After all, police forces across Europe seemed to declare open season on them the second they came within baton reach.

Despite plenty of evidence to the contrary, the authorities, and especially the media, had always treated this simple truth with contempt. In the case of the authorities, this was largely because they were wary of being seen to do anything pro-supporter and anti-Europe, while the media simply preferred to believe that every English football fan was a potential headline and the very idea that any of them could be any kind of victim was preposterous.

As a result, when Chelsea and their huge travelling support headed for Belgium and a match against Bruges just two weeks after Dublin, they were watched by a nervous government and an eager press pack. The club had a huge reputation in hooligan circles so something was bound to happen.

Not surprisingly, given what had taken place in Dublin, and with Heysel still fresh in Belgian minds, the Bruges police were on a high state of alert. However, they were unable to prevent trouble breaking out when local fans began attacking small groups of Chelsea supporters in various bars and cafes across the city.

The police response was immediate. In typical style, they ignored the local hooligans and, instead, simply rounded up as many Chelsea supporters as they could. The ones they didn't arrest, they handcuffed and detained in a warehouse with no food, water or toilets. By the time kick-off time approached, in excess of 500 Chelsea fans had been held. At 5 a.m. the next morning, the entire group, still in handcuffs, were deported.

Tellingly, the media response in England was scathing of the Belgian authorities. News programmes on both the BBC and ITV showed footage of the Belgian police lashing out at Chelsea fans who were simply walking along minding their own business. Equally, tales of people being rounded up and deported for no reason were for once given a sympathetic hearing. However, there was still a lingering sense that somehow the English fans had been to blame and that what had happened in and around the ground had been a result of things that had gone on out of sight of the cameras.

Astonishingly, just a few weeks later on 6 April, the same thing happened again. Once again, Chelsea supporters were the victims when they travelled to play Spanish club Real Zaragoza and were battered senseless by the local riot police.

It is fair to say that some of the incidents at this game defy belief. Four examples of many include: the father of a young boy who was beaten unconscious after he complained about his young son's bag being damaged as it was searched; two young supporters who were brutally attacked by Spanish police when they asked the police for directions to their coach; a man who was hit with a police baton nine times as he sat with his wife and children trying to ignore what was going on around him, and most bizarrely of all, a man who was batoned to the floor when he bent down to retrieve a packet of crisps he'd dropped down a flight of stairs.

Luckily – if that is the word to describe it – much of what went on was shown on British television and once again the condemnation was immediate. However, it wasn't universal. Various newspapers began pointing the finger at Chelsea supporters, including the *Daily Star*, who reported that 'Chelsea's hooligan element shamed English soccer once again with a sickening charge on Spanish riot police'. They quoted one authority who was supposed to speak on the fans' behalf as saying: 'Some of them are not even house-trained let alone fit to be travelling abroad representing our country' and 'I applaud the way the police rounded them up.'

Yet even before the dust could settle, the English game witnessed a third example of supporters suffering at the hands of a European police force. This time it wasn't Chelsea supporters, but Arsenal.

Although not as serious as the events involving their West London neighbours, the problems with the French police at the Arsenal v Real Zaragoza Cup-Winners' Cup final were enough to support the growing belief that provocation and policing were serious and increasing problems for English fans who travelled abroad. The trouble was, despite both Tony Banks and Kate Hoey – two of the most high-profile football fans in the British parliament – voicing their concerns in the House of Commons, the response from the government was simply to point out that out of 17 European games that English clubs had been involved in that season, only three had resulted in trouble and of those, two had involved a particular club. As a Chelsea supporter himself, Banks was furious at the inferred slur, but rather than labour the point, he backed down. It was to be another three years before he was able to say 'I told you so'.

By this time, the papers had turned their attention to Euro 96 and were busily whipping up hysteria about the potential for not just hooliganism, but civil disorder. Centre page spreads of German and Dutch hooligans threatening to wage war on the English featured almost daily, while phone-in shows were full of lads warning about an England superfirm and threatening to bring a halt to the tournament if the English were knocked out.

It was all, of course, bullshit. Everyone who knew anything about hooliganism understood the simple reality that in only a few countries were hooligans able to set aside club differences and follow their national side abroad. Even UEFA had realised this, which was why they had been happy for the tournament to be held in England.

As expected, with the inevitable exception of the Scots and a few Germans, no one came and the tournament passed by almost, but not quite, peacefully. Instead, what happened was that England not only fell in love with football, it fell in love with itself.

The euphoric mood that enveloped the game continued after the tournament and it had an immediate impact on the activities of the hooligans who followed the national side. Home games became the domain of families, face-painting and the corporate empires, while away trips saw a concerted effort to create a more positive and less aggressive atmosphere around the support.

In part, it worked. World Cup qualifiers in Moldova, Georgia and, most notably, Poland passed by relatively peacefully, while for the clubs involved in European competition, life was almost tranquil. Only when Manchester United travelled to Portugal in March 1997 were there any real problems and, once again, they came courtesy of the police, who attacked the English fans outside the FC Porto stadium, injuring several.

The fact that once again English fans were the victims did not go unnoticed. The media were incensed and the Portuguese authorities roundly condemned by supporters' organisations and MPs including David Mellor, who was later to become head of the British government's anti-hooligan task force.

This reaction had a very positive effect on the travelling supporters and there was a genuine feeling that a corner had finally been turned. The police had enjoyed a number of successes in their particular battle with the hooligans and even supporters' groups were starting to think optimistically. With increasing numbers of fans looking to follow England abroad, the future was looking good. Domestically, however, things were not so rosy. Indeed, no one could know it, but real problems were on the horizon.

One of the things that had caused the police some disquiet during Euro 96 had been the number of old hooligans who had made an appearance. Faces that had only been seen on odd occasions since the pre-rave scene days suddenly became regular fixtures at clubs across the country and, increasingly, some were becoming involved in trouble. The big fear was that they would start to travel again and, in October 1997, that fear was realised.

The occasion was a World Cup qualifier in Rome. England badly needed a result and almost 10,000 fans made the trip, many without tickets. Within that number, according to the Italian police, were 700 known (category C) hooligans, and they were soon involved in trouble. On the Friday night, an England fan was badly injured and more were wounded when fighting broke out in the centre of Rome on the afternoon of the match. However, it was in the stadium that it really went wrong.

With so many England fans having bought tickets from unofficial sources, segregation broke down. The result being that when a group of Italian fans held up a banner bearing the legend 'Victory to the IRA', there was an immediate clash.

Inevitably, the police waded in, baton-charging anything that moved, but even as the commentators were screaming at the English scum for heaping shame on the nation once again, someone noticed that the fans taking the biggest beating were all corporate fans, various celebrities and members of the England travel club. The hooligan element were almost all located at the other end of the ground and were simply watching what was going on in disbelief.

That single moment was a watershed for English football. From then on, the English media finally seemed to grasp the fact that there were indeed two distinct groups of English football fans that travelled abroad. The ones who simply wanted to enjoy their football and have a laugh and the ones who would take things a step further if the opportunity arose. Sadly, it was a concept that European hooligans seemed unable to get to grips with.

A month after Rome, Manchester United travelled to Rotterdam and their fans came under sustained attack as they drank in the city centre before the game. Afterwards, Feyenoord hooligans fought with the police as they tried to attack the United coaches but, even as they battled, a group of Manchester lads, having seen and had enough, dived off their coach and fought back. Thirty-eight were arrested.

The next big test for English football lay in France with the 1998 World Cup. The start of the year had seen a huge increase in trouble domestically, including the death of a Fulham supporter during a fight at Gillingham, and fans trying to assault officials at Everton, Barnsley and Portsmouth. As a result, the police put together a huge security operation that included a series of high-profile dawn raids filmed by specially invited TV news crews all designed to deter known hooligans from travelling. As the genuine fans made their way to Marseille for their opening group game against Tunisia, everyone was confident that things were under control.

Interestingly, in the briefings leading up to the tournament, the Football Association's Security Adviser, Sir Brian Hayes, had asked the French police to recognise that the English fans could sometimes overreact to heavy-handed policing. In response, the French made it clear that they would only go in heavy handed if things got really bad. Everyone was happy and confidence was high – sadly, it was horribly misplaced.

The first signs of trouble came on the Saturday night when England fans who had settled into a bar in the Old Port area of the city spilled out onto the street and began showering motorists with bottles and glasses. They were driven back by over 100 policemen, some with dogs, but sporadic fighting continued for over an hour.

The next day, there were more problems when a large group of local Tunisian immigrants who had been chanting and drinking outside a bar close to the centre of town moved along the road towards where a large crowd of Englishmen were gathered. Within minutes, the first bottle was thrown and pandemonium broke out. The police, who had been keeping their distance, moved in very quickly, firing at least five CS gas grenades into the English fans and forcing them away from the area.

The media were furious and launched a scathing attack on the hooligans. Yet it was only a foretaste of what was to come.

On the Monday morning, running battles broke out again in the streets surrounding the Old Port, resulting in 80 England fans being arrested, 24 injured and one hospitalised after an attacker slashed an artery in his neck.

There was also serious disorder later on in the day when local North Africans attacked the England fans who were simply watching the game on the beach. Key to this was that despite the fact the English support included many women and children, the French police stood by and watched events unfolding, only becoming involved when the England fans decided to fight back.

The remainder of the World Cup passed by relatively peacefully for the English although the Germans were involved in a major disturbance in Lens on the day of their game with Yugoslavia. Interestingly, a senior police official pointed out that there was one marked difference between the hooligans of England and Germany. The English were drunk and disorganised while the Germans were sober and very organised.

The aftermath of France 98 was one of close reflection for the authorities. Prior to the tournament they had been convinced that they had done all they could to deal with the hooligan threat and had even gone on record as saying that they knew each and every potential troublemaker, how they were travelling and where they were staying. Yet the morning after the trouble in Marseille, shamefaced figures from both the FA and the British police were forced to openly admit that they had no idea who 99 per cent of the people involved in the trouble were.

It was a terrible admission of failure and a significant factor in the resignation of the head of the National Criminal Intelligence Service. More importantly, with Euro 2000 due to be held in Belgium and Holland and England's bid for the 2006 World Cup still sitting in FIFA's in-tray, a determined government began looking towards the law as a way of stopping potential hooligans from even leaving the UK, a situation made all the more urgent that October when almost 80 England fans were arrested when the team travelled to Luxembourg for a European Championship qualifier.

Less than six months later, English football once again hit the headlines for the wrong reasons when, in March 1999, 8000 Manchester United fans descended on Milan for a UEFA Champions League quarter-final at the San Siro. With over 1000 policemen on duty, security was always going to be tight but, while there were a series of incidents in the city, the biggest problems occurred outside the ground prior to kick-off.

As the United fans tried to enter the ground, panic began to set in as the sheer numbers involved caused crushing to take place at the gates. Pleas for help were simply met with a clout from a baton that eventually provoked a furious response from the United support. Incredibly, subsequent complaints to UEFA were met with a metaphorical shrug of the shoulders as they pointed out that security was nothing to do with them but was instead the responsibility of the local authority who owned the ground. Sadly, the treatment of the United fans was repeated in May at the final in Barcelona and attracted the same response from the game's governing body, despite the presentation of video and documented evidence to support what amounted to police brutality.

Just weeks after Manchester United had been in Italy, a group of foreign supporters actually came to England looking for trouble. The occasion was a European qualifier against Poland and the team arrived with a mob of about 80 lads in tow. They were not, however, looking to fight with the English but with each other. When England travelled to Poland in September, things were very different indeed.

With West Ham having caused significant problems for the French police in Metz in August, the English police were in no doubt that the potential for problems was very real – a sentiment shared by even the most hardened of supporters, who were well aware of the reputation enjoyed by their hosts.

The first major incident took place on the night before the game when a bar full of English lads was attacked by a group of Legia Warsaw hooligans who were apparently supplemented by German hooligans who had travelled to take on the English. This attack was successfully driven off but another incident in the Champions Club at the Marriott Hotel was closer to call, with the Poles claiming a success. However, worse was to come the following day with the now infamous Saski Park battle.

Approximately 100 lads from each side turned up but a number of the Poles had knives and at least one English fan was stabbed during the fighting and hospitalised. It was by all accounts an incredibly violent incident and only the arrival of the police stopped this from turning into something far more serious.

By the time the fans arrived at the ground, the mood was already ugly and it quickly got worse as the England fans found themselves coming under a barrage of coins and flares. Eventually, having simply had enough, they began tearing up seats and hurling them at the locals before a small group broke through a fence and charged at the Poles sending them running for safety. After several minutes of fighting, the police arrived and drove the groups apart.

There was more trouble after the game including a serious incident at Warsaw central station but it is fair to say that the vast majority of England fans were happy to leave Poland behind.

The next away trip for England also saw trouble although, in the event, it was much less than had been anticipated. The reason for this was largely due to the fact that a huge security operation was put in place surrounding the game and, most significantly, that operation was executed by a British police force. Despite this, England's Euro qualifier in Glasgow still saw the fans involved in running battles with Scottish hooligans in Buchanan Street and at Central Station. Over 100 were arrested and, after the game, in excess of 200 police with dogs and horses escorted the England fans back to their trains and out of the city. However, the fact that England had travelled – and in numbers – to the home of their fiercest and most bitter rivals did not go unnoticed, especially with Euro 2000 now drawing close.

But before the national side and its army of supporters would travel to the tournament, two domestic clubs found themselves in trouble on the continent. The first of these was Chelsea who in February 2000 travelled to Marseille in significant numbers and became involved in all kinds of trouble both inside and outside the stadium. Despite a huge police presence, only the use of tear gas managed to bring things back under control.

The second club was Leeds who in March 2000 headed for Rome. The Yorkshire club took almost 7000 fans to Italy and among their number was a tidy-sized firm looking to kick things off with Roma's hooligans, who had a reputation for being fearless fighters. As they waited near the ground, a mob of almost 200 locals turned up but refused to become involved in anything until the police arrived. At this point they suddenly began hurling bottles and coins at the Leeds lads who dispersed to avoid arrest.

Shortly after this, a small group of Leeds scarfers were attacked by approximately 100 Roma fans and badly beaten. Two of them, a 16-year-old lad and his father, received extensive stab wounds to their legs. The Leeds supporters were outraged, especially when it emerged that other Roma fans had been riding around on mopeds carrying knives and trying to slash anyone who looked remotely English.

Tragically, a little over a month later, another group from the Yorkshire club were on the receiving end of a knife attack. This time in Istanbul.

With the Turkish club Galatasaray having beaten Leeds and gone on to make it through to the final of the UEFA Cup in Copenhagen, there was a degree of irony in the fact that their opponents would be another English club,

Arsenal. As a result, the entire hooligan community, not just in England but across Europe, were looking to the North London club to avenge the murders of the two Leeds United fans. It was a responsibility a number of Arsenal supporters were more than happy to accept.

The fear for the Danish authorities was that the large Turkish population who called Copenhagen home would unite behind Galatasaray and become involved in any trouble which might break out. They also voiced concerns that local hooligans would link with the English club and civil disturbances would result. Their fears were well founded.

Some six days before the final, it was reported that a group of Arsenal fans visited Copenhagen to familiarise themselves with the area and make contact with local lads. Two days later, police began erecting crowd control barriers.

The first clashes came the night before the game outside a disco bar called Absalon. Arsenal fans had been drinking inside for some hours when word spread that a group of Turks were hanging around outside. Almost immediately, the Londoners poured out only to find that the group was larger than expected. Undeterred, the Arsenal fans went for it but in the resulting melee, one received a serious stab wound. As more fighting broke out across the city, the police finally made an appearance but, by the time things calmed down, seven people had been badly injured and ten were arrested.

The next day, a mob of Arsenal lads gathered in and around Rosie McGee's bar adjacent to Tivoli Gardens and began drinking. However, on the other side of the square were hundreds of Turkish fans who, goaded on by an eager media pack, soon began abusing the Englishmen. This abuse soon turned to the hurling of missiles at which point, with no police presence and things getting uglier by the second, the Englishmen decided to have a go back.

Although hugely outnumbered, and with many of the Turks using knives, the Arsenal fans crossed the square and dealt out a battering.

By the time it was all over, four people had been stabbed and 64 arrested. Inevitably, the blame was heaped on the English despite the fact that in the majority of incidents they had been forced to defend themselves in the face of overwhelming provocation and a lack of police protection. But with the pictures having been beamed around the globe and Euro 2000 a matter of weeks away, it was the very last thing English football needed.

It is fair to say that there was a sense of satisfaction among the hooligan community at what happened in Copenhagen. There have been many reports that as well as Arsenal fans, there were representatives from Leeds United and various German, Danish and even Swedish clubs involved in the fighting, but whatever the truth of the matter, the Turks certainly came off second best in a series of fights that were invariably weighted in their favour be it with numerical superiority or the fact that, unlike the English fans, they were using knives. Many intended to continue that sequence over into the summer.

In the wake of Copenhagen, the British media went into a frenzy and the police went into overdrive. Feature articles about the potential for trouble and the possible consequences ran in every newspaper in the country, while a series of dawn raids removed various lads from the equation. On top of that, a list of over 1000 known hooligans was passed to the Belgian and Dutch authorities, while magistrates were positively begged to hand banning orders to anyone appearing in front of them for anything even remotely linked to football.

In the event, it was largely a waste of time for there were only two incidents of real note.

The first took place in central Brussels the night before the game against Germany when over 200 English lads kicked it off with some local immigrants. Unable to cope, the local police quickly summoned riot police who were forced to charge at the English and use tear gas to disperse them.

The second incident took place the next day in a small square in the centre of Charleroi.

To say that the trouble here was exaggerated would be a huge understatement. In effect, what happened was that a few lads got drunk, over-reacted to some abuse from a few German fans and threw some plastic chairs around. No windows were broken, no one was stabbed and indeed, no one was even hospitalised. The problem was – since this game had been forecast as the tournament's major flashpoint and the Charles II Square in particular as the likely venue – riot police were keyed up for trouble and, more importantly, every vantage point had been occupied by the world's press. They needed something to happen and when it did they went to town, first with riot police and then with both horses and water cannon. This provided some quite incredible footage which a hungry media sent spinning around the world.

In the 24 hours surrounding this incident, more than 850 people were detained and the majority shipped back to England in a fleet of Belgian military aircraft.

Not for the first time, many of those deported claimed that the Belgian police's zero-tolerance tactic had simply been an excuse for them to use excessive force and make indiscriminate arrests. Tales of quiet bars and cafes being pepper sprayed and any English inside being beaten and arrested were frequent but, once again, they fell on deaf ears. The Liberal Democrats' Home Affairs spokesman Simon Hughes was even quoted as saying 'the Belgian authorities have our full support in being as tough as necessary on the English visitors who are behaving not like fans but like hooligans.' He added: 'English football fans are sick to the back teeth of our fellow-countrymen.'

However, anyone who was there will know how the Belgian police were acting and there have been many reports of Football Liaison Officers (FLOs) from various English clubs actually warning lads to stay out of certain areas because the police were out of control. More tellingly, in one incident, three English fans were walking back to their hotel when they were jumped by a single man who began beating them with a stick. When they fought back to protect themselves, police appeared and arrested them. The man had been an undercover Belgian policeman.

What they didn't realise, however, was that one of the men arrested was a young English MEP who only told them who he was, in Flemish, once they were at the police station. Not surprisingly, all three were released within minutes but only after each had signed a form accepting that they had been treated fairly, an action I still do not understand to this day.

In purely hooligan terms, the tournament was a damp squib. Neither the Belgians nor the Dutch showed and only a few Germans managed to make it although, in their defence, the police operation to stop them leaving Germany was even more draconian than that staged by the English police. What Euro 2000 did confirm was that the Turks had quickly become a real problem for the authorities, yet despite Istanbul, Copenhagen and Brussels – not to mention a number of smaller incidents involving immigrants in various towns and cities hosting games during the tournament – UEFA refused to take any action against them. Something that sent a clear message to hooligans across Europe.

Thankfully, it was not until February that English fans were involved in another major incident of trouble abroad. This time, however, they were very much on the receiving end.

The club in question were Liverpool, who walked into what amounted to civil disorder when they travelled to Rome for a UEFA Cup tie. The previous weekend, an AS Roma fan had apparently been thrown down some stairs by a policeman during a game at Bologna and was still in a coma. As a result, the Roma fans were in an angry mood and rioted before the game, forcing the police to take refuge inside the stadium. They were then attacked by supporters already inside and so had to flee the stadium leaving all their vehicles behind. Various cars, vans and motorbikes were torched.

Caught in the middle of this, five Liverpool fans received serious stab wounds and another three were put in hospital. Yet again, assistance for the injured supporters from the authorities was negligible. As if to justify this, a British Embassy spokesman was quoted as saying: 'It sounds a bit drastic to say they were stabbed. The wounds were very superficial – they were barely punctures.'

The next serious flashpoint came in September when England travelled to Munich for a game that was to go down in history as one of the great team performances. It also handed the German hooligans the chance to prove once and for all that they were capable of taking on the English even if it was only on home soil. It was a chance they grabbed with both hands.

The first clashes came in Frankfurt on the Friday before the game when, despite a huge police presence, some 350 locals took over the subway and caused mayhem as they hunted for any English fans. In the event, there were only a few minor skirmishes and 35 Germans were arrested, but it certainly set the tone for the Saturday.

With almost 9000 English expected, including a sizable mob – despite yet another huge police operation – the potential for trouble was immense. In the event, the German police did a reasonably efficient job in keeping the two groups apart, with most incidents taking place in the afternoon. The worst of these were at the cafe near the main railway station and in and around the Marienplatz in the city centre where fans exchanged bottles and various other missiles. The most serious confrontation of all took place at a bar called the Augustiner where 50 German and English fans clashed.

Despite this, the police regarded the security surrounding the game as being a success, with only 180 arrests of which the bulk were German. The English police were not so thrilled, if only because increasing doubts were being cast on their ability to stop hooligans from travelling with the national side.

Incredibly, in December 2001 more Liverpool fans were stabbed when the team returned to Roma for yet another encounter, this time in the Champions League. In a mirror of events just seven months previously, the victims were people caught in the wrong place at the wrong time rather than hooligans of any sort, but yet again little was done to provide either protection for them or condemnation of the Italians. More worryingly, the build-up to the game saw the Liverpool supporters' coaches attacked with missiles as they approached the Stadio Olympico. There was also a repeat of the fighting between police and Roma fans that resulted in tear gas being used to quell trouble on the Curva Sud.

Unlike the Liverpool fans who were in the main simply victims in Rome, the next English supporters to become involved in trouble abroad were more than willing participants. In April 2002, Manchester United headed for a Champions League semi-final against Bayer Leverkusen which resulted in 128 people being detained of whom 123 were English.

The most serious incident surrounding this fixture took place in the centre of nearby Cologne which was packed with revellers celebrating the German festival of 'May Dance'. Almost 300 fans had to be driven apart by police using baton charges and dogs.

Much to the chagrin of the English police, the Germans refused to charge any of the English fans. Instead they simply took their details, photographed them and then shipped them out. The move incensed the British government who were becoming increasingly desperate for some kind of cross-border anti-hooligan initiative to become more than a pipe dream.

But even before the dust could settle, all eyes turned East to the 2002 World Cup in Japan and Korea.

It is no exaggeration to say that the Japanese, force-fed by a crazed media with pictures of Millwall, Heysel and Marseille, genuinely believed that Armageddon in the shape of English football fans was on the way. As if to confirm this, anti-riot exercises were staged using locals dressed in England shirts and talk was of new technology such as net guns to fire at anyone who became involved in fighting. There were even companies making fortunes selling hooligan insurance to an eager public.

In England, the wave of banning orders reached four figures, while the media were going crazy about hooligans using false passports, organised mobs heading for Thailand and Australia, and even stories of Japanese gangs threatening to take on the English hooligans.

What no one realised, however, was that nothing was ever going to happen for one simple reason: even if there were lads travelling out looking for trouble, a claim which itself is debatable, there wasn't going to be anyone for them to fight with. No other European country exports its hooligans nor does South America, but more significantly, there is no culture of hooliganism in either Japan or South Korea.

As a result, the tournament was a blast and the English will long be remembered not for the trouble they brought with them, but the passion, noise and colour. Sadly, the good news didn't last for long.

Five short weeks after the World Cup final, 3000 Manchester City fans travelled to Hamburg for a pre-season friendly and the night before the game, trouble erupted in the city's red-light district. There were more incidents during and after the game that saw 46 people arrested, although most were German.

Three days later, Everton fans were involved in a series of disturbances in Belgium when the team travelled to Anderlecht. However, in this instance they were certainly on the receiving end of some horrific policing methods, when women, children and, in one case a disabled youngster, were sprayed with CS gas and water cannon.

It was a disgraceful exhibition of police brutality yet, once again, there was no condemnation by the English authorities which, given the circumstances, was equally shameful.

Incredibly, just two months later the FA did finally come out and criticise someone. For once, it wasn't even the England fans but, instead, Slovakian supporters who hurled the very worst kind of racist abuse at Emile Heskey and Ashley Cole during a European Championship qualifier in Bratislava.

However, the FA's indignation, not to mention the subsequent media frenzy, masked the fact that the game saw some of the worst terrace violence seen in recent years.

Tension was already high as a result of an incident the previous night when two England fans received gunshot wounds after security guards fired 16 shots at a group of supporters who refused to leave a bar in Bratislava. The arrival of riot police, who wore not only the usual helmets and armour but balaclavas and uniforms with no markings to hide their identities, helped ensure it wasn't long before things turned ugly.

First missiles were exchanged, and then, following a Slovakian goal, England supporters charged at a fence separating them from the celebrating home fans. Shortly afterwards, as some of the crowd began ripping out seats, the riot police waded in and unleashed some quite horrific treatment on the visitors.

Some England fans have claimed that they were merely responding to missiles being thrown at them from the Slovakians and that the charge was as a direct result of the racist abuse directed at the two England players which, if true, would be ironic, given the history of a section of English fans.

However, although initially supported by the FA, the very idea that England fans could be acting out of such motives was ridiculed by certain sections of the English media. UEFA weren't thrilled either. They charged the Slovakian authorities for the racist abuse and the FA over the conduct of the England fans.

The FA immediately launched an appeal, but even before a date could be set for the hearing, another group of English fans hit the headlines with yet another bizarre incident.

In November 2002, Liverpool, desperately needing a win to progress in the Champions League, headed for Basle accompanied by legions of fans, including an estimated one thousand without tickets. With the local lads having been steadily building their own hooligan reputation, it came as no surprise that a clash occurred on the night before the game. What was surprising was that it happened in Zurich, over 100 kilometres from Basle, and that the bulk of the 'local' support were in fact German.

Although much of the trouble occurred around the main railway station, the incident that received the most publicity occurred at a McDonald's burger bar when a small group of Liverpool fans found themselves confronted by a mob of some 40–50 locals. Having backed into the restaurant and kept the Basle fans at bay by throwing chairs at them, the Liverpool supporters were stunned when a petrol bomb exploded in the doorway, meaning that no one could get in or out. Thankfully, it wasn't life threatening but, by the time the police arrived, the bulk of the Basle group had left and so, inevitably, the English fans took the brunt of their anger, despite only three of the fifteen people arrested being from Liverpool. There were yet more clashes on the day of the match that resulted in over 40 arrests for vandalism and disorder.

Not surprisingly, the trouble in Slovakia and Basle reopened the hooligan debate in England but, as usual, everything was focused entirely on our support and how much blame could be applied to it. As a result, everyone missed the simple truth that among the hooligan community the reputation of our supporters is no longer as feared as it once was. As this and subsequent chapters will prove only too conclusively, there are plenty of lads, not to mention policemen, across Europe who are increasingly willing and able to take on the significant minority of troublemakers who follow our national game abroad.

In part, of course, that is an added attraction to the so-called Burberry Brigade and, with qualifying games for Portugal 2004 and Germany 2006 ahead, as well as continuing success in European competition, it is a cast-iron certainty that we have not yet heard the last of them.

Part Two

WESTERN EUROPE

When putting together a book of this nature, the biggest problem any writer would usually expect to encounter is finding content of sufficient quality to put in it. In this instance, however, it was the opposite. My problem was simply deciding what to leave out.

That was especially true of this section. After all, every major country in Western Europe has a well-defined and recognised football culture and within those exist some of the most organised and violent hooligan gangs in the world. It is also fair to say that in recent years, even countries such as Switzerland have experienced an up-surge in organised hooliganism as has Cyprus where there have been isolated but extremely serious incidents of football violence.

Given that this section is about hooliganism in Western Europe, it is reasonable to assume that all of this and more would have been included and scrutinised, but it hasn't been, for one simple reason.

To have done justice to subjects as diverse as the growth of neo-Nazi activity surrounding Austrian football and the fledgling Casual scene in Ireland would have dis-tracted us from the most important footballing countries, such as Italy, Germany, Spain and Holland.

Therefore, I took the decision early on that in this section, I would concentrate on the four nations already mentioned and touch briefly on two more: France and

Belgium. With Euro 2004 approaching, I had also planned to include something about Portugal but there is relatively little worth writing about. Violence is rare and the Ultra philosophy of rivalry revolving around colourful displays, rather than aggression, seems to have been embraced by Portuguese fans with both hands. In fact, the only negative thing I could find was that some of the graffiti is abusive and usually written in English.

However, to open the section, we will examine a country which was simply impossible to ignore. Over the years it has had a significant impact on the hooligan world and, in particular, the spread of the Casual movement. It is also the only country whose hooligan element have come to England and caused problems on almost every occasion the two nations have met in competition, yet its supporters have managed to cultivate an image of a passionate yet fun-loving group who are welcome around the world: Scotland.

What follows was written by a gentleman known as Steve Simmons and is as comprehensive an examination of Scottish football as you will read anywhere. The accompanying articles on France and Belgium were written with the help of an anonymous Paris lad and Axel respectively and I am hugely grateful to both of them for their time and effort.

CHAPTER THREE
Scotland

Hooliganism in Scotland might seem a bit of a misnomer when you consider the plaudits that are showered on the Tartan Army after every international tournament that the Scots appear in. After all, the traditional image of the Scottish football fan is one of a happy drunk wearing a kilt or even full formal highland dress while going all out to include the locals in the party. Basically they are the extreme opposite to the stereotypical image of the English football fan abroad.

However, just as a stereotype masks the many positive facets to English football supporters (displayed so obviously in Japan during the World Cup), the reality is that there is very little difference between Scottish and English fan cultures. For instance both are based on drinking excessive amounts of alcohol, taking over the town centres of wherever you are playing, and being very noisy and boisterous. In fact, the only difference in the normal behaviours of the two sets of fans is the lack of large-scale violence when Scotland play.

That has not always been the case as anyone who watched an England versus Scotland match at Wembley – or for that matter, any supporters of Manchester United, Aston Villa, Sunderland, Tottenham Hotspur or any of the other clubs who had the delight of entertaining either Celtic or Rangers – during the 1970s and 1980s will be happy to tell you.

It wasn't only English fans that saw the dark side of the Scots in those days, as trouble also flared abroad. Rangers versus Franco's militia in a pitch battle after they won the Cup-Winners' Cup in Barcelona in 1972, or Celtic in the Battle of Cliftonville (although matches involving the Old Firm in Ireland went much deeper than mere football violence due to the religious baggage that both clubs carry), are just two examples of the Scots disgracing themselves abroad in what were major incidents. And no article dealing with Scottish hooliganism can ignore the events at Anfield during the 1977 Wales–Scotland World Cup qualifying tie. The Welsh FA had moved the game to Anfield to cash in on the large Scottish travelling support and they weren't to be disappointed as around 40,000 Tartan Army turned up: in fact the Scots made up about 80 per cent of the crowd. However, in contrast with today's Tartan Army, the behaviour of the Scots support was appalling. Liverpool experienced drunken violence on a massive scale as the Scots rampaged around the city all day. It wasn't much better inside the ground as Scots and Welsh supporters engaged in mass brawls on the terracing with a horrific array of weapons being used. How no one was murdered is a miracle. So what has changed nowadays?

Firstly, the Scottish media and footballing authorities are different. While their counterparts south of the border seem hell bent on painting English fans in as poor a light as possible, the Scots do the opposite. Before any major international tournament the towns that are due to host the Scots are bombarded with positive press and as a result the locals are friendly and welcoming, whereas the English have the exact opposite. All the talk is of banning orders, riot police and zero-tolerance measures. The English have shown in Japan that with the same friendly welcome that the Scots normally receive they can respond favourably. Likewise, if the Scots faced the same level of hostility normally reserved for the English then there would often be trouble. I've travelled away with Scotland on a fairly regular basis and believe me when I say that there are some very volatile individuals who wouldn't be too slow in coming forward if they found themselves under attack.

This brings us onto the make-up of the fans. The negative media received by England over the years has actually perpetuated the problem. The banner headlines and hype-fuelled predictions of carnage every time the English travel in numbers are as effective a recruitment tool as the famous 'Your Country Needs You' poster from the First World War. It's a call to arms to every hooligan the length and breadth of the country. Conversely, the opposite is true of Scotland as very few Scottish hooligans have any interest in following the national side abroad due to the friendly image. However, where the opposition seems appealing from a hooligan perspective, the Scots do occasionally turn out. With the exception of the matches against England, the most notable example of this was the Holland–Scotland friendly in Utrecht in 1994 when the two main hooligan groups in Scotland at the time – the Aberdeen Soccer Casuals and the Capital City Service who are attached to Hibernian – called a truce and travelled over to Holland together. There they engaged in a series of running battles with Dutch hooligans both in Amsterdam and Utrecht, much to the dismay of the Tartan Army. There have also been many incidents involving Scots clubs abroad – for instance, Anderlecht–Hibs, Standard Liège–Hearts and PSG–Rangers – which, strangely, have done little to taint the Tartan Army image in the eyes of the media.

Basically, the same potential problems so often on display with England are bubbling just under the surface of the Scots fan culture. That they don't show as often with the Scots is nothing to do with any perceived difference in the racial mentality of the nations, but has a lot more to do with the image promoted of the respective fan groups in the media. After all, there is a very strong case to put forward that says that the Scots actually invented football violence.

The Old Firm of Glasgow Rangers and Glasgow Celtic have dominated Scottish football from the late 1800s all the way through to the present day with brief interludes in the 1950s – when the Edinburgh sides dominated – and in the early to mid 1980s – where Aberdeen and Dundee United stole the spotlight. The Glasgow giants are, in comparison to the other Scottish clubs, massive, and as a result no one has been able to mount a sustained challenge to their dominance. As well as enjoying the backing of Scotland's largest city, due to the cultural background of both clubs they also enjoy nationwide support to the detriment of the other teams.

Celtic, like Hibernian from Edinburgh, were formed by central Scotland's large Catholic Irish immigrant population to represent them, often in the face of prejudice and racism from the indigenous Scottish Protestant population. Rangers, as a result, were always considered to be *the* quintessential Scottish establishment club representing the hard-working Protestant population. Thus the two teams became representative of the two sides in a bitterly divided Scottish workforce and this rivalry has continued throughout the history of the clubs. Nowadays both teams try to distance themselves publicly from the religious bigotry attached to their fans; in reality, however, both could surely have done more to address the problem. For instance, the two Edinburgh sides also had a degree of religious baggage attached to them – Hibs, as previously mentioned, represented the Irish immigrant population and Hearts the Protestant establishment – and even though Edinburgh was generally more racially integrated than Glasgow, the two rivals identified that there was a problem within their respective supports, especially during the troubles in Northern Ireland in the 1970s and 1980s, and both took action to deal with it. For instance, the flying of potentially inflammatory symbols, such as Irish Tricolours, the Ulster and Union flags, have been banned from Easter Road and Tynecastle and persons caught chanting sectarian songs are quickly ejected and banned from the stadium. Rangers and Celtic, despite their assurances that they wish to dissociate themselves from sectarianism, have failed even to take those relatively straightforward measures.

As previously indicated, at the turn of the twentieth century the working-class communities of Glasgow and indeed the whole of West Central Scotland were bitterly divided by religion. This, coupled with the high levels of violence that you would expect in the appalling slums that existed in Glasgow at the time, ensured that with football becoming the main pastime for the working classes, violence wouldn't be far behind. There are reports of crowd disorder in Glasgow from the 1890s all the way to the present day. Of course this wasn't uncommon in other parts of Britain and matches between city rivals elsewhere in the country also witnessed crowd disorder. However, some of the worst examples seemed to occur in Glasgow. For instance the *Mercury* newspaper reported a major riot that occurred after the 1909 Scottish Cup final at Hampden Park between the Old Firm. Fans armed with knives invaded the pitch, damaged the stadium, built barricades which they set on fire before attacking the fire brigade and the police in battles which raged for over two hours and resulted in police officers being stabbed.

This was obviously a particularly serious incident but the levels of violence in Scotland remained far higher than in England particularly in the period between the wars. Much of this can be attributed to the fact that there are a high number of clubs situated relatively closely together, but another key factor was the emergence of the Brake Clubs. These were the forerunner to supporters' clubs and were almost certainly the first instances of fans organising collective travel to away games. Many of those Brake Clubs' memberships were decided on religious backgrounds as well as footballing and this wasn't just a problem for the Old Firm, as the Edinburgh Brake Clubs had the same sectarianism.

Glasgow as a city has also obtained a great deal of notoriety due to the violent street gang culture that has existed for many years. Many of those gangs in the early days were formed on sectarian lines and the most famous of all, from a footballing context, were the Bridgeton Billy Boys. Formed in the mid 1920s, they took their name from their leader Billy Fullerton and according to legend could number in excess of 800 members for Orange Walks and Rangers matches. Ironically, the area of Bridgeton that the gang hailed from is very close to Celtic's Parkhead Stadium and many Celtic fans were attacked by the Billy Boys even when they weren't playing Rangers. This area is staunchly Protestant to this day and the recent murder of a young Celtic fan on his way home from a game shows that not a lot has changed in Glasgow in 70-odd years. The Rangers fans still even sing about the exploits of Billy Fullerton and his followers on a weekly basis to this day in the song –

> Hello Hello we are the Billy Boys,
> Hello Hello you'll know us by our noise,
> We're up to our knees in Fenian blood,
> Surrender or you'll die,
> For we are the Bridgeton Billy Boys.

The post-war period until the mid to late 1960s is generally accepted as being the golden age of British football. It was a time before rampant professionalism crept into the sport and when huge crowds turned up at matches and generally behaved well. After six years of war the population of Britain had had enough of fighting and it is because of this largely peaceful period that many ill-informed commentators describe football hooliganism as a modern-day problem when you can see that, in reality, spectator violence is as old as the sport itself. However, by the mid 1960s things were changing again.

The Mod movement had caught on among the youth of Britain and in many areas it had become very gang-based. Once again Glasgow in particular achieved a degree of notoriety here, and their Mod gangs became well known as the exotically named Fleets and Tongs (common gang names) clashed in the city and also at the football where pitched battles on the terraces of Rangers and Celtic became commonplace. Often, due to the gang influence, this trouble would be fans fighting among themselves but, with the increasing working-class affluence of the time, travelling supporters were becoming more prevalent.

Up until this time the Glasgow giants ruled the hooligan scene in Scotland as much as they ruled the league tables; however, other clubs were now beginning to catch up. As Rangers and Celtic supporters travelled in ever increasing numbers to other towns, the resistance was beginning to get stronger and it would eventually see other teams taking the fight to the Old Firm in their own back yard. As the 1970s began, Scottish football would enter into its most violent period. Not only was there heightened tension between Rangers and Celtic due to the troubles in Northern Ireland, but the emergence of large hooligan groups within other Scottish clubs – in particular Hearts and Dundee – together with the new fad for 'taking the opposition end', would plunge Scottish football into a depression that it has never really recovered from. The 1970s would become the era of the boot-boys.

As the Mod movement hung around in Scotland for much longer than in England, Skinheads didn't really appear on the Scottish terraces until about 1971 when they were already on the decline in England. Indeed they didn't last too long and by the end of 1972 the Scottish football thug would be turned out in bovver boots, flares, wing collar shirt, star jumper and long hair – a look which would last in much of Scotland until 1977 when Punk finally began to take over.

The craze for taking weapons to matches was also at its height in the 1970s and fans fought on the terraces armed with anything from knives to machetes and axes. Stab wounds were common in battles, in particular between Rangers and Celtic fans. If anything, the hatred between those two sets of fans was getting worse, although things did calm down a little after the Ibrox Stadium disaster of 1971 when many fans from both teams lost their lives when a staircase barrier collapsed. For a while that tragedy did seem to bring the football family in Glasgow a bit closer, but it wasn't for long and soon the fans were at war again.

Until now we have concentrated on Rangers and Celtic but, while their fans were a major problem throughout the 1970s and to a lesser extent into the 1980s, it is important to look more closely at other teams whose supporters were grabbing the headlines for the wrong reasons, namely Hearts fans in the 1970s and Aberdeen and Hibs supporters during the Casual era of the 1980s.

The Hearts team in the early 1970s was far removed from the entertaining and successful side of the 1950s and early 1960s, when both Hearts and Hibs ensured that for a brief period the power base in Scottish football moved east towards the capital. Hearts had suffered two blows in the mid to late 1960s when, on the last day of the 1964–65 season, they lost the championship to Kilmarnock by a goal-average difference of 0.042, and then in 1968 lost the Cup final to Dunfermline. These two events seemed to knock the stuffing out of Hearts, and team performances went into a steady decline which would take about 15 years to turn around.

The crowds dwindled as well and, in common with all other grounds in Scotland at that time, large empty spaces appeared on the terraces at Tynecastle while supporter discontent was at an all time high. Mirroring Glasgow's street gangs, Edinburgh – like most cities – also experienced a huge rise in gang culture in the 1970s, many of which had loose religious/football attachments. For instance, areas of Edinburgh were very much defined on a football basis and you wouldn't have found many Hearts fans in gangs such as the Young Lochend Shamrock and, likewise, Hibs supporters in the Young Clery Derry. Back then, street gangs from estates to the west of Edinburgh such as Clermiston, Wester Hailes, Sighthill, Broomhouse and Gorgie would have almost certainly been at war outside of a football context, but on the terraces they would have mostly put their rivalries aside to come together and fight for the club.

The key word there is *mostly*, as Hearts did gain a reputation for their fans fighting among themselves on occasions and this was solely down to rival gangs. Indeed, the book *Bring Out Your Riot Gear – Hearts Are Here* by C S Ferguson mentions rivalries between Edinburgh-based hooligans and Hearts supporters from the new overspill town of Livingston erupting into violence at Hearts games in the early 1980s.

At first the fledgling Hearts firm stuck to defending their home territory against the invaders of the Old Firm. Although there was, surprisingly, trouble with both Glasgow teams (when you take into account the Protestant background of many Hearts fans), the biggest battles, even more surprisingly, always occurred against Rangers. Their fans would get into the ground early and try to take the Hearts territory, a large open terrace at the Gorgie Road end of the ground and a covered terrace opposite the main stand. Hearts would normally be able to defend the Gorgie Road End but the battling under the Shed usually ended in stalemate until the end of the 1976–77 season when Hearts eventually managed to run Rangers all along the Shed in some of the most vicious fighting ever seen at Tynecastle. It was around that time that the Hearts support was at its peak and, despite the yo-yo performance of the team, with relegation followed by promotion then relegation again, it would be fair to say that Hearts had the most notorious fans from then until around 1982–83 when the new kids on the block from Aberdeen would take over.

However, it took years of chaos to reach the top and Hearts started taking the Gorgie Aggro on the road all the way through the 1970s, from Ayr United – when the Hearts fans charged across the pitch and chased the home support out of their end – to Aberdeen, where the supporters' buses would stay until midnight and the evening would be spent battling in the city centre. When Hearts visited my local team, the talk in school in the run-up to the match was all about the expected violence, and they were never disappointed. There seemed to be certain teams where Hearts would put on a show, and as well as the obvious targets of Hibs, Celtic and Rangers, some of the more provincial teams got it bad. There always seemed to be trouble, especially in the late 1960s and early 1970s when they visited St Johnstone, with their local Perth Pac gang, while games at Motherwell and Kilmarnock always seemed to descend into full-scale rioting all the way into the 1980s. One place where Hearts came unstuck a few times was in Dundee, mostly when the opposition was Dundee FC, who had a gang calling themselves The Hilltown Huns. Both the Dundee and Dundee United stadiums were situated close to the Hilltown area, which was a rough council estate. Dundee, like Hearts and Rangers, had a large loyalist element within their fan base and any team with a decent travelling support got a very warm welcome from the locals.

The city rivals, Hibs, were also doing a bit of damage on their travels, and when the two teams played each other the atmosphere was poisonous. Although Hibs in the 1970s weren't a match for Hearts (their time would come in the 1980s), they always put up a show when they played Hearts at home, with all the hardcases from the Leith area of Edinburgh turning out for them. There were numerous riots involving Hearts fans at Easter Road, the worst being during a game in the late 1970s when the Hearts hooligans, unable to get at their Hibs rivals due to police segregation, left the ground halfway through the second half and gained entrance into the home end when the gates were opened, scattering the Hibs Cave End terrace. As previously mentioned the atmosphere at the Edinburgh derbies at this time was hate-filled. As well as the violence in the grounds, both sets of fans had aligned themselves to the opposing paramilitary groups in Northern Ireland. It was like a mini Old Firm game with Union and Red Hand of Ulster flags commonplace in the Hearts end and Irish Tricolours in the Hibs end. It was a highly politicised era and the troubles in Ireland were at their peak, which was obviously rubbing off on the Edinburgh football fans.

Some of the best stories I've managed to trace about the Hearts support relate incidents which seemed to have occurred on visits to England in the Texaco/Anglo-Scottish Cup competition. A classic story appears in a book about Oldham Athletic fans called *We Are The Famous Football Hooligans* by Carl H Spiers, about Hearts' visit to Oldham in 1974 for a Texaco Cup match.

Oldham had a bit of a reputation back then and, from the mid 1960s to the early 1970s, they were one of the top mobs outside the English First Division. The Gorgie Boys had heard this and had taken quite a large travelling support down, many making a short holiday of it with a trip to Blackpool. The story begins with, 'We were drawn to play Hearts, a Scottish team. Surely there would be no trouble against them. How wrong I was to be; it was one of the most violent games ever at Boundary Park.' The passage describing the game then basically sums up what football violence and the Hearts support were like in the 1970s as it describes a mass battle raging in the home end of Oldham's ground for almost the whole match. Despite being heavily outnumbered and being up against one of the biggest mobs of boys that Oldham would ever pull together, Hearts managed to stay in their end for the entire game. The writer describes how many of the Hearts fans were tooled up with coshes and that it was even rumoured that one of the Hearts fans had a double-barrelled shotgun!

Another trip over the border took Hearts to Newcastle where they managed to stay on the Gallowgate terracing for the full 90 minutes despite the Geordies' best efforts to move them. However, things didn't always go in their favour and a group of Hearts fans had to escape onto the pitch when they tried to take the home end at Everton. They also took a hiding on the streets of Middlesbrough at a pre-season friendly in 1976.

For most of the 1970s the trouble at Hearts' away matches came from a few supporters' buses which had gained a certain reputation. Groups such as The Pivot and The Manor and slightly later and most notorious of all, The Gorgie Sons of William, were always in the thick of the trouble. This supports the image of Hearts being very much a collection of localised gangs who tended to keep themselves to themselves most of the time. It was also unusual – as it certainly *was* the trend elsewhere – for hooligan groups to travel by train. There were of course the football specials which were laid on for bigger matches, and the people who used them often caused trouble, but it wasn't really until the late 1970s that a proper firm appeared at Hearts who used the service train on a regular basis to travel away. This firm was called the Hearts Service Crew and were mainly Punks and the new wave of Skinheads that had surfaced at Hearts between 1977 and 1979. It was only with the arrival of the Casuals that large and organised groups of hooligans began travelling by service train. The Skinhead element among the Hearts support also obtained notoriety from a different source. As most of them were very pro-Loyalist it wasn't surprising that they would show support for the far-right and in particular the National Front. *Bulldog*, the newspaper of the party's youth wing, was openly sold outside the ground and the Hearts thugs, together with their Rangers counterparts, were often mentioned in a regular article called *On The Football Front*, which glamourised racist football hooligans.

For a last word on Hearts I have included below a short paragraph from the Hearts fanzine *No Idle Talk* which sums up the 1970s rather well.

In the mid to late 1970s nearly every game had some sort of violent scene, whether it was inside or outside the stadium. Chants of 'You're gonna get your fuckin' heads kicked in' were mandatory if there was any away support present. Of particular note was a trip to Dumfries for a match against Queen of the South in April 1978. We had a reputation and they knew we were coming, resulting in many Rangers scarves appearing in the crowd. A Hearts fan stabbed someone in the street and the violence carried on throughout the game. There are numerous occasions when a riot was narrowly avoided in games against Rangers. In April 1976 with us already relegated we spent the whole match chasing their fans along the Shed, the front line started off under the pie stall and ended up near the toilets. On another occasion at Ibrox with Hearts fans in the enclosure, their mob in the stand above started throwing anything they could get their hands on, down on us. This provoked an extremely violent reaction. Probably the best stadium battle was at Kilmarnock in 1978. A big crowd and little policing meant running battles on the terracing from start to finish. The best street battle I can remember was at Falkirk in either the 1981–82 or 1982–83 season and it lasted some considerable time after the match. Another major riot was at Clydebank on a Wednesday night as Hearts were going for promotion which they eventually lost on the last day of the season at home to Motherwell. This was a case of good prevailing over evil as the police took such a kicking that day that consequently until the Shed was demolished (1995–96) there was a lack of police presence among the fans.

The 1980 Scottish Cup final dragged Scottish football to its lowest ebb. The watching nation on TV witnessed a battle between hundreds of Rangers and Celtic fans on the Hampden pitch as bottles and cans rained down from the terracing. The introduction of mounted police was required to contain the fans. This was the SFA's showpiece of the season and it had been ruined by hooliganism of the worst kind. As well as the trouble, the most shocking part of the afternoon was the fact that people all over the world now knew that Scots were still, in 1980, tying scarves around their wrists and wearing flares! The nation's fashion police were in mourning and something had to change. To see what that something was you have to travel up to the Granite City of Aberdeen.

Aberdeen had always had more than a few guys who were prepared to mix it in the 1970s but by their own admission they used to be turned over by the Old Firm. However, in 1980 the team were doing the business on the park, crowds were up and among their number was a new breed of fans who were no longer willing to tolerate this invasion of their town. The fans were also travelling to the club's European away games and, after a match against Liverpool at Anfield, the Aberdeen hooligans had their first experience of the style and fashion of their English counterparts. Shortly afterwards was born one of the most notorious gangs in the history of football hooliganism in Scotland: the Aberdeen Soccer Casuals (ASC).

Just as the terraces of Tynecastle had been home to Skinheads and Punks, Aberdeen's Pittodrie Stadium became home to youths sporting wedge haircuts, Slazenger and Pringle jerseys, Lois jeans or cords, Adidas windcheater jackets and smart Adidas trainers. It was like a continuation of the Mod movement of the 1960s and was far closer to the original ideals of this movement than the 1979 revival was. Fashions were constantly changing and one-upmanship ruled supreme. The competition between firms of dressers was as fierce when it came to fashion as it was when it came to fists. In the absence of any competition on the clothes angle in Scotland the Aberdeen fans took part in the war of words that raged on the letters pages of *The Face* and *Sounds* music papers, as Casuals from all across Britain tried to outdo each other in the fashion stakes.

As this competition hotted up, more expensive brands came in. Designer sportswear is what the Casuals are best remembered for, and the labels more commonly found on Centre Court at Wimbledon such as Fila, Ellesse and Sergio Tachinni became essentials – these would later be replaced by top designer-house makes such as Burberry,

Armani, Aquascutum, Stone Island, etc. Of course, when you were wearing hundreds of pounds' worth of gear you wanted to show it off a little, and the ASC began travelling to away games on service trains to avoid being marched directly to the grounds when they arrived in the host towns or cities. This play allowed them time and space to put on a bit of a show for the local lads.

It was also a useful way of avoiding detection by the ever more effective policing of football. The police watched supporters' buses and football specials, not service trains. They were also looking for Skinheads decked out in their clubs' colours, whereas Casuals cast aside the traditional dress code of football fans as no one wore anything identifiable with the team. This caused a few problems at other clubs with already established hooligan cultures (mainly Hearts, Celtic and, to a lesser extent, Rangers), as it was thought that not wearing your team's colours was nothing less than an act of cowardice.

However, the lack of similarly dressed opposition at the time didn't stop the ASC building up a reputation for themselves. After all there were plenty of Skinheads who were more than happy to indulge in a bit of toe to toe with those strangely dressed men from the North. But, in 1983, another Casual mob finally appeared on the scene. And it came from a totally unexpected team.

Motherwell has always been known as a rough town, but due to its close proximity to Glasgow many of the town's hooligans did their fighting at Ibrox or Parkhead. As a result the local side never really had much of a firm. That was until the Saturday Service appeared on the scene bedecked in Italian designer sportswear. A rivalry quickly developed between the self-proclaimed (but at the time, more than accurate) 'best dressed in the west' and the ASC, that would result in a number of confrontations between the two mobs. The main incident was in February 1984 when the ASC entered the Motherwell end of the ground on a visit to Fir Park. The resulting trouble ended up with the Motherwell Casuals being chased onto the pitch as other gangs of ASC fought with police in the Aberdeen end. The game was halted for about ten minutes and the resultant media hysteria saw to it that the Casuals were front page news all across Scotland. It also sent shock waves through the clubs and Motherwell FC even went so far as to ban fans wearing sportswear such as Kappa Kagoules from their ground – a story which was carried by the Scottish *Sunday Mail*.

By the end of the 1983–84 season small groups of Casuals were appearing at other clubs and these would grow in number throughout the 1984–85 season. Dundee and Dundee United hooligans formed a joint mob called The Utility, Rangers had the Inter City Firm (ICF) – named after the legendary West Ham firm – Celtic had the Roman Catholic Casuals who would soon become the Celtic Soccer Crew, Hearts had the Casual Soccer Firm (CSF) and Hibernian fans formed the Capital City Service (CCS). The latter would rise during the 1984–85 season to become the main challenger to Aberdeen for the Casual crown in Scotland and, depending on who you believe, some would claim that the Hibs firm did rule the roost in Scotland in the latter part of the 1980s. As well as those main firms most of the smaller teams had a few Casuals following them as well. A few examples were the Arbroath Soccer Society, the Montrose Soccer Unit – soon to become Portland Bill's Seaside Trendies – St Mirren's Love Street Division (LSD) and Airdrie's notorious Section B, which was originally a Punk/ Skinhead firm in the late 1970s but had gone Casual by 1985. Even lowly Meadowbank Thistle had the Thistle Soccer Boys (TSB) who numbered about 15 maximum, all in their mid to late teens. They had their moment of glory away at Hamilton one Sunday when they stood their ground against their Hamilton counterparts.

The first real problems for the Casuals came during the 1984–85 season when the ASC had 47 members arrested for trying to ambush visiting Motherwell Casuals. These arrests, some of which were for planning the violence, sent the media into a frenzy as for years they had painted football hooligans as mindless morons who'd have trouble writing their names. Now they were confronted with smartly dressed, generally inoffensive looking youths who were capable of organising things such as an ambush of visiting fans. Soon they had journalists travelling with the firms to try to get even juicier stories and the *Sunday Post* did a feature on a visit by the ASC to Celtic, which was written in the required sensationalist style.

As previously mentioned, the CCS at Hibs would soon become the ASC's main rival and would replace the Saturday Service at Motherwell as Aberdeen's main target. One of the two groups' first confrontations involved the ASC travelling in numbers to Easter Road and, during fighting before the match, a young Hibs fan was given a severe beating and he almost lost his life. Interestingly, in Jay Allan's excellent book, *Bloody Casuals*, he confirms the relief that the ASC felt at the news that the Hibs fan made a full recovery as no one wanted to see fatalities due to football violence. However, it didn't stop them producing newsletters to wind Hibs up about the incident.

The growth of the Hibs firm came out of the blue for people who had an interest in the Scottish football scene at the time. Although they had always had a fairly useful fan base (and a pre-Casuals organised train firm called the Inter City Fleet), Hearts had a larger and far more active hooligan support and many had suspected that they, rather than Hibs, would have provided the main Casual firm from Edinburgh. One reason put forward for this not happening is the fact that the early Hearts

Casuals faced a lot of physical opposition from the existing hooligan groupings at the club – a fate also suffered by the Casuals at Celtic. As a result neither club was able to compete with Aberdeen and Hibs when football violence in Scotland came to be the sole preserve of the Casuals. In fact, many hooligans who were Hearts supporters and wanted to adopt the new styles started turning up at Easter Road, quickly swelling the ranks of the CCS. As word got round the Edinburgh estates about this, more and more people followed suit and the CCS soon became a real force.

Hibs also had a reputation for taking things to extremes. In the mid 1980s they threw a petrol bomb at visiting Aberdeen Casuals in Edinburgh's main shopping street at 5.30 p.m. on a Saturday. A few years later they attacked a nightclub in Dunfermline armed, allegedly, with axes and machetes. They also conducted a campaign of terror on rival Hearts Casuals in Edinburgh 24 hours a day, seven days a week. The level of violence in those incidents often turned Edinburgh city centre into a war zone on a Saturday evening as running battles were fought and pubs attacked and smashed up. The CCS was a full-time occupation for its members.

The Hibs lads also gained a reputation for themselves in England after they ran riot at various friendlies in England. Oldham, Aston Villa and, more impressively, Millwall were all put on the back foot when they were confronted by the CCS. The game at The Den was played prior to the 1990–91 season on a Friday night, and despite police attempts to stop them travelling – which involved cancelling bookings with coach companies – the CCS turned up on the Old Kent Road with around 150 lads. Hyped up they ran amok, attacking a couple of Millwall pubs along the way. A small firm of Millwall emerged from the Crown & Anchor to confront them but came out of the encounter second best. Interestingly, Millwall have always contested Hibs' claim that they were turned over, arguing that they didn't know the CCS were going to show and therefore they didn't have a firm out. However, that is hardly Hibs' fault. They showed, took liberties, and Millwall have only themselves to blame. The CCS reputation was further enhanced with a couple of riotous European trips to Anderlecht and FC Liège in the UEFA Cup which once again grabbed the headlines in the Scottish media.

Although the Casual movement continues to exist – in Scotland, after it reached its height during the 1984– 85 and 1985–86 seasons, it went into a slow but steady decline. The heavy policing and strict sentencing put many off while others simply lost interest. Changing fashions also had an impact as many lads turned towards the club scene, which was growing under the influence of Hip-Hop and House music from America. Clubs such as The Tunnel in Glasgow and The Hooch in Edinburgh became popular with Casuals. And while many would continue to combine both the football and clubbing, others would leave the football behind to concentrate fully on Ecstasy abuse. Of course the new club-and-drug scene was ripe for exploitation and there is little doubt that some football lads got involved in that. It was rumoured that a few of the CCS were more than willing to use their muscle on Edinburgh's underworld although it is important to point out that not all the Hibs lads were happy about that direction.

The clothes aspect which had always been an integral part of the Casual movement also stagnated during the 1990s. Whereas previously there had been a great deal of one-upmanship with the fast moving fashions, the current labels have come to resemble a football lad's uniform: Stone Island, Burberry, Aquascutum and Adidas Old Skool trainers seem to be the standard look year in and year out – a look blighted by the English 'chair throwers' of Charleroi and light-years away from the original style-obsessives. Similarly, in the old days, getting hold of the relevant clothes was often incredibly difficult as there were very few outlets stocking designer fashions and hardly any more people wearing them. Your average Saturday night crowd were still dressed in Burton's latest range, so when you walked into your local disco pub, resplendent in your new Tachinni top, Lois cords, Diadora trainers, jewellery and wedge haircut, you stood out from the crowd. Nowadays every wannabe drug-dealer from Torry, Dennistoun, Hilltown or Leith is kitted out in Stone Island and the obligatory Burberry baseball cap. Who in their right mind would want to be associated with that?

Although the rivalry between the ASC and CCS is intense, the two firms have always had a mutual respect for each other and, with the possible exception of the ICF at Rangers in the latter part of the 1980s, regard themselves as the only two decent firms in Scotland. The rest they felt were a waste of time. It was therefore only natural that the other Scottish gangs would look to the big two to lead any national firm when Scotland had a potentially troublesome fixture. More often than not, this meant games against England for, despite the friendly Tartan Army image, there has always been trouble with their near neighbours and it was only natural that the Casuals would want some of that. I can remember small groups of Hibs and Aberdeen Casuals largely operating separately from each other at Auld Enemy matches both at Hampden and Wembley in the early/mid 1980s. However, it was at the last two matches between the nations in the 1980s, where Hibs and Aberdeen fought alongside each other and actually did very well. This alliance was more noticeable when Scots Casuals travelled in numbers for a fixture against Holland in Utrecht as mentioned earlier. Trouble erupted with rival Dutch thugs, with Scotland getting the upper hand, resulting in over 50 Scottish lads being arrested.

Other firms were also present in Holland, such as Dundee and Airdrie – albeit in small numbers – and the alliance was repeated at Euro 96 for the England–Scotland match. The media coverage in the run up to the tournament was all about how hooligans from Germany, Italy, Holland etc. were coming over to teach the English a lesson. Not surprisingly none of them showed and it was left to the Scots to prove once again that they are the only hooligans who always turn out against England. Scotland's firm was around 300–350 strong and, although they were pulled from a variety of clubs, inevitably Aberdeen contributed the biggest numbers. Trafalgar Square became the focus for the fighting, which involved running battles with both the police and English hooligans. A Scots mob of around 200 strong also attacked a pub full of English thugs in Leicester Square before the game.

In the aftermath of Euro 96 and with the police now very much in control of the domestic football scene in Scotland, some faces from Hibs, Hearts and Rangers tried to form a Scottish National Firm (SNF). The idea was to turn up unexpectedly at English league games and also to follow the national side abroad. However, despite showing at both Manchester City and Middlesbrough – where they were involved in disturbances with both sets of fans – it must be stressed that not everyone was happy with the idea. Indeed, the resulting arguments at Hibs split the CCS in two and, when the SNF tried to recruit the ASC, they were turned down flat – a move that resulted in a great deal of friction between the two groups, culminating in violence after Aberdeen played a cup match at Tynecastle. The fact that a number of ordinary Aberdeen fans were injured in the fighting made matters even worse and things got so bad that during the France

98 World Cup the ASC and the SNF called it on for Bordeaux prior to the Scotland–Norway match. However, the SNF never made it. For, having travelled via Spain, a joint operation involving Scottish, Spanish and French police saw 50 of them stopped in a coach en route to the meeting. After returning to the Spanish resort of Salou, the SNF were involved in a series of disturbances with the locals and were subsequently thrown out of Spain. Their return to Scotland made the front pages of the tabloids.

Towards the end of the 1990s and the beginning of the new millennium there were very few incidents to report. Even the ASC had quietened down and were picking and choosing their games. There were some battles prior to a pre-season match against Everton at Pittodrie and the ASC also travelled to away friendlies at Rotherham (where they clashed with the Blades Business Crew of Sheffield United in Sheffield city centre) and Hartlepool where they fought with rival fans inside the ground. A visit to Kilmarnock for the last match of the season in 1997 also saw a violent day as 70 ASC attacked a pub used by the Kilmarnock firm and also fought with police. Further trouble flared in Glasgow as the ASC were on their way home with Rangers fans returning from an away match at Hearts.

Recently it would be fair to say that a certain rivalry has developed between the ASC and Rangers ICF. After a few smaller scale incidents this boiled over early in 2002 during a live televised match. When Rangers fans threw coins onto the pitch injuring an Aberdeen player, the ASC spilled onto the pitch and charged up the touchline towards the ICF situated in the Rangers end. The fact that it was broadcast live on television ensured that once again the media reaction was extreme and – alongside outbreaks of trouble between Hearts and Celtic fans, Rangers fans in Bradford, Airdrie and Motherwell supporters, and also Airdrie fans at Ayr United – prompted hysterical headlines about a return to the dark days of football violence. However, the reality is much different. When the Casuals began, it was a movement made up of teenagers. Nowadays there is no interest among teenagers to fight at football and so the people who are getting involved are mainly men in their mid 30s – the same men in fact who grew up with the Casual era. As a result, eventually the incidents will become fewer although I don't think that they will ever die out completely. Football by its very nature brings out tribal instincts which always carry the likelihood of spilling over into violence.

But while the future is uncertain, the past remains as a testimony to the passion of Scottish football and particularly its supporters. These supporters are much more than a media-friendly Tartan Army or groups of religious bigots, but are instead a part of a culture which has a long history of its own, which might yet be added to.

CHAPTER FOUR
France

It would be reasonable to expect that France, as one of the largest countries in Europe, would have a sizeable hooligan problem, but in fact the opposite is true. Incidents involving French clubs are relatively rare and certainly nothing like on the scale of near neighbours Holland, Germany or Belgium.

The reason, quite simply, is that France is not a footballing nation. No city, including Paris, is home to more than one major team and attendances at games are, on average, a third of their equivalents in Italy, England and Spain. The French have always thought of attending games as a leisure activity rather than a way of life.

That is not to say that the country hasn't got a football culture, it has. It just hasn't got one in which violence is a major element. Where hooliganism does exist, the numbers involved are relatively small and often politically motivated. Indeed, of all the French clubs, only Paris Saint Germain (PSG) have a group which could be considered comparable to some of the larger more well known mobs across Europe.

It was not always thus. In the 1970s and early 1980s, French football was the domain of the Skinhead culture, and at times that was very violent indeed. One of the most well known examples of this occurred in 1984 when England – at the time home to the most notorious hooligans in Europe – travelled to Paris and were met by a combined force of skins from a number of French clubs. In the event, and not entirely unexpectedly, the French came off second best but they certainly made their point.

However, just as it looked as if hooliganism was about to explode in France, the nation's terraces experienced a huge sea-change out of which developed not one, but two specific cultures.

The reason, in part, was the demise of Skinhead and the growth of Casual. Over a relatively short period, fans of clubs situated in the north of France began to adopt the English style of supporting and this developed into what became known as the Kops culture (at PSG for example, the most prominent group was the Kop of Boulogne).

In the south, however, supporters began looking towards Italy and the Ultra. Groups such as Ultras Marseille and Brigade Sud (Nice) quickly embraced the theatrics of the Italian terraces with one significant difference. From the outset, the French Ultras' attitude towards rivalry revolved not around aggression, but creativity. For them, it was all about who could stage the biggest and best displays rather than how much grief they could give each other.

As time passed, this approach began to attract supporters from the north and has now reached the point where almost every French club has groups that have moved away from the almost subversive Casual culture towards this more proactive, visual and less aggressive style.

For many, one of the attractions of the Ultra groups is the fact that they are relatively well organised. Not only do the majority of them have well defined links with their clubs, but they also have a structure within the group that will include such positions as a president and a treasurer. Equally, they will often take a week to prepare what they are going to do during a match which, for the individual members of groups such as the Boulogne Boys (PSG), Magic Fans (St. Etienne) and Ultramarines (Bordeaux), adds a whole new dimension to the football experience and their involvement within it.

Yet despite the growth and success of the largely non-aggressive Ultra movement, there are still a number of hooligan groups in France some of whom are more than capable of taking on all-comers. The most famous of these are to be found on the Kop of Boulogne stand watching PSG.

The reputation of the PSG hooligans is long, and well deserved. Domestically, they have been at the top for many years, while on the international stage, Juventus (1989 and 1993), Anderlecht (1992), Arsenal (1994), Bayern Munich (1994), Liverpool (1997) and Glasgow Rangers (2001) have all had first-hand experience of their capabilities. These incidents aside, two episodes in particular show how powerful and dangerous they can be if the circumstances are right.

The first happened in 1993 when Caen, a club with no real history of either Ultra or hooligan behaviour, came to Paris. With the upper terrace of the Kop under development at the time, the PSG fans had gathered on the lower tier when, from among their number, a shoe was thrown onto the pitch. Almost immediately, the owner jumped onto the pitch, retrieved it and then climbed back in among the home support.

Within a minute or so, the CRS [the French riot police] appeared and moved onto the terrace to arrest the individual concerned. However, the fans weren't so willing to let one of their own be taken out and started to put up some resistance. Almost immediately, the struggle escalated and, within a few minutes, had deteriorated to the stage where the CRS were forced to fire tear gas in order to facilitate their retreat from well over 250 battling hooligans.

The problem was that the hooligans managed to keep hold of three members of the CRS who were badly beaten before being released. At this point the PSG fans rioted and drove the CRS out of the stadium entirely.

Unfortunately for French football, the incident was filmed and the pictures broadcast across Europe. But, for the PSG hooligans, it was a huge result and one that enhanced their burgeoning reputation as a group able to raise significant numbers at a moment's notice.

The second incident of note occurred on 13 March 2001 and, like the first, happened in Paris. However, this one had far more sinister overtones.

Like many hooligan and Ultra communities across Europe, French supporters had been outraged by the murder of the two Leeds United fans in Istanbul. This was especially true at clubs with strong nationalist elements among their support of which PSG is one. As a result, less than a year later when Galatasaray and their army of fans – including many who were actually resident in France – headed for the French capital for a Champions League tie, they were met by in excess of 200 Parisian hooligans intent on extracting some kind of revenge.

From early afternoon, the mob hunted down and attacked anything even remotely linked to Turkey, including individuals, vehicles and property. This witch-hunt continued until kick-off time approached when the mob headed for the stadium.

With the police seemingly unable to control them, they forced their way through a roadblock and into the ground where almost every section experienced sporadic outbreaks of violence and missile throwing. However, as the second half started, things got even worse when the Turkish fans tried to steal a PSG banner from supporters on the Auteuil terrace.

Almost immediately, PSG surged towards the police lines which were keeping the two sets of fans apart. After a major battle, 100 of them managed to fight their way through, and set about attacking the visiting supporters.

At the same time as this was going on, PSG fans at the other end of the ground, having seen what their comrades in the Kop were doing, tore down a fence and invaded a second section full of Turkish supporters. This resulted in yet more violent assaults and a number of the visiting fans being forced to jump onto the pitch to escape.

It was an horrific incident and received a great deal of media coverage across Europe. It also added yet another chapter to an already bad reputation.

Strangely, for a nation as fiercely patriotic as France, the national team have rarely had any kind of hooligan following attached to it. There have, however, been attempts at starting a national firm, most notably against England in 1984 – as mentioned above – and in 1992 when a group led by the PSG hooligans fought with Belgian fans prior to an international fixture between the two nations. But it is fair to say that even during the build-up to the 1998 World Cup, and certainly since, the French hooligan and Ultra scene has remained largely apathetic towards the national side. Even the violence that took place in Marseille involving England fans was largely orchestrated by Tunisians protesting against the French police – and, in a few instances, reaction to some racist abuse from the English support. The only French hooligans involved were a relatively small number from Marseille.

Instead, support for the national team has become the domain of the totally non-threatening Les Bleus culture. They were present in their thousands in Japan and Korea and, with the French team seemingly recovered from their Far East humiliation, that looks set to continue right through to Portugal 2004 and beyond.

CHAPTER FIVE
Belgium

Like the majority of countries in Europe with serious hooligan problems, Belgium found that it was only during the early 1980s that the phenomenon began to have a significant impact on its football culture.

While this was fairly typical of football across Europe at that time, what is almost unique about Belgium is that as a result of its landlocked position and the involvement of its various clubs in European competition, the nation's hooligans began to draw inspiration not simply from the more traditional scenes in England and Italy, but also from those of its near neighbours, Germany and Holland. One of the more interesting consequences of this was that as groups began adopting names, alongside the more traditional tag of 'firm' (as for example the East-Side Firm at FC Brugge) other groups used 'side' – Hell-Side of Standard Liège being one of the first.

Despite this burgeoning culture, the Belgian media remained largely apathetic to what was going on as, to a certain extent, did the police, who rarely provided anything other than token security at games and certainly nothing by way of segregation inside grounds. This changed dramatically on 29 May 1985 when 39 football fans died at Heysel.

The impact of Heysel on Belgian football was immense, primarily because of the condemnation heaped upon the authorities by the world's media. Almost immediately, the country woke up to what had been going on and, as a consequence, the police began to go on the offensive. The number of officers employed at games increased dramatically – for one international fixture against Scotland, 600 police were on hand to monitor just 300 Scottish fans – while escorts to and from train stations became the norm. More importantly, segregation became compulsory as did the searching of fans entering grounds, while the photographing and filming of supporters became routine.

By 1987, the aftershocks of the tragedy had lessened but the grip the police were exerting on the activities of the hooligans continued to strengthen. The consequence of this was that the Belgian hooligan scene was forced to become more organised and more cunning. They had realised quite early that the only way they were going to be able to avoid the attentions of the police was to travel in small numbers and independently of the non-violent fans. That meant that they invariably travelled to games in cars rather than on buses or trains – something which also enabled them to disperse quickly and easily after incidents. At the same time, to avoid drawing attention to themselves on their travels, they began discarding the traditional club colours and instead adopted a more English-style approach to their clothing. A move that eventually led to the formation of groups such as the Brugge Casual Firm (FC Brugge) and K4 Casuals (Anderlecht).

Of equal importance to the still-emerging Belgian scene was the continuing ban on English clubs from European competitions. For, as a result, the influence of the Dutch scene became even greater, which led to various alliances being formed between hooligan groups, among which were Den Haag and FC Brugge, Anderlecht with Ajax and Antwerp with Feyenoord.

In the late 1980s, the Belgian scene experienced a

notable period of expansion. Up to that point, the vast majority of incidents had involved just four clubs: FC Brugge, Antwerp, Anderlecht and Standard Liège. Now, hooligans at various clubs, including Charleroi, Beerschot and RWDM, began making an impact. Equally, a number of hooligans, primarily from Antwerp and Standard Liège, began following the national side.

One of their first significant appearances was in Germany in 1991 when two coachloads appeared in Hanover and became involved in a serious disturbance outside the ground. So shocked were the Germans that when the return fixture came around, three train-loads of hooligans headed for Belgium and, despite having been tailed by the police, were allowed to enter Brussels. The sheer scale of the invasion was such a shock to the Belgians that very few of them were willing to take a stand and so the Germans turned their attention to the police with the result that over 800 German fans were arrested.

Bizarrely, despite their continuing efforts at combating hooliganism on the ground, at this point the Belgian police still had little in the way of legislation to deal with the people arrested. Often, those detained would remain in jail for a few hours, while stadium bans were still unheard of. This only began to change towards the end of the 1990s when the joint bid with Holland for Euro 2000 was successful. In an effort to send a message to both the hooligans and UEFA, the number of officers involved at high-risk games was increased by 30 per cent while CCTV was installed at all of the top-flight stadiums. Alongside this, clubs began compiling blacklists of known troublemakers and banning them from stadiums. However, as it did in England, this simply forced the hooligans to take their battles out of the grounds with the result that trouble in town and city centres increased markedly on match days.

Interestingly, in an effort to ease the tension that existed between the security forces and the hooligans, the police adopted a new tactic and tried to forge direct contact with the leaders of all of the known groups. It had little or no effect. Instead, things got so bad that in September 1999 a single weekend saw three top-flight fixtures, including the clash between Anderlecht and FC Brugge, cancelled because of fears of crowd trouble.

The consequence of this was that by the time the tournament came around, the Belgian police had decided that the only tactic that they dare employ was one of almost zero tolerance. During the build-up, various groups were hit with dawn raids and the police made it clear that if anyone stepped out of line during the summer months, they would be dealt with quickly and severely – something England fans who were in Brussels and Charleroi will readily testify to. With the exception of major incidents at these last two venues, it was a tactic that was largely successful although it attracted a huge amount of condemnation from among the football community, particularly in England.

Since Euro 2000, the Belgian scene has continued to cause problems for the authorities on a regular basis. As recently as April 2002, police foiled a planned clash between hundreds of hooligans from Antwerp and Beerschot on an industrial estate car park the night before the two teams were due to meet. Furthermore, in October 2002 a Champions League tie between FC Brugge and Galatasaray ended in violence in the city centre despite it being policed by 800 officers and two helicopters.

So concerned are the authorities about this type of confrontation that the Belgian parliament recently passed a law which means that anyone arrested within five kilometres of a stadium on a match day will be considered a hooligan and dealt with accordingly.

For the hooligan groups this simply adds to the attraction of the game, as it does in every other country that is home to a similar problem. There is, however, one aspect of the scene in Belgium that is, as far as I know, unique. They apparently have a social conscience.

The first incidence of this occurred at Standard Liège where the Hell-Side organised a collection among the fans to raise funds for Kosovan refugees. However, in March 2002, the Kiels Hools gang from Beerschot went one further when they organised a pub quiz-night to raise funds for the son of a supporter who had contracted cancer.

The teams, who were all specially invited from Belgian mobs at clubs including Antwerp, FC Brugge and Groningen, answered questions on hooligan history based on the Kiels Hools' extensive archive of related books and videos collected from across Europe.

Despite police fears, the event passed by without any hint of trouble, while the first prize, a framed picture of hooligans from Poland and England fighting in Warsaw, was won by a team of lads from Antwerp. Over £10,000 was raised.

CHAPTER SIX
Holland

M ention Dutch football and the first thing that will spring to many people's minds is Orange. Whenever the Dutch national side play, the colour is simply everywhere and, together with a sense of carnival, has come to symbolise the Dutch game and its fans. Indeed, it is fair to say that a number of nations look enviously at what the Dutch have done and wish they could replicate it in some way.

The practice supposedly began back in the early 1980s when fans started wearing bomber jackets inside out to celebrate their national colour. But however it started, following the defeat of the USSR in the final of Euro 88, the practice quickly spread until it got to the stage where the fans at tournaments would actually adopt a theme to reflect the host nation. USA 94 saw them wearing Indian tribal headgear or hats made to look like the Statue of Liberty while for France 98, it was the Eiffel Tower. All in bright orange of course and all designed to raise a smile. During Euro 2000, a tournament co-hosted by Holland and Belgium, the entire Dutch nation caught the bug. Houses, cars, dogs and even an entire herd of cattle were painted in the national colour, while in Rotterdam the fountains even gushed water dyed orange for the duration. If the Dutch know one thing, it's how to enjoy themselves.

However, this image hides a few simple truths about Dutch football. For as anyone who knows anything about hooliganism will be well aware, Holland is home to some of the most fanatical and violent football supporters in Europe. And the only reason why the international stage has not witnessed them in action is quite simply because the groups at the various clubs hate each other too much to set their differences aside. The one exception to that is games against Germany and German teams which, for fairly obvious historical reasons, have seen serious trouble in the past involving mainly groups from Feyenoord, Den Haag and Groningen. The domestic scene, however, is a different thing entirely.

Like many European nations, violence really only began to impact on the Dutch game in the early 1970s. Key to this was the evolution of the 'sides' – groups of lads who took their names from the section of the ground where they stood and watched games. Although at that time more of an irritation than a problem, mobs such as F-Side (Ajax) and North-Side (Den Haag) sprang up all over Holland. Initially, the violence that did occur was directed at players and officials, but in 1974 their activities took on a whole new meaning.

The catalyst was the second leg of the UEFA Cup final. Tottenham Hotspur travelled to Feyenoord and left the next day with their fans having rampaged through Rotterdam. With over 70 arrested and almost 200 injured – including a large number who had been stabbed – the Dutch media were outraged, but for the 'sides' it was an introduction to a whole new scene. Almost immediately, hooligan groups began appearing at clubs across the country and violence between them was most definitely on the agenda.

Inevitably, some clubs were worse than others, but it is widely acknowledged that the most violent at that time were Bunnik-Side of Utrecht. So bad did their reputation become that the mayor of Bunnik actually asked the club to change the name of that section of the ground. The club refused, much to the delight of the fans who by now were routinely fighting rival gangs with weapons including hammers, clubs and knives.

Incredibly, despite this violence, the Dutch FA still refused to take the problem of hooliganism seriously. Security at games was minimal while segregation was all but unheard of. That was to change on 24 October 1976 when the TV channel NOS broadcast the first pictures of a riot inside a Dutch football ground. Not surprisingly, Bunnik-Side were involved.

Having travelled to Amsterdam for a game against Ajax, the group entered the De Meer stadium and, having seen the TV cameras, realised that they were being handed an opportunity to give their already bad reputation a huge boost. As the players came out for the match, some of the group ran onto the pitch and headed towards the F-Side. In many respects, this in itself was a first as no one had ever invaded the De Meer pitch before, but with only a few police present – none of whom seemed to know what to do (so they simply did nothing) – the Utrecht fans were soon joined by a small number of F-Siders. The subsequent fighting was actually quite humorous. In one bizarre incident, an Ajax fan waving a bicycle chain around his head crashed into the Ajax keeper Heinz Stuy who angrily held out his hand and demanded that he hand over the weapon. Suitably chastened, the fan handed it over. Indeed, it was the intervention of the Ajax players that actually resolved the problem as they screamed at the fans to get off the pitch so that they could get on with the game.

The following day, the trouble made front-page news across Holland. There were even questions asked in the Dutch parliament who, for the first time, began to take the matter seriously. For the fans, however, whom the media had labelled 'a disgrace to Holland', this would simply prove to be the start.

By the 1980s, the Dutch game had witnessed a massive upsurge in violence in and around its stadiums. Damage to property and assaults on innocent members of the public were routine as were attacks on the police. In 1986, the authorities realised that something had to be done and established the Centraal Informatiepunt Voetbal Vandalisme to take action against the hooligans. Many were blacklisted and given stadium bans, but the effect was negligible. Not even the increased use of segregation inside grounds calmed the situation as the fans simply took to hurling missiles and flares at each other. In one incredible incident in 1987, a fragmentation bomb was thrown onto the pitch during an international fixture against Cyprus, while in 1989 Ajax received a one-year ban from European competition because an iron bar was thrown at the keeper of Austria Wien.

It is fair to say that the problems surrounding Dutch football could fill a book of their own and to document them here would merely skim the surface as well as serve little purpose. There are, however, two specific incidents which do need to be examined because, not only do they illustrate just how bad things have become in Holland, they also highlight just how difficult a job the police face as they try to combat the hooligan threat. The fact that neither incident happened anywhere near a football stadium makes them all the more astonishing.

Although both are entirely different, they do have one thing in common: they both involve Ajax and Feyenoord. To say that these two clubs are rivals is an understatement of unimaginable proportions. These two clubs hate each other with a passion that few football fans outside Holland can really understand.

As with most rivalries of this ferocity, there is much more to it than simply football. There is also an element of identity best illustrated in the contrast between the two cities. Rotterdam is very much an industrial metropolis with a tough, working-class population while Amsterdam is both a beautiful place and a cultural delight.

On the terraces, the mutual hatred had been festering for years. But as the police finally began to make some headway in combating potential problems inside grounds, the two groups – in common with all of the other Dutch football gangs – simply took their activities outside with, it must be said, a great deal of success. Key to this was the arrival of that modern-day phenomenon, the mobile phone. Suddenly, the groups were able to plan fights well in advance and change venues at a moment's notice. This led to huge problems for the police who were now all but powerless to prevent confrontations and were, instead, forced to resort to being simply reactive. However, no one could predict where the next major confrontation between the two groups would take place.

Concerned at the rising tide of violence in and around football grounds, a Dutch TV show, *Lief en Leed* (Love and Sorrow) decided to try to get to the root of the problem by staging a live studio debate. It invited various politicians to take part as well as a selection of fans from Utrecht, Ajax and Feyenoord. However, the Ajax fans refused to take part, claiming that they had nothing to say to people who they regarded as the scum of the earth. In response, the Utrecht and Feyenoord fans made it clear that they were the top boys in Holland anyway so what could the Ajax fans possibly have to say that would be of any value!

The show was to be broadcast on 28 May 1995 and, as the guests arrived at the studios in Hilversum, what they didn't know was that hurtling towards them in a convoy of cars was a group of F-Side, many of whom were wearing balaclavas and some of whom were carrying guns.

As the guests readied themselves for the broadcast, the Ajax fans steamed through the gate and after initially entering the wrong studio, burst through a second set of doors and found themselves in a large room dominated by a soundproof glass window on the other side of which was the studio filled with their arch-rivals. Immediately, they realised that the window was darkened meaning that while the F-Side could see into the studio, no one on the other side could see them.

Concerned that the police would be there any second, the group simply shot the window through, spraying the guests with glass and debris and leaving an astonished group of Feyenoord and Utrecht fans staring down various barrels held by masked gunmen. After what seemed an age, the Ajax fans, having made their point, turned and ran. None was ever caught.

The watching public, completely unaware of events, were treated to a blank screen and then a re-run of an Oprah Winfrey show.

Not surprisingly, things got much worse after that, and tensions were heightened in 1996 with the release of a book called *Hand in Hand*. Written by Dutch journalist Paul van Gageldonk, it documented two years spent shadowing Feyenoord's hooligans. Ajax fans – in particular the F-Side – were outraged. They accused Van Gageldonk of portraying them as being an inferior firm and promised not only to increase the severity of their attacks on Feyenoord, but to deal with him as well. Some even christened him 'Fatwah' and advised the journalist to get in touch with Salman Rushdie and ask him for advice on hiding.

The problem was that in almost every meeting between the two groups Ajax were outnumbered and all too often came off worst. One of the most serious examples occurred on 16 February 1997 when 50 F-Siders found themselves having to back off from 300 Feyenoord hooligans during a pre-arranged fight on the Amsterdam ring road. But if people thought that things were already bad, they were about to get a whole lot worse.

On Sunday 23 March 1997, Dutch football reached its lowest ebb when 35-year-old Ajax fan Carlo Picornie was beaten to death in a field just outside the small town of Beverwijk.

The events that led up to this murder are nothing short of astonishing. Both sets of fans had made it clear that they wanted to settle things once and for all and, with Feyenoord due to play AZ in Alkmaar just 35 kilometres from Amsterdam and Ajax not due to play RKC Waalwijk until that evening, plans were made for a fight at a location to be settled on the day.

The police got wind of things almost immediately but were forced to sit back and wait until eventually they knew for sure where the fight would be. As Feyenoord fans headed for Alkmaar in their hundreds, all they could do was shadow them and hope that they would guess right. But once again, they were outsmarted.

As almost 300 Feyenoord hooligans gathered at a motorway service station near Schiphol airport, the police became convinced that Ajax and the F-Siders would turn up at any minute and sent 40 riot police to contain things. However, Ajax weren't on their way at all. They had been slowly drifting into Beverwijk – a small town 20 kilometres west of Amsterdam and on the route to Alkmaar – and to avoid detection had travelled in tiny groups.

It was a tactic that worked perfectly and, fairly soon, Ajax had almost 200 lads milling around the marketplace among the Sunday morning shoppers.

As soon as contact was made, the decision was taken to have the fight in the marketplace and so the Feyenoord fans dived into their cars and headed for Beverwijk just a short drive along the motorway from where they had been waiting.

At this point, the police, having spotted the F-Siders and having realised what was happening, took the decision to close a tunnel on the slip road leading into the town, effectively cutting off access to, and from, the market. What they didn't do, however, was to close the slip road itself and, when the Feyenoord fans left the motorway only to find the road ahead blocked, they simply put their cars in reverse and backed up.

Seeing this and assuming that the Feyenoord hooligans had given up and were simply going back to the motorway to head for their game in Alkmaar, the police sat back and let them go. But the Feyenoord fans had other ideas.

With incredible speed of thought, they grabbed their mobile phones and contacted the F-Siders to tell them what had happened. Immediately, the two groups agreed that rather than call it off, they would simply change the venue and have the fight in a field adjacent to the A9 motorway just outside the town. By the time the Feyenoord convoy arrived and stopped their cars by the side of the road, almost 150 Ajax lads were already waiting for them. The police, meanwhile, were all over the place. Some were still at the tunnel, others at the motorway service station and yet more were waiting in the marketplace wondering where everyone had gone.

By the time they arrived at the field, the fighting was over and among a variety of seriously injured hooligans, Carlos Picornie lay dead. He had refused to back off when the Feyenoord fans had begun to gain the upper hand and had simply been beaten to death with a hammer.

The aftermath of the fight was equally astonishing. The police rushed to the stadiums in Alkmaar and Waalwijk in an effort to arrest anyone who had any sign of an injury or the merest trace of blood or even mud on their clothes. But some had changed while others had simply stayed away from the games. Meanwhile, the injured, after having been treated in hospital, simply melted away while others were allegedly 'rescued' by fellow Feyenoord fans later on in the evening. In the event, only 28 people were detained on the day.

Although not the first football-related murder in Holland – on 8 December 1991 an FC Twente fan named Erik Lassche died after being stabbed by a Feyenoord fan the night before the two teams were due to play each other – the ferocity and shocking nature of the incident stunned the public and there was an immedi-ate outcry and a demand for action. But if anyone thought that the rivalry would ease off, they were sadly mistaken.

The F-Siders launched a furious verbal attack on their enemy, accusing them of breaking the sacred rule of hooliganism: when a man is on the floor and unconscious, you leave him alone. Even Paul van Gageldonk became a target and was forced to leave his home as the Ajax fans wrongly believed he knew who had killed their man.

Most worryingly of all, the F-Siders even gained support from the Amsterdam underworld who made public an offer to help them avenge the murder.

The Feyenoord hooligans, meanwhile, mindful of the fact that the police would be all over them, immedi-ately adopted a low profile. Games went unattended and mobile phones remained unused for fear of them being traced. However, other Feyenoord fans weren't so reluctant to make an appearance and, at the first game after the incident, a number infuriated the mourning F-Siders by taking huge inflatable hammers onto the terraces.

In an effort to put an end to the rivalry, the chairmen of both clubs got together and sent an open letter to both groups asking for three representatives from each side to come along to air their differences and explain why they continued to wage war with each other when everyone else – from the directors to the playing staff – could seemingly get along with no problems. Sadly, neither group responded.

The police, meanwhile, adopted a bizarre approach. For years they had been hampered, and frustrated, by a lack of legislation allowing them to infiltrate the gangs or even stop them gathering together on match days, and it showed in their response. They publicly stated that in the light of what had happened in the field, they were simply relieved that the fight hadn't happened in the marketplace where the consequences could have been disastrous. The chief of the Waalwijk police even stated that 'if hooligans have to meet and fight each other, let them do it in a field on their own'. It was an opinion shared by a great many fans and commentators, one of whom is quoted as saying 'if those assholes want to kill each other, please let them'.

In the event, less than 10 per cent of the people involved in the fight at Beverwijk faced any kind of legal action and only a fraction of those were convicted. But the consequences for Dutch football were far-reaching.

Increasingly convinced that the hooligan problem was all but insoluble, the Dutch authorities, in a frightening echo of pre-Hillsborough England, began treating everyone as a potential problem. Calls for the introduction of an ID card system and a ban on away fans became frequent, while the police adopted an even more draconian approach to security at games.

However, the groups simply withdrew in on themselves to the extent that they even began to become detached from the clubs they followed. Their main aim was now simply to fight opposing fans, which they continued to do with monotonous regularity.

But if the authorities thought things couldn't get much worse after Beverwijk, recent years have seen the activities of the hooligans reach a startling and sinister low point.

Key to this was the arrival of a new and outspoken voice on the Dutch political scene in November 2001.

Pim Fortuyn hit Holland like a whirlwind. The openly gay politician was savage in his condemnation of the establishment, accusing it of ruining his country and letting down the people. He demanded that the Dutch borders be closed to any more immigrants and even labelled Islam a 'backward religion'. Not surprisingly, his opinions sparked off a number of fierce debates but they also attracted a great deal of support, including a substantial amount from among the right-wing element of the hooligan community.

Tragically, on 6 May 2002, Fortuyn was assassinated. Riots that broke out outside the parliament building that night saw hooligans from ADO Den Haag's North-Side at the forefront of the trouble while supporters left scarves and flags on the fence surrounding his villa in Rotterdam. Just two days later, during the UEFA Cup final between Feyenoord and Borussia Dortmund, the Dutch fans chanted Fortuyn's name repeatedly throughout the game as if he were one of their own.

Yet even as Holland was still struggling to come to terms with the murder of a major political figure, the world of football was further stunned when the manager of Sparta Rotterdam, Frank Rijkaard, was sent a letter blaming him for the club's impending relegation from the first division and warning him that if he didn't resign, he and his family would be hurt. The letter contained two bullets. Rijkaard resigned.

The next victim was Feyenoord manager Bert van Marwijk and, soon after that, PSV manager Guus Hiddink. Fresh from his success with Korea in Japan, Hiddink's bullets came with a letter warning him that 'everybody who hinders Feyenoord's progress to becoming champions will be eliminated'. It was signed, 'Feyenoord Hooligans'.

The most recent reported victim was the head of the Dutch FA, Henk Kesler. But it is almost certain that there have been more. Indeed, so feared are the hooligan groups becoming in Holland that one club chairman was reported as having said that some clubs dare not ban known hooligans from their grounds because it is simply too dangerous.

For the Dutch game, this is nothing short of a disaster. And the ones suffering most are the average football fans. The new Prime Minister, Jan Peter Balkenende, is again talking about banning away supporters, the railways have threatened to stop carrying them and an ID card scheme looks imminent. Ajax have already stated that they will allow fans to enter their ground only if they show a passport, driving licence or an ID card first.

Supporters' groups are naturally up in arms about this and are calling for the de-criminalisation of genuine fans and a tougher stance against the hooligans. To ensure that this message gets across, protests have already been staged at games including the international fixture against Belarus on 7 September 2002 and more are planned, but quite what happens next is anyone's guess.

What follows is a passionately written article about the current state of the game in Holland and the impact the hooligans have had upon it. It was written by 'Ruben' and perhaps the ultimate message is one that the authorities in the Netherlands would do well to hear.

In this article you won't find many stories about confrontations, revenge or acts of vandalism nor will you read any anecdotes about pitch invasions, battles with the police or discover which firm is hardest. This chapter isn't even about which firm is called what and why.

The reason for this is because almost everybody

knows that hooliganism in Holland still exists and might become a bigger problem than it is already, so what would be the point? What people really want to know is what is happening now on the Dutch scene and what might happen in the future.

To do that, we need to look at the truth and ignore the lies of the media, the clubs, the KNVB [the Royal Dutch Football Association], the police, the Ministry of Justice, City Councils and so on. I say that because together they are running a smear campaign against Dutch football supporters and the so-called hooligans. The result of this is that true supporters are being silenced, which is breeding frustration and anger among even peaceful fans. Of course I can't speak for every supporter, but I know that a lot of fans agree with what I shall say here. I will simply tell the truth, nothing more, nothing less.

It is difficult to discuss hooliganism in Holland when there is no real and comprehensive definition of what hooliganism actually is. For someone who doesn't know anything about football, almost everyone who visits a match is a hooligan. People who sometimes watch games in the stadium, on television or who read about it in the newspapers will think that hooligans are those people who sing and curse while others will say that hooligans are football supporters who throw bricks, break windows and kick the shit out of the opposing supporters. And if we believe the politicians in Holland, everybody who wears a replica shirt is a hooligan.

So what is the real definition? Well, to me, a hooligan is someone who is fanatical about his team and is really concerned about the club and everything that happens to it. The club is part of their life and no one can take that away. This may also apply to other supporters, but the difference lies in the way they will defend the honour of their club. The hooligans will go much further then the average or even the fanatical supporter, and will literally fight for their club and just as importantly, their mates. But they also know how to stay out of trouble with the police, because they know the law and the way it works. Because of that, they normally avoid the stadium or any crowded area so if there is a confrontation with other hooligans, the chance of being arrested or of innocent bystanders getting hurt is almost zero.

In the old days of course, everything was different. Football was played in stadiums that exhaled warmth, nostalgia and enthusiasm and there was a feeling that 'we are one'. Everyone knew everyone, not only the supporters, but also the players, the technical staff and the management. There was also a strong bond between the supporters, especially the hooligans. Incidents happened frequently and were designed to let the other groups know that we [Ajax] are the toughest and no one fucks with us. If you do, you're in serious trouble.

But it was also a game: trying to break into each other's stadium to steal the centre spot or paint your club's name on their seats was all just harmless fun. For us, from the 1970s to the early 1990s, the stadium was the playground. Yes there were battles, and they were fought either on the terraces or just outside, but things changed as time went by. Now, together with pitch invasions, it has almost all disappeared. And there are two reasons for it.

The first was the introduction of Closed Circuit Television (CCTV) which made it very easy to catch the bad seeds in the crowd. This lesson was quickly learned by the hooligans, who began to make sure that they behaved inside and outside the stadium or at least kept a low profile.

The second has been the introduction of the 'combi' which is a ticket and a travelling voucher. This stops you making your own way to away games and also lets the police treat you like cattle as they are the ones who take you to the away ground. It also means that the chances for confrontations are very limited.

The consequence of this is that the last few years have seen the hooligans moving their battlefields from inside or near the stadium to places far away, and not only on match days. More and more, hooligans from different clubs are arranging meetings hours or even days before kick-offs and at specific, secret locations. It has also seen a new phenomenon arising: hooligans at music festivals, in particular house festivals.

To many of us, these are the new terraces and our new home. What you find there is an interesting mix of alcohol, drugs and music together with lots of hooligans from other clubs. In a way this is not surprising. If you can't fight in or near the stadium, you just find a new location where you can. The fact that there are almost no police or CCTV at these festivals means that the number and frequency of these confrontations is likely to increase simply because the chance of being caught is so small compared to at the stadium or in the town centre. What it also means is that the number of lads involved in these fights is much smaller.

It is not easy to discuss numbers of hooligans in Holland because of the semi-organised structure of the firms. At the core, of course, things are very well organised, but around them will be a large number of people who simply follow the main lads. They will fight for sure, but not lead or plan. For example, Ajax's hardcore is about 200–250 strong but, when something kicks off, hundreds more will join in. However, for a pre-arranged off, the numbers will be much smaller –

anywhere between 20 and 150 on each side. That doesn't mean that those meetings are less violent. The opposite is probably true because those people on both sides are the ones who are more fearless and won't back down.

Some people of course will read this and think that it is all lies. They are the ones who have seen the Dutch national team and watched the fans in their orange face-paint and bright wigs and say that we have no hooligans in Holland at all. But they are wrong. The reason we don't follow Holland is because we all hate each other too much. We would never sit beside each other like you do in England because whenever and wherever we meet, a fight is always likely.

This is why the plans to form a Dutch Army for Euro 2004 in Portugal and the 2006 World Cup in Germany are a waste of time. It will never happen because Ajax will never work with Feyenoord, FC Utrecht will never work with Ajax and FC Den Haag will never cooperate with PSV. And those hatreds are only intensifying, so a Dutch Army is further away than ever.

This is not what the media want to hear. They would love a Dutch hooligan army because it would give them so much more to write about. The reason for that is because they love football violence – as nothing sells newspapers and attracts viewers more than people fighting or throwing bricks, and that's all they care about these days.

Unfortunately this means that more and more only the negative aspects of football supporters are high-lighted and the positive things are ignored. This has a very bad effect when it comes to forming people's opinions because men and women who never go to football or attend only occasionally don't know what is really going on. Their opinion of football supporters and hooligans is based on what they read, what they hear and what they see in the media. And that is always perceived as the whole truth even when it is not. For example, if a newspaper publishes a story that includes pictures of football supporters who are fighting, people will sooner or later believe that every supporter is a hooligan. While in fact, it might only have been a very small group of supporters causing problems.

For supporters it is very hard to defend ourselves against inaccurate and false news coverage. If you send an e-mail or a letter to a newspaper or a television station to explain what is really going on, they either ignore you, laugh at you or accuse you of sending threats. Another problem is that the media copies itself. If one newspaper pays a lot of attention to hooligans, another newspaper will follow and will try to bring 'better' news coverage of the problems. And, while this continues, there is nothing we can do about it. The media exposes only one side of the story and that's almost never the side of the supporter. There have been many examples of this recently.

On 1 September 2002 the FC Groningen–Ajax match was played without the Ajax supporters being allowed entry to the stadium. This was because the mayor of Groningen had forbidden the Ajax supporters to attend the match simply because FC Groningen supporters said that they would cause trouble. This meant that the Ajax supporters were punished undeservedly and about 150 of them decided to protest against this decision. On the day of the match they went by car to Groningen and stopped on the main highway where they played a game of football, negotiated with the police and then went home. The protest was totally peaceful and a TV crew of the NOS [public network] was there all the time. But what did we see that evening? Images of the protest and interviews with a couple of angry people stuck in the traffic jam. After this coverage the reporter then said that this protest was a disgrace to Dutch football and that it would be better if all away fans were banned. This was a very strange statement because the people who protested weren't allowed to see the game anyway.

On 11 August 2002 Ajax played against PSV in the Amsterdam Arena for the Dutch Supercup. The PSV supporters were allocated only a fraction of the 10,000 to 15,000 tickets they should have been and so, on the morning of the game, they decided to protest by locking the entrance gate to the PSV training ground meaning that the players couldn't get out to go to the stadium. The game eventually started an hour late but even though the protest was entirely peaceful, the media (and the KNVB) portrayed the PSV fans as the scum of the earth. The head of the KNVB even accused the fans of not simply trying to disrupt football, but the whole of society.

Yet another example of this bias occurred on the live television talk show *Rondom Tien* ['around ten'] on 5 September 2002. The idea was for supporters from different clubs to talk about the criminalisation of football fans. The unique thing about this was that supporters from different clubs normally don't appear in the same programme because of the rivalries and potential problems. But in this case they wanted to show that they weren't hooligans but normal supporters and they wanted a serious debate in which they were (finally) allowed to give their opinions.

Unfortunately the presenter had other ideas. He just wanted to talk about violence and continuously silenced the supporters when they wanted to talk about the real issues. In the end the Ajax supporters simply got up and walked out. Their response, although perfectly understandable, simply played into the hands of the media and the politicians.

After all, they never come to games as supporters, they are always VIP guests in luxury boxes and so they have no idea what's really going on. Instead, they read the sensationalist media and come up with ridiculous measures rather than look at the reasons why the trouble takes place. For example:

– Janssen van Raaij (Member of Parliament, LPF party):
'It should be made possible to confine football hooligans to military barracks so they can get military training. The people who perform best should get a job within the armed forces.'

– Rijpstra (Member of Parliament, VVD party):
'We need a more effective way to deal with the hooligans. We could use a mobile judge who can pronounce a verdict straight away.'

– Balkenende (Prime Minister, CDA party):
'It would be better if we don't allow away supporters anymore. We have had enough of all the problems and this is the best solution.'

The politicians and the members of the Royal Dutch Football Association want to take drastic measures to reduce football violence and hooliganism. But will measures like banning away supporters, higher fines and more stadium bans help to reduce it? The answer is no, it won't. First of all, most of the hooligans keep a low profile during matches and secondly, nothing will change if the non-violent supporters are not taken seriously and are punished for things they are not responsible for. All this will do is fuel anger and things will just get even worse.

If the politicians, the KNVB and the media really

want to solve hooliganism, all they have to do is listen to what those people have to say and act on it.

CHAPTER SEVEN
Germany

My first encounter with German football fans took place in 1980 while I was serving with the Royal Air Force in northern Germany. It was actually quite a surreal affair for it occurred one Saturday morning as my mate and I were standing in the middle of Bielefeld town centre watching a man standing on a box berating passers by. The fact that he was dressed in the uniform of a soldier from Rommel's Afrika Korps complete with a pair of desert goggles clamped firmly over his eyes and a tank driver's helmet on his head made it all the more bizarre.

Out of the blue, the sound of chanting football fans caught our attention and we turned to see this mob of scruffy Herberts approaching; they turned out to be Armenia Bielefeld fans. Suddenly mindful of the fact that we were English in a foreign land, we took a step back and let them pass. They were all fairly young and typically German – all denim jackets with sewn-on patches and dodgy moustaches – and when they had gone, we looked at each other and laughed. Not because we were relieved, but because compared to what we were used to seeing at home, their appearance was almost comical. It certainly wasn't threatening.

However, seeing them reminded us that at heart we were both football fans and, as we hadn't seen a game for weeks, we decided to follow and see what their place was like. What we found was that while they were enjoying a rare spell in the top flight, they were a pretty poor side. But we also discovered that among their crowd were a sizable number of squaddies from the various army units dotted around the region. They had adopted the club simply because, like us, they loved their football. This initial visit turned out to be the first of what became a regular occurrence for us and it was actually quite a giggle. Interestingly, we were warmly welcomed by the German fans who made no secret of the fact that they thought we were all a bit mad.

Seven years later, having returned to Germany for another spell courtesy of HM Forces, things were very different. Although still years behind what was going on in England, hooliganism had begun to take a grip on the German game. So much so that when the England team headed for Düsseldorf in 1987, the threat in terms of German fans looking to fight with the English, was considered very real. Indeed, every British serviceman stationed in Germany at the time was warned about the consequences of becoming involved in any trouble at the game and our travel was very closely monitored. In the event, incidents were limited to a few skirmishes including one just outside the turnstiles as we left the ground. But with Germany due to host Euro 88 the following year, the message many English fans took home with them was that the local lads had the potential to be a genuine problem.

As it happened, the group who came out on top were the police. From the outset they had warned that they wouldn't tolerate any trouble and they were certainly as good as their word, clamping down quickly and effectively on anything that looked even remotely threatening and reducing problems to just the odd confrontation despite the best efforts of both the German and the English groups. The one exception was the riot in

Hamburg following Germany's defeat by Holland, which is widely acknowledged as being one of the most violent incidents of hooliganism ever seen in Europe.

For the German hooligans, Euro 88 was a significant success. Not only did they prove that they were no mugs on their home ground but they showed that they were more than capable of taking the fight to anyone who wanted it including the English. Confirmation of that came some weeks later when the police released the final arrest figures. Out of just over 1200 supporters detained, over two-thirds were German. They might not have won the tournament, but the nation's hooligans were now firmly on the map.

These days, as we shall see, there is much more to the German hooligan scene than the appalling haircuts and bad dress-sense we tend to ridicule so much in England. In many respects, it is actually one of the most interesting in Europe because, thanks to the fall of the Berlin Wall in 1989, it has in effect two distinct cultures running within the same league.

There is also increasing friction between the hooligan and Ultra groups who follow the same clubs. The Ultra disciples try to replicate the Italian style of watching the games while the hooligans regard them as nothing more than simple poseurs. However, much of this conflict has its origins in the make-up of the respective groups. At most clubs, the Ultra, who are semi-violent, tend to be between 15 and 20 while the true hooligans are older – usually 25–40. Yet another source of conflict is the fact that the older hooligans try to stick religiously to the recognised and accepted code of fighting while the younger ones are becoming increasingly prone to using weapons to protect themselves – a reflection on German society perhaps.

In terms of numbers, the bigger hooligan gangs in Germany certainly stand a comparison with their English counterparts. Clubs such as Hamburg, Dynamo Berlin and Schalke 04 have no trouble putting together a mob of 400–500 lads with many more turning out for the bigger games. Surprisingly this is also true of a number of clubs in the lower divisions, such as Offenbach, Mannheim, Leipzig and Dresden, and those groups can be frighteningly well organised. It has even been reported that on at least one occasion, a gangleader was seen handing out armbands to his lads so that when things kicked off, they wouldn't end up fighting each other!

However, it is fair to say that in recent years the German police have enjoyed a great deal of success in their war with the hooligans. Most recently, their operation during the build up to Euro 2000 was hugely successful in stopping the German mobs from crossing the border, although it was certainly not without its critics. In yet another echo of England, German civil liberties groups were outraged that restrictions were placed on the free travel of individuals with seemingly no proof of intent to do anything. But the fact is, it worked. And after France 98 and the horrific assault in which German hooligans almost beat French policeman Daniël Nivel to death with an iron bar, that has to be seen as a positive result.

An equally encouraging consequence of the trouble during France 98 was an increased awareness of the *Fanprojekts* that exist at most major clubs in Germany. They had actually been around since the 1980s and were initially formed as a way of helping the fans forge relations with their clubs and the police, as well as friendships with other supporters' groups.

For example, in 1991, the *Fanprojekt* at Borussia Mönchengladbach organised a series of events that raised DM 21,000 for the Hillsborough disaster fund. As a result, there are now strong links between both clubs and, just as the red shirts of Liverpool are often observed

on the Nord Curve, so the green, black and white of
Borussia have frequently been seen at Anfield.

The success of these initiatives has been immense and
key to this is the fact that the majority are well run and
properly funded. For instance, the project at Bayer
Leverkusen is supported by the DFB [German Football
Association], the Federal State of North Rhine-Westphalia
and the city of Leverkusen. As a result, its influence
extends way beyond football and it is directly involved
with all of the football institutions, the police, schools
and even the social and employment services.

One of the core aims of the *Fanprojekts* is to facilitate
a reduction in football-related violence both inside and
outside stadiums, and it was this anti-hooligan aspect in
particular that appealed to many German supporters
post-France 98 because it provided a relatively simple
way of registering their feelings about what had been
going on.

However, while their continued existence can only
be for the good of German football, given that hooliganism is once again on the rise in Germany, it is difficult
to see how they can be regarded as any kind of long-
term solution.

What follows is an article that looks in greater
depth at the German scene and examines where it is
today. It was written by someone I have got to know
reasonably well over recent years but who, for a variety
of reasons, has asked to be credited by his nickname:
Laxel, KA–Germany.

However, before I close this introduction, I would like
to pass on one more anecdote that was told to me quite
recently. If only because it must have been one of the
most hilarious sights ever seen inside a football ground.

These days, due to the police, stewards, CCTV and
so on, trouble inside the big German football grounds
is all but unheard of. One of the last major incidents

took place on 6 December 1992 at Schalke 04. The visitors were FC Köln whose supporters had chosen the game to celebrate Christmas and in typical football-fan style, many of them went to the game dressed as Father Christmas.

Unfortunately, during the match trouble broke out which resulted in a couple of hundred Köln fans tearing down a fence and heading for the main stand where the Schalke supporters were housed. Not surprisingly, the sight of numerous Santas steaming towards them was a source of much humour to the home support, but the resulting violence saw many of them take severe beatings.

The problem for the Köln fans was that the Schalke ground was one of the first in Germany to have a decent CCTV system and, as a consequence, many were identified and ended up receiving harsh sentences for their indiscretions.

One can only imagine what the reaction was when the film was shown in the courtroom!

'*Deutschland Hooligans, Deutschland Hooligans . . .*'. Football fans across Europe will be familiar with this chant from games involving the German national team. For us, it is a rallying call. A common bond for the lads and the troublemakers.

The German hooligan scene only really began in the 1970s but the last 10–15 years has seen it go through many important changes. As in England, many of these were forced upon the game by commercialisation. The first division of the Bundesliga has become a big family event where upper-class mums and dads show off their well-educated kids who happily wear their Bayern München, Dortmund or even Manchester United shirts as they watch games. This, along with more aggressive policing and the switch to all-seater arenas where the clubs can make more money from their new audience has driven the traditional fans away. Angry that their songs, chants and passion are no longer wanted.

The result of this is that the first division has almost nothing in common with division two. More importantly, most of the top hooligan firms are in the Bundesliga 2 or even in the Regionalliga (third division). This is because football there has managed to survive commercialisation and keep hold of its working-class roots. The fans still have the old passion and rough behaviour, while abusive language and aggression aimed at the visiting teams isn't branded as unsportsmanlike conduct. It is also here that the major incidents of violence inside grounds happen.

One recent example took place in 1999 when Mannheim had to make the trip to Offenbach – a distance of only about 50 miles. Around 4000 Mannheim travelled, with about 400 being hooligans, and during the game Offenbach (who had a mob of almost 500 hooligans) tried to get at the Mannheim stand. Only the arrival of the riot police kept the two rival groups apart for the rest of the game.

Afterwards, the Mannheim fans were attacked by Offenbach with the result that the police were forced to use water cannon to drive the local fans away. But they simply moved into the surrounding streets where trouble started again. After a police car was attacked and badly damaged by fighting fans, they were even forced to fire warning shots at the angry mob.

By the time it had all calmed down, more than 100 people had been injured, including 25 police officers, one police dog had been killed and 28 fans arrested. The authorities described it as the worst violence German football had seen for many years.

Unlike in other countries across Europe, this was one of only a few incidents where the German police have come under direct attack. This is largely because, in Germany, the police are treated with a great deal of respect and an assault on an officer of the law is treated as a very serious offence which can easily result in jail. That is not to say that the police do not treat the activities of the hooligans any less seriously. Even using a mobile phone inside a ground can result in big trouble if they think you are up to no good.

Many people actually think that the police, together with the German government, regard hooliganism as a way of showing the country how dangerous anti-social groups can be and how hard they will come down on them. This is perhaps one reason why sentences for hooligan offences are so high in Germany. It is often said that you will get fewer years in prison for molesting children than you will for being involved in football-related violence. It also explains how the police are able to force through laws restricting the free movement of people – as used during Euro 2000 to prevent German hooligans travelling to Belgium and Holland – and gain permission from the courts to install CCTV cameras anywhere they want to; two things that many German people are afraid of because they are tools that could allow the government to control them. Control of that kind means power.

Another thing of concern to the German public is that the media almost completely ignore what is going on in football. Even very serious incidents will only receive a few lines in the newspapers, and the television news shows almost nothing. They claim it is because they have adopted a policy of not giving the hooligans any publicity, but many believe it is because they are under pressure from the authorities not to show the truth.

Of course to the hooligans themselves, this simply adds to the excitement. It is fair to say, though, that the German scene is far less organised than in England

and Holland. Spotters and scouts are almost unheard of and while mobile phones are used to arrange fights on the day, the supposed love affair German hooligans are having with the Internet is nothing more than a media myth.

It is also true to say that even the style of fighting among the hooligan groups is different. In Germany, fights between hooligan groups are known as 'matches' and they are fought under a well-respected code. Almost nobody uses weapons such as knives or base-ball bats, and attacks on normal fans or even Ultra groups are not acceptable. It is about *hool* versus *hool* and that is why most of our matches are 'fair'. That is not to say bad things do not happen, they do. But for the most part they are done in the heat of the moment rather than being planned.

Sadly, it isn't the same when you play teams from other nations. They do not use German rules and so you are forced to use theirs. Often, that means weapons – which isn't fair at all.

It could even be argued that the German hooligan scene is actually developing a specific identity by leaving behind some of the more usual hooligan behaviour. For example, the fashion of adopting names that was copied from the English scene has begun to die out. The main reason for this is because the modern-day hooligans respect what went on in the 1980s and 1990s at groups such as AdlerFront (Frankfurt), Destroyers (Karlsruhe) and GelsenSzene (Schalke 04) and do not want to undermine that history. Now the lads simply call each other by the name of their clubs.

Another aspect of the English scene that never caught on in Germany is the obsession with clothes. Although style is important, it is felt that hooliganism is about what you do with your fists rather than what label you have on your trousers. Germans actually find it quite funny that the English classify an enemy by their clothes! That is not to say that certain companies have not tried to get the hooligans 'labelled up'. Pitbull, Hooligan and Category C are three labels that have tried but in truth only the wannabes are wearing it.

Yet another difference is that recent times have seen more and more hooligan groups forming alliances with firms at other clubs. For example, Stuttgart and Karlsruhe, Offenbach and Leverkusen, Schalke 04 and Nürnberg and, most amazingly of all, Bayern München and 1860 München. There are even some that have been formed with Dutch clubs. Schalke 04 with Twente Enschede and Bremen with Kerkrade are two of the better known ones.

The English scene is still, however, regarded as the best, and many German hools have a great deal of respect for firms such as the ICF, Soul Crew and the Service Crew. This is as a result of the fact that they will never back down and are always absolutely determined to get a result both at home and abroad. One famous story among German hooligans involves Leeds at Stuttgart in 1992 when about 30–40 Service Crew scattered a good 100–150 German wannabe hooligans before the match. The funny thing was that as the wannabes were trying to get inside a bar to escape, all of the German top lads were inside trying to get out to confront the Leeds fans!

When they did finally manage to get out, the fights were more evenly matched, but it was still a humiliation for the Germans because of the numbers involved.

This respect is of course carried over to the international stage where England are one of the huge rivals. The German hooligans know that if an English club side or the national side are in the country, they will almost always have a mob with them. This highlights one of the big differences between the two scenes. For the English hooligans, games are seen almost as wars whereas the Germans see them as adventures – it is also true that whereas most English fans are born into the love and loyalty for their team, German fans simply choose theirs without any real pressure from parents, brothers or friends. This is especially true of the hooligans who follow the German team. At international matches there is a strong comradeship that melts even the worst of enemies together to stand their ground against opponents. This means that often Germany have very large mobs when they travel. Six hundred in Belgium in 1995, slightly more in Rotterdam in 1996 and almost 700 in Lens during France 98. It was here that the French policeman Daniël Nivel was almost beaten to death during a fight.

The one place German hooligans do not travel to is England. There is obviously some concern about what will happen when they get there but the main reason is because of the travelling. Driving around Europe is easy but to get across the Channel you have to take a ferry or a train. This makes it very easy for the authorities to control what the hooligans do and where they are going and, in the past, many lads have been stopped and turned back at the borders. Now, they simply do not bother although that is something not unique to Germany! When England come to Germany, however, the German fans will always try to take them on.

But the English are not the biggest rivals. That honour is reserved for Holland. The root of this lies, of course, in the Second World War when Germany took over their country in just three days. Naturally, they harbour resentment for that and also they feel guilt that so many of them collaborated with the Nazis. Now, it all comes out mostly in football. The first big confrontation was during Euro 88 when, after years of trying, their team finally beat us on German soil. The Dutch fans went crazy in celebrating but, just after the game, it was rumoured that one player had used a German team shirt to wipe his backside. All of Germany went crazy and, that night, hundreds of hooligans fought with the Dutch in Hamburg. There were also riots when we played them later that year and again in 1989.

It got even worse in 1990 when we played them during the World Cup. Germany was outraged when Rudi Völler was sent off after Frank Rijkaard, who was also dismissed, spat at him, and fighting broke out at towns all along the Holland–Germany border. There were also riots when the two countries met in 1996 and in 1998.

Mention of the Nazis leads on to one of the biggest and most important aspects of the scene in Germany: the politics. Many people believe that hooligans are all goose-stepping neo-Nazis or extreme right-wing orientated, but that is not true. For sure they will put on a show if provoked, for example when the abuse from the other side gets too much. But the war ended nearly 60 years ago and even the German people are finally starting to show a kind of national pride again. During the World Cup 2002 every German flag was sold out nationwide and that has been unthinkable for decades.

Obviously there is a right-wing element in Germany (as in every country), but it is important to understand that much of that comes from the east. In the west, we have many hooligans with foreign blood but, in the east, non-Germans are hard to find so a lot of the DDR [German Democratic Republic] lads are very right wing and they have a lot of Skinheads in their ranks.

The reunification of Germany in 1989 was also very

important for the German scene. Afterwards, football went through many changes and a lot of hooligans from the west travelled to clubs in the east to cause trouble because the police there were hopeless and fights were easy to find. But the eastern lads learnt fast and now they are very strong opponents who hate the clubs from the west. The hardest of all are the hooligans from Berlin and especially the ones who follow BFC Dynamo Berlin, the former club of the STASI [secret police]. But not far behind are Magdeburg, Dresden and Leipzig. However, like all the clubs from the east, they do not travel very much so most of the trouble takes place when firms from the west go there. The strange thing is, even though many are right wing, they will often try to provoke us with songs and flags from the old days when they were the communist DDR!

For many German hooligans, a fight between the east and the west would be the ultimate contest. It has been talked about many times but has never happened. Maybe that will change one day because only when the two sides meet head-on will one truly know who in Germany are the hardest.

'DEUTSCHLAND HOOLIGANS!'

CHAPTER EIGHT
Italy

In 1980, when hooliganism in England was still approaching its zenith and I was a lowly Junior Technician in the Royal Air Force, I was lucky enough to spend a few weeks in Sardinia working with a squadron of Harrier aircraft.

The day after our arrival, we discovered from one of the locals that Cagliari were at home to Juventus on the Saturday and, as most of us were football fans and none had ever seen a game in Italy before, a decision was taken to get on down there and show the Italians what English football supporters were really like.

Sadly, come the weekend, the demands of broken aircraft and desperate hangovers meant that only three of us made the trip: a Glaswegian known universally as Jock, who seemed to have a Celtic shirt tattooed on to his body, a six-foot-six Gooner named Tiny (obviously) and yours truly.

Since we didn't even possess enough Italian between us to order the traditional three beers, our journey to the stadium was not without its moments but, having purchased various scarves and flags as souvenirs, we settled down behind the goal to watch the game.

We quickly realised that Italian football fans are mental. Even corners were met with some extremely worrying exhibitions of passion and, at one point, I genuinely thought a fella in front of me was going to top himself when Cagliari hit the bar.

More used to watching our football in an atmosphere of abuse and violence, we began to treat these displays of emotion with something approaching ridicule but, as the second half kicked off, Tiny pointed out that a small gap had opened up around us and, even as the game was being played, angry eyes were focused not on the pitch, but on us.

We were in the shit. Confirmation of which came when one of the locals walked over and spat on the ground in front of us.

As we were busily trying to work out how to escape from an end full of crazed Italians, many of whom no doubt recalled that a few months previously hordes of our fellow countrymen had laid waste parts of Turin, a middle-aged bloke approached and said, 'They think you are the enemy. Wave your flags.' Torn between the desire to have a pristine Cagliari banner hanging on my wall and making it out of there alive, I was soon waving for all I was worth, as were my two colleagues, and although the gap around us remained, at least they stopped glaring at us.

Heading homeward, I was struck by one thing. Like most English football fans, especially back then, I genuinely believed that we weren't simply a cut above every other football fan on the planet, we were invincible. The very idea that anyone would dare take us on was laughable and, even if they did, we'd have no problems spanking them because . . . well, we were English. It's what we did.

I have absolutely no doubt that there are still people who think like that – one only need watch some of the footage of England in Marseille during France 98 as proof – but my afternoon in Cagliari taught me a valuable lesson.

It also ensured that I kept a wary eye on Italian football and, while I have little real interest in the game out there, events off the pitch have been nothing short of staggering. The Italian terraces have seen some quite astonishing developments over the years and, even today, things happen which are simply unthinkable here in the UK. And at the forefront of everything are the Ultra.

To many, the term Ultra equates simply to hooligan but, in reality, this isn't always the case. Hooligan has only one real meaning and that is 'aggressive', while in the football sense, Ultra is an all-embracing term that has its roots in the political history of the Italian nation. Indeed, politics has been at the heart of the Ultra movement since its birth in the late 1960s.

Key to this was the fact that in post-Second World War Italy, political conflict involved every aspect of society including sport. In a footballing sense, this led to particular teams being regarded as either left- or right-wing, based on the social status of its supporters. In Milan, for example, AC became the team of the traditionally left-wing working class, while Inter represented the more affluent middle classes and, as a result, attracted a more right-wing support.

Not surprisingly, the political leanings of the terraces proved to be a breeding ground for extremist views and this was especially true of the right wing. When the Italian Social Movement was banned from campaigning on the streets, the movement targeted the antisocial elements on the terraces to boost membership and support. The result being that numerous clubs, including both Lazio and Inter Milan, became hotbeds of right-wing extremism.

A consequence of this political influence was that particular rivalries and alliances were forged. One example of this was Bologna whose left-wing Ultra group fought with the extreme right-wing Ultra at Lazio yet became friendly with the left-wing Ultra at AC Milan. It also led to various Ultra groups adopting the typical uniform of the political activists: green parkas or camouflage combat jackets, jeans or combat trousers, and caps with bandanas tied around their necks which were quickly pulled over faces in the event of trouble breaking out.

Another aspect of the political scene that was adopted by the Ultra from the very early days was the organisation of the membership. This allowed the group to develop into much more than a simple supporters' club and, instead, it became a social group. One that had the support of the team as its core value.

The Ultra also took up the typically political practice of chanting slogans and making flags and banners to display their thoughts and feelings, a practice that continues to this day. Indeed, as recently as February 2000, the Ministry of Interior went so far as to ban all political flags from stadiums after the Irriducibili at Lazio exposed a banner praising the Serbian leader Arkan.

It should, however, be pointed out that in the main, the displays staged by the Ultra at games are very much apolitical. Indeed, the planning and execution of these amazing spectacles, which can include anything from banners, flares and choreographed chanting right through to laser shows, highlights one of the fundamental differences between the Italian and English styles of supporting.

Whereas in the UK supporters' clubs are usually nothing more than drinking dens or ticket outlets, and the links that supporters have with their clubs are at best tenuous and at worst non-existent, in Italy, things are very different.

The reason for this is quite simply because the planning of the match-day activities is both time-consuming and hugely expensive, and therefore the Ultra have to raise significant funds. As a result, a typical Ultra group will raise money by organising special buses to away games and selling souvenirs such as scarves, hats and stickers all of which will carry the name and symbol of the group. So lucrative can this be at the bigger clubs that some now have retail outlets and sell merchandise alongside official products.

Generally speaking, the profits from these activities are ploughed back into the group to fund the creation of flags and banners and to pay for the purchase of flares.

Alongside this, many groups have set up membership schemes that raise substantial funds at the start of each season. One of the additional benefits of this is that it allows everyone who joins to feel that they are an integral part of the Ultra and have a role to play, however insignificant that might be in reality.

Obviously, the organisation behind the continuation of such activities is extensive, which brings us on to another important aspect of the Italian Ultra scene, the structure.

At the larger clubs, a central core of older and respected members will decide everything from the design of the flags to the nature of the songs sung on match days. Around these will be people responsible for dealing with the finances, booking transport, purchasing merchandise and even obtaining tickets from the club. Perhaps surprisingly, it is not unknown for some of these individuals to be women.

There is no doubt that the Italian style of support has had a huge influence on European football and, while the level of organisation in Italy has not been replicated in many countries, it does show what can be achieved if supporters have the will and desire to organise themselves.

Sadly, while much of the Italian example is positive, the Ultra do have a darker side.

Like the English game, clashes between supporters had been a permanent fixture of the Italian game for decades, but the birth of the Ultra movement and the associated rivalries in the early 1970s saw the problem take on a new dimension. As a consequence, on 21 December 1975, the Italian Soccer Federation called for a 'friendship day' – the aim being to set aside all established rivalries and start afresh.

To an extent, this was reasonably successful, but much of that can be attributed to the decline of the various political movements during the mid 1970s, which left many Italians feeling isolated.

However, within two seasons problems had not only returned to their previous level, they were actually getting worse. There were a number of significant factors involved in this. One of the most important was that the Italian public began to vent their political frustration through a series of street battles between the left and right wing. Alongside this, Italy experienced an explosion of youth culture – in particular the Skinhead style – that, as a result of the xenophobia and racism attached to it, led to a growth in the right wing, particularly at clubs whose Ultra groups had leanings in that direction.

Of equal importance was the fact that the police were becoming a big problem for the Ultra as they had become determined to exercise some degree of control over what was going on inside the stadiums. The result of this was simply that the groups were increasingly forced to take their fights out of the stadiums and onto the streets, something which culminated in the death of a fan at the Roma–Lazio derby in 1979.

By the early 1980s, the Ultra phenomenon took hold at clubs in the lower leagues and, as the political scene declined, the emphasis began to switch to more provincial-based rivalries. Ultra groups at clubs such as Verona, Atalanta and Brescia based their ethos very much on the defence of their turf and their colours.

This was also the case at many of the larger clubs who suddenly found themselves sharing the Curva (terrace or end) with smaller groups largely comprising younger lads who looked upon football simply as an excuse to fight.

These Italian Casuals, better known as Cani Sciolti (loose dogs), had no time for alliances or 'rules', preferring instead to cause as many problems as they could – not just for rival fans but for the police who, as a result, took a renewed interest in what was going on.

The following article gives a clearer insight into what is happening in Italy and why. It was written by Lorenzo Contucci and I am indebted to Stan Thain of the Aberdeen Gialloblu and Yvonne Scott for the translation.

However, before that, I need to pick up on three significant points relating to Italian football, and the first is to do with the Italian media.

With a country as fanatical about its sport as Italy, it should be no surprise to discover that the sporting press is huge in Italy and this is especially true of football. However, as in many countries across Europe, journalists seem loath to report on anything positive happening in and around the nation's football stadiums, preferring instead to focus on the negatives.

This process began in the early 1970s when any violence received only a cursory mention. But from the mid 1970s on, entire sections were devoted to events on the Curva and the activities of the Ultra outside the confines of the grounds. This coverage eventually began to attract the attention of the police, who became increasingly concerned that it was acting not as a deterrent, but as a catalyst.

As a result, the papers became critical of the police who, in turn, were forced to become more aggressive in their policing of the Ultra.

However, the sensationalist nature of the reporting led to accusations from among the Ultra that journalists were embellishing, or even making up, stories and this led to the Ultra actively targeting various journalists. Some groups even began naming them on banners, and one of the more famous examples of this involved Aldo Biscardi, the presenter of a popular sports show Il Processo del Lunedi (The Monday Trial).

Following the death of a Roma supporter before a game with Milan, Biscardi was scathing in his condemnation of the Milan Ultra and, when three fans were arrested not long afterwards, the Ultra were furious and blamed him directly. As a result, at the next home game they displayed a special banner which read 'Biscardi you are a son of bastards'.

The next point we need to examine is the support of the Italian national side. In short, the Ultra groups tend to treat it with a degree of apathy simply because they are unable to set aside their hatred of rival groups and refuse to sit alongside them.

One well-documented example of how far this can be taken reaches back to Italia 90 when Napoli fans refused to support the national side, preferring instead to back their hero Maradona. As a consequence, many other clubs took to supporting any team Argentina were playing against, which even resulted in the bizarre sight of racist Skinheads cheering on Cameroon.

These days things are slightly less extreme but the basic ideal remains the same and support for the national side is almost entirely the preserve of families and corporate money.

The final aspect of the Italian scene that needs to be examined is the future. For while there are many positives to be taken from the amazing support the Ultra groups give their teams, there are also many negatives. These extend way beyond the often extreme violence which for example, in February 1995, saw all Italian sport cancelled for an entire weekend in protest at the murder of a Genoa fan prior to a game against AC Milan.

Primarily, I am talking about the power the Ultra exert on the clubs. Stories of groups threatening to misbehave if they are not given free tickets or travel are legendary, despite the Federazione di Calcio (the Italian FA) declaring such practices illegal. Similarly, it is well known that certain groups have directly influenced the signing and selling of specific players and have even ensured that certain decisions relating to the club are made in their favour.

The problem for the clubs is that having allowed this situation to develop, they are now unable to deal with it, but with a number looking to float on the stock exchange, the activities of the Ultra will have a direct impact on the future prosperity of the club. After all, what corporate image is going to be enhanced by the sight of chairs being ripped out, fans rioting and flags being burnt on the terraces?

Quite how clubs are going to resolve this complication is impossible to guess, but given the status of the Ultra, it would not be a surprise if somewhere along the line, they were directly involved.

The Ultra phenomenon began in Italy in the late 1960s and grew out of the culture of political protest that enveloped the country from the mid 1960s when various student and blue-collar groups began registering their disquiet at the way that Italy was being governed.

In an age in which fights between political factions in the streets were the order of the day, the groups were formed more or less in alignment to political ideals, even if the most important thing in the minds of many who stood on the various Curva at grounds across the country was the absolute and unconditional support of the team.

Equally important to this development was the transfer of the organisational skills the Italian youth had learned in the squares and on the streets. Something which quickly led to the formation of groups such as La Fossa dei Leoni (The Lions' Den) at AC Milan in 1968 and, later, the Boys S.A.N. Inter and the Red and Blue Commandos at Bologna.

The first use of the term 'Ultra' is claimed by two clubs, Sampdoria (Ultras Tito Cucchiaroni) and Torino (Ultras Granata), but it is the fans of Torino who really made a mark on the Italian game as their theatrical and colourful performances on the terraces were truly spectacular.

From this beginning, the Ultra groups spread like wildfire to all the major clubs and, with one eye on the English terraces and the other on Italian culture, the new terrace style quickly took shape.

Unlike the largely spontaneous English style, however, everything the Ultra did was planned in advance and the groups carried with them drums, trumpets, flags and banners. This almost warlike style even spread to the names and symbols they adopted, as the intention was to intimidate or even scare their adversaries who might not perhaps have been used to the 'militarisation' of support.

There were still, however, some groups who followed the English style of crowd noise, humour and banter, and the most important of these was Brigate Gialloblu at Hellas Verona. The forerunner to similar groups at Lazio and Inter, the members of the Brigate were the only Ultras at the time to say they supported the group first and the team second. This *esprit de corps* made them a formidable enemy for their rivals.

The heroic deeds of the Veronesi came to an end when the leaders of the group were arrested *en masse* and accused of being the heads of a criminal gang responsible for looting, vandalism and aggression. Despite protesting that they could hardly be held responsible for the behaviour of everyone in the group, their days were numbered and, eventually, the original Brigate Gialloblu ceased to exist.

At a time when supporters still identified with the players and the team, before the ills of modern football arrived, the support the Ultras gave to the team was regarded as more important than any violent intentions they might harbour towards opposing fans. However, on a few occasions, trouble did occur and the various groups soon began to understand the power they had and increasingly they embraced the idea of proving that they were tougher than their adversaries – something that was helped by the continued inability of the police to understand the new Ultra phenomenon.

Occasionally, however, incidents would be more than simply fights inside grounds. The groups would stage properly planned raids into enemy territory with the aim of humiliating the opposition by stealing their precious flags and banners. This basic level of organisation, typical of the early 1970s Ultra scene, was fine-tuned and improved upon from the end of the decade onwards.

Inevitably, as the Ultra scene developed, there were certain clubs who proved to be more significant than others and one of the more important was Commando Ultra Curva Sud (CUCS) of AS Roma. Formed in 1977 from the union of various smaller groups, the CUCS were the group who introduced the idea of choreographed displays to the Italian stadiums – an idea subsequently copied around the world – as a way of improving the support given to the team.

Unfortunately they were also the group responsible for the first death in an Italian stadium. On 28 October 1979, a Lazio fan was killed on the Curva Nord when he was hit by a rocket flare fired from among the CUCS.

Following that incident they were declared an 'armed group' by the judiciary and were prohibited from showing their banner at any game. A few years later, the ban was revoked and this kick-started the idea of the fans' magnificent displays.

The decline of the CUCS began in the 1990s when, following some internal divisions, they began to lose their grip on the Curva Sud. At the start of the 1999–2000 season, they were replaced by a new group, the AS Roma Ultras.

By the end of the 1980s, the level of violence associated with the Ultra scene had increased dramatically and many of the original groups began to fade as the more senior members became disillusioned with what was happening around them. One of the most important reasons for this was that many of the new groups didn't follow the principles and ideals that had been at the heart of the original Ultra movement. At Lazio, for example, the traditional 'Italian style' of support that had made the Eagles Supporters so popular was abandoned in favour of the 'English style' that had by now begun to inspire other supporters across Europe. This is how, in 1987, the Irriducibili were formed.

This new group, who made no secret of their radical far-right ideals, soon won over control of the Curva Nord at Lazio and adopted songs taken from the English terraces – obviously with most words translated into Italian.

Initially some groups were sceptical and, even though they proved they had good organisation and strength, some other groups accused their leaders of betraying the Italian movement and being more interested in making money for their own personal gain.

This late 1980s shift in Italian terrace-culture spawned other problems for the larger Ultra groups. Traditionally there had always been one principal organised body with an active decision-making directorate of between ten and fifty people. These would be followed by hundreds if not thousands of rank and file members. However, the move towards the English style of support saw a number of small, violent groups developing alongside some of these larger groups. These splinter factions even began to adopt the Casual style of dress to avoid attentions from the police and were involved in several serious incidents where the stated aim was to defend the reputation of their city and the group.

Several of these groups are worthy of mention but one of the most feared were the Opposta Fazione (Opposing Faction) of Roma. Formed in 1989 they were a breakaway group from the predominant Commando Ultra Curva Sud and counted a number of hardened criminals among their membership. They were also not averse to using weapons and created problems in stadiums all over the Italian peninsula. Unlike other Ultra groups they didn't produce many souvenirs or wear any signs of attachment to the group. They just did things that no one else dared to. Inevitably, they ended up under close scrutiny and, eventually, police attention decimated their numbers, although some of their members are still active.

Another group who operate along similar lines are the Gruppo Brasato of AC Milan. Although they haven't been around for as long as the Opposta Fazione, they have learned from their example as have the Teste Matte (Crazy Heads) of Napoli, who have even taken to travelling independently of the other Napoli fans thus hopefully evading police escorts.

However, the violence associated with these splinter groups began to attract increasing attention from both the media and the police – two groups whom the Ultra have come to regard as real enemies.

The problem of football violence in Italy is made up of many things including politics in the stadiums. A number of Italian Curva, although not the majority, have sympathies that lie with the right wing. This has led to the display of various right-wing symbols, such as the Celtic Cross, being displayed in certain stadiums much to the anger of the left wing. Those that understand the life of the Curva realise that the exhibition of such flags is not organised by the Ultra groups with any secret intentions or political motives but is merely used for the most part simply to show their political leanings to rival Ultras.

The problem for these right-wing groups was that the newspapers, who have always had political ideals and are for the most part orientated to the left, see these symbols as a throwback to history. As a result, they initiated a massive press campaign to stamp out racism in the stadiums. This in turn led to a police crackdown against the displaying of any political symbols in Italian football stadiums.

Obviously the people who have to enforce this law are the police who, at least in a football context, are largely dictated to by what is written about Ultras in the newspapers. For this reason the link between the mass media and the police is important in the sense that if a paper reports an incident, be it true or false, the police have to do something about it even if that means finding culprits for reported crimes even when no crime has been committed.

This relationship has had other implications for the Ultra who increasingly find that the word itself equates to either 'hooligan' or 'guilty' in the eyes of the general public.

Ironically, in recent years, there has actually been a decrease in the number of incidents between sets of fans. This can be proved by a simple check of the statistical data available. But, thanks to the media, this is not the perception of the Italian public, who actually think that incidents are on the rise. This has set alarm bells ringing and has led to the general public being behind special government legislation that allows fans to be banned and ordered to sign-on at local police stations at the time that matches are played. This was originally used in 1989 but became an unpopular method of dealing with the Ultra groups. However, little by little it has become more common and changes have even been made to the law, which means that it is now possible to be banned from stadiums even if you haven't committed any actual offence.

The enforcement of this law sent the Ultra groups into a rage. This was primarily because it handed the police the power to get rid of anyone they wanted to, even though in 90 per cent of cases they were innocent of any crime.

But the fact that they had this amount of power without ever seemingly being held accountable for what they were doing with it, also saw the police becoming even more brutal. Hitting out at people without reason, firing tear gas canisters at head height, throwing back seats that had been thrown at them by Ultras, and likewise with flares and fireworks.

This caused increasing problems between the police and the Ultra who quickly came to regard the police as an adversary with the privilege of impunity ('Who bans the Ultras in uniform?' read one banner in the Curva Sud). It has also led to a reduced feeling of hatred between rival supporters. In one incident, the Ultras of Roma and Lazio joined together to fight the police when they arrived to break up a fight the two groups were having with each other before a derby match.

Inside grounds, things were even worse. Unlike in England, in Italy the state and not the clubs are responsible for security inside the stadiums, a role that has traditionally been carried out by the police. There was an attempt made, based on the English model, to introduce stewards onto the Italian Curva, but they were forced to abandon the project as they were constantly attacked. Even the police – who were at one time able to stand alongside supporters on the Curva – very rarely entered into the areas housing the Ultras, preferring instead to keep their distance, film everything and then arrest any possible offenders after watching the tape playback.

However, there were some politicians who were unhappy with this style of policing and, following a number of incidents in the latter half of 1999, two ministers – Bianco and Melandri – decided that 'stadiums should not be lawless places'. This forced the police to go on the offensive and they decided that the best way to approach the problem of football violence was with an iron fist.

This led to a huge backlash from the Ultra and there were wild scenes all over the place culminating in the famous battle of Roma–Liverpool on 15 February 2000 when there was a real and proper revolt by the Ultra groups of the Curva Sud.

In Bologna, a week before the Liverpool game, a Roma Ultra named Alessandro Spoletini went into a coma after being knocked down a steep stairway inside the stadium by police, who claimed it was accidental. This was the last straw for the fans and, on the night of the Liverpool game, the Roma Ultra attacked the police with rockets, home-made bombs and clubs. The police were forced to abandon the stadium, and with the Ultras clearly having the upper hand they were free to set fire to several police cars and police transportation buses.

That episode made the police and the authorities reflect on things and it was thought that a better way to control the fans might be to begin a dialogue with small groups of known and respected Ultras in the hope that they would effectively police their own Curvas. But this idea was soon found to be unworkable as most Ultras would have nothing to do with it.

These days, it's much more common to hear about incidents between Ultras and the police than Ultras versus opposition Ultras. The only regular hotspots of fighting between rival Ultra groups happen in the lower leagues where far fewer police are present and the press attention isn't so overwhelming.

However, even in Serie A, from time to time, there are still incidents that are every bit as violent as the scenes back in the 1980s. In 2000–01, one of the most high-profile incidents involved a game between Napoli and Roma, two teams who have a long and bitter rivalry.

Roma needed to win to clinch only the third league championship in their history, and 10,000 supporters travelled south to Naples in three special trains and a long trail of buses and cars.

Those that made the journey knew what they were letting themselves in for. Naples is never a safe place for visiting Ultras, as the whole Neapolitan population is against you, not just the local football fans. The Romans were not disappointed as, even before they had reached Naples, there were problems with the trains being pelted with rocks and other objects as they passed through stations to the north of the city. Once they arrived in Napoli Centrale station, the scene was set for the day when Roma fans threw a home-made bomb. Thankfully, it failed to explode.

Outside the stadium there were numerous fights between Neapolitans and Romans, with the police having to resort to firing tear gas in an effort to control things. This led to injuries for many fans, who were hit by missiles as they struggled to see through the smoke.

Inside the stadium the Roma fans were gathered in a large cage, and this treatment was severely criticised by the media (one paper ran the headline 'This is football?'), but the truth is that it saved many fans from being hit by objects which included flares, fireworks, coins, and even a dead mouse.

During the game there was continuous fighting and the Romans at one stage got the better of the police who had to flee for their own safety.

Afterwards it was even worse, with the local train station 'Campi Flegrei' being literally razed to the ground by the Roman Ultras. On the train back to Rome there was more violence and a police officer was stabbed.

Another memorable fight involved two trainloads of Milan and Sampdoria Ultras who for some reason stopped alongside each other in open countryside. With the trains being miles from anywhere, it took the police a considerable time to arrive and stop the fighting, which had broken out almost at once. Thankfully, both groups had followed the old Ultra rules of 'no weapons' and so nobody was seriously injured.

The rules of the Ultras are hard to explain. The Mentalita Ultras (Ultras mentality) doesn't allow for the inappropriate use of excessive arms such as knives or guns but sticks and belts are permitted. However, the knife is used relatively frequently, not to inflict serious injury but to humiliate the opponent by scarring them or stabbing them in a non life-threatening place such as the buttocks or sides of the legs. It doesn't always work out like that of course and in 1995 a young Genoa fan was stabbed to death before a Genoa versus Milan match. Sadly, he wasn't the first to have been killed in this way nor will he be the last.

However, in the majority of cases these days, thanks

largely to the massive police presence at games, it is almost impossible to get close to opposing Ultras and so any trouble is usually conducted at a distance with reciprocal throwing of objects. This can make the whole thing seem more 'virtual' than real.

In all honesty, I can't see that ever changing.

CHAPTER NINE
Spain

I have a confession to make: I have never been to Spain. To be honest, I'm not sure why that is. After all, plenty of Brits go there on holiday and the football is obviously world class. However, as a consequence of my ignorance, my knowledge of the place, the people and the sporting culture is severely limited. So much so that when I set out to write this book, I had already placed Spain firmly in the 'also ran' category.

Clearly, that would have been a huge mistake. For not only is the culture surrounding Spanish football phenomenally interesting, the political side of it – aside from being amazingly complex and influential – is almost unique. Similarly, the relationship between the Ultra groups and the clubs is incredible. Can you imagine the leader of the Blades Business Crew or the Zulu Army not only being given free tickets, free travel and even cash by the board of their club, but a parking space in the private car park at the ground, and even some office space under the main stand! Yet just that has happened at Atlético Madrid and at various other clubs in Spain. Certain groups have even been given funds by individual players in the past, as happened when Frente Atlético at Atlético Madrid received money with, it must be said, the full support of the club, who saw such assistance as an investment in the fans and, therefore, of benefit to the team. For in Spain the Ultras do not have anything like the bad reputation of the hooligan crews in Britain.

What follows is an article looking in depth at the evolution of Spain's football culture and particularly the role that extremist politics have played in it. It was written by someone who wishes to be credited as Mr Licor Café (R.C. Celta Firm. Por Galiza Polo Celta), and I would also like to thank Karen Warner, Thomas Gravgaard and Brighton 90 for their help.

However, before I move on to that, there are a few things that need to be explained and highlighted. The first is that the organisation of the Ultra groups in Spain is unlike anything we see in the UK. Aside from the close relationship many have with their clubs, as touched on above, most raise substantial funds by selling merchandise ranging from T-shirts and scarves to photographs and videos.

Similarly, it is important to understand that although the Spanish Ultra groups have (or had) a hardcore membership, the most dangerous aspect of the movement – and one which provides another distinction from the British hooligan scene – is that potentially all members of the group, even the ones who are peaceful 99 per cent of the time, can be brought in to the violence if orchestrated by the leadership. This is why on derby days, groups such as Frente Atlético and Ultras Sur have a potential 'super-firm' of more than 1000 people. And make no mistake, the violence they have become involved in over the years has, on occasions, been simply incredible.

There is little doubt that hooliganism exploded across Spain in the early 1990s for this was when groups such as Frente Atlético, Boixos Nois and Ultras Sur enjoyed something of a renaissance following a post-Heysel clampdown by the Spanish authorities. Indeed, during this period almost all the Ultra groups started to expand and become more organised, easily packing the ends of their home stadiums with hundreds of members – even thousands in the case of Frente Atlético and Biris.

The most extreme rivalry at that time was between the Ultra groups from the two La Liga teams in Barcelona – Boixos Nois (FC Barcelona) and the Brigadas Blanquiazules (Espanyol) – and was based on their traditional identification as pro-Spanish (Espanyol) and pro-Catalan (FC Barcelona). Increasingly, however, confrontations began to be influenced by other factors: the growing number of Skinheads in both groups and the desire for revenge being just two. More worryingly, incidents began taking place not just on match days, but also during the week. In Barcelona, for example, the feud between members of Boixos Nois and Brigadas got so bad that people were being hunted down and attacked in their homes and even at work. The end result of this spiral of violence was that, somewhat predictably, one of the Brigadas was murdered.

Thankfully, violence of this nature happens with less frequency than it used to, but it does still happen. And as the fans embrace the technology of the Internet and the cellphone, it occasionally takes on a whole new dimension.

Vallecas, with nearly a million inhabitants, is a working-class area of Madrid with a fairly large proportion of left-wing inhabitants. It is also home to Rayo Vallecano, a small football club that against the odds has managed to maintain a place in La Liga. The most radical group of Rayo fans go by the name Bukaneros and are famous for their anti-fascist tradition – a notable achievement given that both Real Madrid and Atlético Madrid have large fascist followings who regard Bukaneros as an enemy.

Not surprisingly, the anti-fascist supporters at both Real and Atlético have taken the opposing path and have aligned themselves with Bukaneros and, when a group of left-wing supporters at Real secretly discovered that the Ultras Sur were planning to attack two bars frequented by Bukaneros before the two teams met in a local derby, they had no hesitation in passing the information on.

The plan they uncovered was that the Ultras Sur intended to infiltrate the area in small groups and then come together to hit the two bars they knew would be full of people they considered to be 'reds' and 'supporters of ETA' – the Basque separatist terrorist group. But, having learned of the plan, the Bukaneros began organising their defences.

On the morning of the game, spotters were placed at various points around the area and, when they detected the arrival of a small group of around 40 hardcore Ultras Sur, they immediately phoned through to the two bars and then began shadowing them to see which one they would hit first.

When the group finally arrived at their target, they still believed that they hadn't been detected and immediately steamed towards the entrance only to discover that the steel door was locked firmly shut. What they didn't realise, however, was that on the other side was a bar packed full of Bukaneros and a number of Athletic Bilbao's left-wing Herri Norte's group, all of whom were tooled up with a variety of clubs, bottles and, in the case of one individual, an axe.

As the Ultras Sur began trying to break down the door, those inside poured out of a back door and, after mobbing up in a side street, hit them from the side. The resultant battle left numerous people seriously injured, including one of the Ultras Sur who had been stabbed in the buttocks.

Having vanquished the Ultras Sur, the Bukaneros relaxed, and plans to defend the second bar were all but forgotten as they became convinced that the right-wing group would never dare stage an attack after taking a beating. More importantly, no one had the forethought to keep track of them which meant that vital phone calls were never made.

Inevitably, the Ultras Sur had other ideas and, determined to exact almost instant revenge, headed for the second bar where they managed to catch the Bukaneros in the plaza outside. So ferocious was the attack that the left-wing fans were forced to retreat into the bar and lock themselves in. Unfortunately, two of their members were left outside and both received serious wounds when they were assaulted with bottles.

The fact that the Ultras Sur were so single-minded is significant. For it proves that even the most dangerous and feared of groups can suffer defeat and humiliation if it's inflicted by a small but well organised group of rival fans. It also confirms the simple truth that within the hooligan culture, the protection of a reputation is a major factor, especially when that reputation is as considerable as that of the Ultras Sur.

Besides the typical clichés of sun, fiesta, paella and the sadly all-too-well-known bullfights, Spain is also recognised internationally for having one of the best football leagues in the world. But what do we know about its hooligans? What happens in the stands of the Spanish stadiums? And what goes on in the heads of its most violent fans?

There is of course no single answer to these questions. Primarily, this is because they involve a complex mixture of politics, rivalries, nationalist movements, drugs and an infinite number of styles and subcultures. This sometimes-explosive cocktail has been constantly evolving since the early 1980s and at times has put Spanish football in the spotlight for the wrong reasons.

Violence on the terraces of Spain is, however, a relatively new phenomenon. For Franco's coup d'état and the resulting dictatorship (1939–75) meant that the country was effectively isolated from the rest of Europe for almost 40 years. During that time, severe censorship laws meant that only extremely limited news and culture from outside made it to Spain, while the football league, with the exception of a few players who came from Eastern Europe and South America, was closed to the outside world.

The major exception to this was Real Madrid who enjoyed great success on the European stage. However, while the Franco regime realised the propaganda value of this and exploited it to the full – as they did when the country hosted the 1964 European Championships and beat the USSR in the final – the nation's fans remained almost totally ignorant of the Ultra and hooligan movements that were developing in Italy and England at that time. Spanish stands were simply full of 'normal' fans with no greater wish than to spend a quiet Sunday watching their favourite team play.

Following the death of the dictator in 1975, and the restoration of democracy, Spain began a process of opening itself to the world. During these early years of transition a key event occurred that was to have great significance on the evolution of Spanish football culture: Spain hosted the 1982 World Cup.

The presence of thousands of Italian, South American and especially English football supporters inside Spanish stadiums allowed the young fans living in Madrid, Barcelona, Bilbao, Valencia and the other host cities to witness at first hand these new styles of supporting the game, while the numerous incidents in the streets of Bilbao and its stadium, San Mamés, allowed them to experience at close quarters something that up until then had been largely alien to them. Football violence.

Suddenly, they realised that football could be more than a quiet Sunday pastime. It could be a true and genuine experience. This realisation was augmented by the arrival of the new youth fashions and subcultures, particularly from England. Mods, rockabillies, rockers, Punks and Skinheads began appearing on the terraces, and they brought with them a degree of colour and style that until then had been absent from Spanish football.

This led almost immediately to the formation of a wave of radical supporters' groups including Boixos Nois (crazy boys) at FC Barcelona, Ultras Sur at Real Madrid, Frente Atlético at Atlético Madrid and Supporters Sur at Real Betis. Although not the first Spanish supporter groups – that honour was claimed in 1974 by Brigada Norte Biri Biri (also known simply as Biris) of Sevilla FC while Ultras Sur, Boixos Nois and Supporters Sur all appeared after splitting away from previously existing supporters' clubs – the decision to adopt the more 'European' style of animated support brought a dramatic and very positive change to the atmosphere on the Spanish terraces. It was also warmly welcomed by the clubs and, in exchange for this passionate and animated support, marked by the first organised usage of large flags, drums and banners identifying themselves, a number of these early Ultra groups were actively supported by the clubs.

Despite this dramatic change in culture, the terraces remained relatively calm until the mid 1980s. However, as time passed, friction between rival groups began to become apparent and the number of confrontations increased. One of the most famous of these was the historic battle surrounding the 1986 King's Cup final between Zaragoza and Barcelona which erupted when the two main Ultra groups from the capital (Ultras Sur and Frente Atlético) united to attack Barcelona's Boixos Nois on the streets of Madrid.

What characterised these pioneering groups of Spanish hooligans was the enormous diversity of the member-ship. They were invariably young (the average age was 19–20); however, they came from right across the Spanish social spectrum. Middle- and upper-class lads mixed with those from working-class families and even with simple thugs. The one thing they all had in common was that they were passionate, energetic and vocal in support of their club and were ready to defend it both on the terraces and in the streets. However, by the 1990s, a new factor began to emerge that was to provide perhaps the most distinguishing factor among groups from different teams; it would come to determine rivalries, spark violent confrontations and establish alliances among hooligans of different teams across the country and even the rest of Europe: the politics.

In the mid 1980s groups like Ultras Sur and Frente Atlético were already establishing their identity as advocates and protectors of a singular Spanish nationalism. Conceived as basically consistent with Franco's vision of what Spain should be, the ultimate aim was a country unified (by force if necessary) by right-wing politics and the Castillian Spanish language. As a result, they openly professed and demonstrated their hatred of any and all groups that defended regional identities and, specifically, Catalan, Basque and, later, Galician nationalism. However, it should be said that among their ranks these largely extreme right-wing groups contained a few anarchists and communists who got along based on their support for the same team. A little-known example of this coexistence could once be found on the terraces of Real Madrid where legend has it that among the Ultras Sur were heard occasional shouts in support of Herri Batasuna (popularly recognised as the political wing of the terrorist group ETA) as a way of protesting against the beatings and intimidation by baton-wielding police in their section of the stadium. Nowadays, such a thing would be impossible.

During these early years as the terraces became unreservedly political, the primary target for the right-wing clubs were the Boixos Nois, who were regarded by the rival groups as being anti-Spanish due to their leftist ideologies and support for Catalan independence. In the southern end of the Nou Camp they supported Barcelona with as many Catalonia flags as Barça flags and, alongside their unwavering passion for the team, proclaimed their support of the Catalan nation and its language as much as they protested against the police and the Spanish government.

As the 1990s progressed, the Ultra groups began to solidify ideological divisions among themselves, creating two rival blocks. Those advocating fascist ideologies (also known as Spanish nationalists) and those aligned to the left (which included anti-fascists and the supporters of independence movements, including the Basques, the Galicians and the Catalans). To make matters even more complicated, two of the main right-wing groups, Ultras Sur (Real Madrid) and Brigadas Blanquiazules (Espanyol) established friendly contacts with each other and provided an example of unity that was soon being copied by others who shared the same beliefs. Key to their success was the extremeness of their convictions and their lack of hesitation in using violence against everything they believed to be their enemy.

On the other side of this ideological divide, the majority of anti-fascist and leftist groups began to adopt practices and positions that would disassociate them from the right-wing hooligans. One example of this was the rejection of the word 'Ultra', a term that had come to symbolise the extreme-right and everything it stood for. Instead, they adopted the expression 'Hinchas', which is Spanish for supporters.

At the same time they began to distance themselves from the Tifosi or Italian style of support that had been adopted by their Ultra enemies. Instead, little by little these leftist fans began to follow the English style, which concerned itself less with spectacle and merchandising and more with vocal support and alcohol. These days, this style has been adopted by all but two of the largest, most colourful and perhaps less violent groups aligned to the left, Riazor Blues (Deportivo La Coruña) and Biris Norte (Seville FC). For the others, efforts are concentrated on singing and shouting their support for 90 minutes and demonstrating their toughness on the street.

Two left-wing hooligan groups, Herri Norte Taldea (Athletic Bilbao) and Celtarras (Celta Vigo) have been particularly successful in establishing themselves as solid ideological opposition to the right wing and have consistently backed up this reputation with violence. To their right-wing enemies they are among the most hated and at the same time most respected groups on the left. Both contain a notable presence of anti-racist, leftist Skinheads, which has become fairly typical of the Spanish scene where the smaller groups – on both sides of the political divide – tend to be more violent and more committed.

One exception to this politically fuelled division is that of the Boixos Nois, mentioned above as a model during the 1980s for their radical leftist and independence-minded members. Today as a group they are practically isolated from, if not in direct confrontation with, other groups on both left and right wings. The reason is the infiltration by right-wing Catalonian Skinheads which has angered the anti-fascist members to such an extent that many have actually left the group. As a result, the Boixos Nois today find themselves in a strange situation. Their historical enemies (the pro-Spanish Ultras Sur and Brigadas Blanquiazules) still hate them for being Catalan nationalists while they are now also despised by the majority of the anti-fascist groups for the violence and aggression of the Boixos right-wingers.

The third and equally complicated political aspect of

the scene in Spain involves the four clubs from the Basque region: Real Sociedad, Athletic Bilbao, Osasuna and Deportivo Alavés. For while the average supporters hate each other with typical football-fan rivalry, the hooligan groups invariably turn derby games into huge parties simply because their feelings against Spain are bigger than the rivalry between each other. This has become a source of much anger to the Spanish people because it is another indication that people from the Basque region hate them so much. Interestingly, while the groups' hatred of Spain extends to the Spanish national football side, they do come together under the name Euskal Hintxak (Basque supporters) to support the unofficial Basque team who play at least once a year.

Inevitably, the anti-Spanish feelings of the clubs from the Basque region have had an impact on the way they are policed. Something that is also true of many clubs in Galicia and Catalonia. Although in the case of the Basque clubs it is the Basque police force who are responsible for security at home, when they travel, the forces of law and order are a very real enemy – one which they have come to regard as nothing more than a repressive, foreign force defending the interests of fascist groups. Ironically, the police, who have been known to accuse the Basque fans of being nothing more than terrorists, are often forced to defend them from the aggression of the home supporters when they have travelled to away games.

However, though it may seem incongruous, the majority of fan groups on the far right (ie Atlético Madrid, Real Madrid, Espanyol and Betis) are also distrustful of the police. Indeed, in the opinion of many Ultras the biggest and most dangerous group they might meet in a stadium is not the Ultras Sur, Brigadas Blanquiazules or Boixos Nois, it's the group made up of hundreds of uniformed men who are all well-equipped for fighting.

Since the implementation of Sport Law and the Antiviolence Commission in the early 1990s, certain restrictions on what can be brought into the stadiums have caused some groups to feel especially targeted. Besides prohibiting alcohol, flares and flag poles, and requiring the installation of closed-circuit television to monitor and record what goes on in and around the stadiums, the ban on racist, Nazi and other hate-inciting symbols have made the Ultras in general – and especially groups with a more explicitly racist character – feel especially harassed by the police. As a result, confrontations, both inside and outside stadiums, are common in local derbies and games between big rivals. Many have even been broadcast on television and have become unforgettable in the history of Ultras in Spain. For example, the Ultras Sur fighting the police in the stands of Zorilla (Valladolid) in the 1980s and the police attacking Basque fans from Real Sociedad in the King's Cup final in the Bernabeu. Others that particularly stand out are those of the police unloading against Chelsea supporters when they came to Zaragoza in 1995 and, most recently, in November 2001, fans of Celta and Athletic Bilbao who came together and succeeded in forcing the Spanish police to retreat in a spectacular fight in Balaidos (Celta).

Like the police, television and the rest of the Spanish media have become important players in the culture of Spanish football. Initially, in the post-Franco era, they treated even the most radical of fans with respect and objectivity but since the first serious incidents of violence inside grounds – and especially post-Heysel – the policies and practices (and maybe even politics) of the press have been consistently the same: silence the positive and emphasise the negative.

Successes worth reporting such as the passion and colour the fans bring to the stands, the friendships between the various Ultra groups, the numerous campaigns against racism and hooliganism, have all become insignificant footnotes compared to even a minor exchange of fists between opposing fans or throwing things onto the field. For the press, the socially valuable activities of these groups are not worth mentioning. Instead the word 'Ultra' only appears in the headlines as the equivalent of guilty even though on occasions their own pictures have proved that those responsible are 'respectable' fans who smoke their cigars in their expensive seats.

The consequence of this type of reporting is that it is now almost impossible to find anyone from the Ultra groups willing to take part in television debates or give interviews to the press. This, in turn, has led the media to adopt a new approach to its reporting of the fans, the use of hidden cameras and undercover journalists.

The most successful example of this happened at Real Madrid when a reporter managed to film an exposé of the Ultras Sur which proved what many people had always suspected: that they were being supplied complimentary tickets by the club and were selling them on to fund their activities; that they were staging violent attacks against rival fans; and that they were extremely racist, active in fascist politics, and that they hated the police and the press.

The impact of this programme, not to mention the way it was obtained (considered unethical by many), was immense. Not only did it result in a number of senior Ultras Sur figures being identified and arrested, it also ensured that the press in general and journalists specifically have become prime targets for the Ultras Sur. However, this isn't just limited to Real Madrid. For the tension between young fans across Spain and the increasingly sensationalist press have placed journalists, their cars and their equipment on the list of prime targets around the stadiums.

It is fair to say that since the end of the 1990s there

have been many changes to Spanish football and, taken together, they have resulted in a huge reduction in the level of violence that had previously dogged the game. Stricter policing, higher ticket prices, all-seater stadiums and pay-per-view television have all had an impact, but the most important, and successful, has been the tendency among the younger Ultra fans to remove politics, racism and violence from their sporting culture.

This apolitical, non-violent style has been remarkably successful, with newly formed groups such as Orgullo Vikingo (Real Madrid), Gol Gran (Valencia), Colectivo 1932 (Real Zaragoza), Penya Juvenil (Espanyol) and Juventudes Verdiblancas (Racing Santander) adopting a style of support based simply on total loyalty to their teams and the creation of colourful terrace spectacles in the Tifosi mould. More importantly, when they travel they try to avoid confrontations – not always successfully – with local hooligans; sometimes, by looking to establish direct and friendly links with like-minded groups in other cities.

It has not, however, been universally welcomed. Many of these new factions have been established by dividing from older and more violent groups. Not surprisingly, the left-wing Ultra groups doubt the sincerity of these apolitical newcomers, considering them to be largely made up of formerly violent fascists who are trying to avoid coming under attack while at the same time looking for the club to help them travel to away games. The same distrust comes from the Ultras on the right who regard them either as traitors or simply leftists who are afraid to admit to their political beliefs.

Sadly, despite the success of the new groups, neither serious crowd violence nor politics have disappeared from the game in Spain, nor will they. Recent years have seen the Spanish Ultra groups develop increasingly close relations with hooligan groups in other countries primarily as a result of their shared politics. For example, Ultras Sur (Real Madrid) and Brigadas Blanquiazules (Espanyol) maintain a strong, friendly relationship with fascist and racist hooligans at Lazio. A similar situation exists with the Riazor Blues (Deportivo La Coruña) and Biris (Seville) with the Ultras from Olympic de Marseille and Oporto, while anti-fascist hooligans from Celtarras (Celta Vigo) and Herri Norte (Athletic Bilbao) have linked with both Glasgow Celtic and St. Pauli in Germany. Even the apolitical groups are at it with the most well-known example being between Orgullo Vikingo (Real Madrid) and various Ultra groups at Greek club Panathinaikos including Gate 13.

Similarly, as recently as 6 October 2002, police were forced to use rubber bullets and tear gas to control serious disturbances which broke out at the local derby between Seville and Real Betis.

The one area of the Spanish game that has yet to see any significant hooligan or Ultra activity is the national side. This is due largely to the fact that supporters are reluctant to travel abroad, which was true even at the height of the Ultra movement in the mid nineties. It is most certainly not due to lack of interest or national pride as, when they play at home, the support for Spain, especially in Seville, is incredible.

However, there are signs that this may finally be changing. Far-right supporters from a number of groups have come together under the name Orgullo Nacional (National Pride) and have begun causing trouble at games. For example, there were serious problems in Madrid when Spain played Israel in 2002.

Quite what will happen next in Spain is a mystery. The game has become very fashionable and stadiums are filled with people who come only to watch the match. This means that it is only the Ultra groups who are keeping the noise, colour and passion going and that is starting to cause some frustration. This has meant that trouble inside grounds, much of which is directed at the police and the stewards, is showing signs of an increase. And although it is unlikely to ever reach the levels of the 1980s and the 1990s, the Spanish parliament are so concerned that they have said that they intend to introduce new legislation to combat the problem.

For the fans, and especially the Ultra groups, that could be very bad news indeed.

Part Three

SCANDINAVIA

While Scandinavia is not necessarily the first region that springs to mind when talking about the culture of hooliganism, there is little doubt that the region provides some of the most interesting examples of the different ways in which the issue can impact on the game. For not only does it contain two countries where football violence is all but unknown, it is also home to two of the most infamous and active hooligan groups in European football.

More importantly, at least for the purposes of this book, the influence of English hooliganism upon the region is both obvious and acknowledged. In Denmark, for example, having seen the damage done to the English game, the authorities made a conscious effort to try to create a fan culture that would make football-related violence totally unacceptable to Danish supporters. In Sweden, however, the fans did all they could to try and make sure that exactly the opposite took place. When they saw hooliganism at first hand, they decided that they wanted it!

However, before we look in depth at what happened, and why, in those two countries, it is worth examining two of the other footballing nations in the region because, while neither has a hooligan culture to speak of, there are worrying signs in both that things may be heading in that direction.

Of the two, Norway is the more interesting given that they were involved in a joint bid with Sweden to stage the 2008 European Championships. This is a tournament at which security is bound to be a prime concern.

For the majority of Norwegian football fans, hooliganism is something that rarely impacts on their supporting pleasure. Games have a history of being remarkably passive affairs and it is fair to say that ice hockey matches are far more likely to see violence than football. There are, however, a small but growing number of lads at clubs who seem intent on establishing a Norwegian footballing culture akin to that in England. One of the main reasons being that English games are beamed live into Norwegian homes every week and, not only is the football of a better standard than the domestic game, but so is the atmosphere and passion generated by the crowds.

Inevitably, these lads have begun to form themselves into small supporter groups and chief among these is VIF Waffen who follow Oslo-based club Valerenga. Although their numbers rarely exceed 40, they have been active on a small number of occasions particularly against the bigger Norwegian teams, such as Brann and Lillestrom. They also have one spectacular claim to their name. For it was allegedly one of their number who was responsible for the England fans rioting in Malmö during the 1992 European Championships. Having climbed onto the roof of a beer tent and blown a whistle, he supposedly sent the signal for England supporters to go ballistic.

Despite this small but growing problem, Norwegian football has so far remained remarkably hooligan-free and many people suggest that the main reason for that is the role of the police. For while they have total responsibility for security at games, they are rarely present in significant numbers and almost never in any kind of riot clothing. The result is that the mood at games generally remains calm and good-natured with what rivalry there is revolving around songs and banter. That is not to say the police do not take the problem seriously, they certainly do. But they prefer to use their resources to target individuals away from the football environment, a tactic that, to date, has proven remarkably successful. Quite how they would have fared if their Euro 2008 bid had been successful we will never know.

The other Scandinavian nation who have a small but growing hooligan problem is Finland.

Finnish fan culture first saw the light of day in the late 1990s when, for the first time, the nation's players began making their mark in Europe. From seemingly out of nowhere, Litmanen, Hyypia, Forssell and numerous others became household names and football suddenly became hugely popular.

The problem for the Finnish authorities was that up until that point, crowd numbers had been relatively low (usually between 2000 and 2500) and hooliganism was something only ever seen on the news. As a result, security at domestic games was unheard of but, within a short time, the game in Finland was seeing the first indication that things would have to change.

The first incident of note took place in 1998 and involved a group of supporters allied to Inter Turku: the Ultraboyz.

With the team battling for promotion and playing away against Ilves Tampere – the side at the top of the division – about 25 Ultraboyz travelled to Tampere in the hope of seeing their team secure a victory. At that time travelling supporters were almost unknown, so their appearance was not only something of a shock, it created a degree of tension inside the ground.

Inter scored after just nine minutes and, as Ultraboyz celebrated, flares were lit and one of their number set off with one in his hand intending to do a lap of the stadium. However, he was quickly detained and, almost unbelievably for a Finnish game at that time, thrown out of the stadium.

In the second half, the home team scored twice, but of more importance was the fact that having seen one of their number ejected, their team looking like they were going to lose, and suffering a stream of abuse from the locals, the mood among the Ultraboyz was not a good one. With just two minutes to go, a smoke bomb and a flare were thrown onto the pitch forcing the referee to stop play while the smoke dispersed. Immediately this happened, the few police present steamed forward and attacked the Inter fans, throwing one of them down a flight of stairs before calm was restored.

As one of the first cases of football-related violence in Finland, the incident received huge publicity in the media and both teams were fined by the Finnish Football Association (SPL) – almost certainly the first time any team in the country had been fined for the behaviour of its supporters. It also led to an increase in security at all stadiums and a total ban on all kinds of fireworks.

It was a warning that seemed to work for it was almost three years before another incident of domestic hooliganism was reported in the Finnish press. However, the impact this one had was immense. For while it was a relatively small fight involving only about 15–20 supporters of Tampere United and the FC Lahti fan group FCLK, the whole thing was filmed and shown repeatedly on national television.

Almost immediately, a huge debate began in the media warning the country that it was about to see an explosion of hooliganism. Unsure of what to do but certain that they had to be seen to be doing something, the authorities once again clamped down. Security at games was increased and all travelling supporters were treated as a potential threat.

This time, however, the over-reaction didn't work. For

only a few weeks later, there was yet another instance of violence at a game. This one was far more serious than anything the country had ever seen before.

The 116% Boys of FC Jokerit – so-called because they stand in section 116 and give 100 per cent support to the team – had already been given a warning by the SPL for chanting racist abuse at foreign players, so when they travelled to FC Haka for what appeared to be just a routine fixture, security around them was naturally tight. But when Haka scored in the last minute to secure a 2–1 win, about 50 of them managed to get onto the pitch and began fighting with the police.

Two officers were badly injured before reinforcements arrived and forced the 116% Boys out of the ground and onto their buses. However, rather than head for home, they headed towards the local bars where more fighting broke out – this time resulting in only minor injuries but some serious damage to property. For the police that was enough and, as the fans headed towards Helsinki and home, their bus was stopped and everyone detained. However, following complaint and counter-complaint by the fans, only one made it to court where he was charged with assaulting a police officer in the course of his duty.

The media were incensed and demanded even more action against the hooligans with the result that security was stepped up even further. For the first time, away supporters were allocated specific sections and everyone attempting to pass through a turnstile was searched, a practice that continues to this day.

However, while the domestic scene is one thing, the international scene is another. Strangely, home games against Hungary and even Moldova have often involved serious crowd violence, although it has to be said that almost every incident involved local fans fighting with the police and stewards. However, in 1999, a game against Turkey saw some of the most serious fighting

Finland has ever witnessed and the national stadium was set on fire after police failed to stop some Turkish protestors invading the pitch and planting a political flag in the centre circle.

Quite why the national side have attracted this problem to a greater degree than the domestic league is something of a mystery, although there is a belief that they appeal to a number of people who do not necessarily follow football but, rather, support ice-hockey teams. Indeed, it is fair to say that just about every hockey club in Finland has lads who are more than willing to become involved in trouble, although it is usually unorganised and spontaneous.

However, the fact remains that given the rising popularity of football in Finland and the increasing profile of some of its overseas stars, there is little doubt that unless the authorities get hold of things, it is only a matter of time before hooliganism, and the culture that surrounds it, begins to take a serious hold on the game.

It should be stressed, however, that the problems in Norway and Finland are tiny compared to those of their near neighbours Denmark and Sweden – two countries whose hooligans we have to examine more closely.

CHAPTER TEN
Denmark

Danish football fans have a reputation for being among the most boisterous groups of supporters to be found anywhere in the world. But it is a little known fact that this reputation was actually born at Wembley stadium in London.

In the autumn of 1983 almost 20,000 Danes were inside the historical home of English football to witness Denmark secure a famous 1–0 victory in a qualifier for the 1984 European Championships in France. They were drunk and colourful, but above all, they were well-behaved. The Danish press rewarded them with the label 'Roligans' (rolig means calm), which cemented a huge and still all-dominant desire within the Danish football society to distance itself from any association with hooliganism.

This desire had first originated in the days following England's visit to the old Idraetsparken stadium almost a year previously. The behaviour of the English support in 1982 had provided the Danish press with their first real taste of football violence on the international stage and it was not well received. As a result, they decided that rather than follow the English media's path of condemning their own supporters, which would almost certainly create a negative image that would actually help to create a bad reputation – as it had in England – they would instead concentrate on the positive side of the Danish support.

This they believed would be the way to help the decent fans build a strong image for themselves and the Danish game, and it worked perfectly.

Among the lads on the club scene, however, things were different. That same visit had provided an inspiration that many felt was somehow long overdue. For while there is no doubt that the English certainly showed the Danish fans how to indulge in violence, it has to be pointed out that the domestic club scene already had intense rivalries which provided a strong foundation from which hooliganism could build. In the capital, games between KB, AB and BK Frem attracted huge crowds, while in Aarhus, AGF and IK Skovbakken could not stand the sight of each other – a relationship only slightly better than that between fans of OB and B1909 in Odense.

While the Danish national following throughout the 1980s built on their new-found reputation as colourful and peaceful, the club scene also remained largely unaffected by violence. However, while two of the historically dominant sides, KB and AGF, had a limited core of fans who would occasionally cause small amounts of trouble, especially at away matches, things were to change with the arrival of Brondby IF as a major footballing force. For their domination of the Danish game – including the five championship titles they secured between 1985 and 1991 – was to play a significant role in the formation of an organised hooligan scene in Denmark.

To try to counter this dominance, in 1992 KB merged with another Copenhagen club, B1903, to form the highly ambitious FC Copenhagen. Suddenly, the Danish league had not two but three big clubs looking for honours. More importantly, it also found itself with three supporter factions which, by 1995, thanks to the formation of organised hooligan groups at each of the clubs, had developed a vicious rivalry.

However, there is more to these rivalries than simply

football. Politics and even regional differences play a significant role and, for that reason alone, it is important that we examine each of them separately to understand just what drives them along.

The mentality of AGF supporters is provincial and they are proud of it. Their home is in Denmark's second largest city Aarhus, which is situated on the mainland, Jutland. The rivalry that exists between Copenhagen and Jutland in general is obvious to anyone who visits the country, speaks to the locals, and is not completely ignorant. It is largely verbal and humorous, and mainly manifests itself in banter. But in the bigger cities of Jutland, such as Aarhus, Aalborg and Esbjerg, it is not always a joke. People from Copenhagen cannot automatically expect to be welcomed in the local bars or nightclubs and, if all of the inter-regional fighting that has taken place over the years had taken place on the football stands, Denmark would have a very active hooligan scene indeed.

The supporters of AGF – violent as well as non-violent – find a large part of their motivation and identity in their dislike of the teams from the capital area. This antipathy has not exactly been curbed by the fact that the growth of both FC Copenhagen and Brondby IF has coincided with a decline in their own clubs' fortunes. Although it is FC Copenhagen that has come to personify the cheeky and arrogant capital, fans of AGF always consider Brondby IF to be their main rival. There are two reasons for this. First, the rivalry with Brondby IF dates 'all the way' back to the mid eighties (Copenhagen FC was founded only in 1992 and quickly obtained sufficient charisma to disengage itself from the memory of KB) and second, when Brondby IF took over as the new dominant force in Danish football, it was at the expense of AGF.

It was these feelings, together with the frustration of

having to endure occasional violence at the hands of the Brondby firms, that in October 1994 made a group of AGF fans split from the official supporters' club to form Ultra White Pride – a firm that would not have to rely on police protection to survive a trip to the capital area.

Within a season, the group had become an established part of the AGF support but, due to their necessarily exclusive nature, their numbers were limited and so, on occasions, they would join with other groups to boost their size. These would include members of the semi-violent AGF group, Aarhus White Angels for home games and, on away trips to Copenhagen, they would often be backed-up by hooligans from BK Frem. However, to put things into perspective, the size of the firm at that time rarely exceeded 30.

One possible reason for this is that Ultra White Pride has always had the stigma of Nazism attached to it. Although officially the name relates to the team's white shirt, it also reveals the political dimension of the group, or at least of some of its members. Aarhus is a town that has had its share of trouble with organised gangs of Palestinian, Somalian and Turkish immigrants and, from this perspective, Ultra White Pride stretches beyond the football ground. They have left right-wing propaganda and swastika stickers inside more than one Danish ground and infuriated the supporters of Dutch side Twente Enschede when they displayed Nazi symbols during the away leg of their 1997 UEFA Cup tie.

Other instances have included members of the group standing guard at gatherings of the right-wing Den Danske Forening [The Danish Society] and an Ultra White Pride presence at a Nazi-party gathering in Jutland in 1999. The group have also been saluted on the website of the Blood and Honour organisation and, as recently as the early summer of 2002, some of its members were involved in clashes with local immigrants on the streets of Aarhus. Interestingly, of the eight people arrested on that occasion, two were English.

There is no doubt that Ultra White Pride means business, and apparently not only when it relates to football rivalries. From an international perspective – and even compared to their main domestic rivals – they struggle to find the numbers which could cause the damage they aim for. But they are ambitious and, even in small numbers, have proved that they are more than capable of causing trouble inside and outside many domestic grounds. Once AGF return to the top of Danish football, supporters across Europe are almost certain to witness them in some sort of action.

The second group in Danish football are the Southside United of Brondby IF. The club takes its name from a small village that became engulfed by the spread of Copenhagen in the latter part of the 20th century but, whereas FC Copenhagen draws most of its support from the centre and the wealthy areas in the north of the capital, the majority of Brondby followers come from the more inflamed western suburbs.

The group's origins date back to the early nineties when a small group of supporters adopted the name Southside Brigade after the stand where the hardcore fans gathered. Trouble at derby games against FC Copenhagen quickly became the norm and, in 1994, the group took real trouble to their rival's home ground for the first time when, in what quickly became known as 'Black Friday', more than 40 were arrested. Over the next few seasons, things were to get considerably worse.

In 1993, the club had formed an official supporters' movement with the idea of replicating the kind of fanatical but peaceful support enjoyed by clubs in Southern Europe. However, just as at AGF, a number of fans were unhappy with this and set out to distance themselves from the official supporters' club by forming small groups of their own. Since many of these groups were up for trouble, particularly when FC Copenhagen were the opponents, it was only a matter of time before they all came together under a single banner and, in 1996, an umbrella organisation entitled Southside United was created. Suddenly, Brondby IF had a united firm that could outnumber any domestic opposition and, from that point on, the threat of violence was present every time Brondby played, especially against either AGF or FC Copenhagen.

One of the most interesting aspects of Southside United is the way that they showed a high level of recklessness and little respect for the law. On one occasion, they even stormed a police station to attack a group of Ultra White Pride who were themselves waiting to collect a group of their own lads who had been detained before a game. They also hold the record for arrest figures: in June 2001, 54 were detained when the club met FC Copenhagen to decide the Danish league title.

As one of the strongest groups in the region, Southside United have not been slow in forming links with other firms across Northern Europe. Relationships with the Black Army of AIK Stockholm are such that some of their number are known to visit and even fight alongside their Swedish friends, while at one stage they even set up a joint home page with hooligans from FC Brugge.

Inevitably, the Danish authorities are less than thrilled with some of their activities, and the club have come down strongly against them, blaming them not only for causing trouble, but for giving visiting hooligan groups an excuse to cause problems in and around the city on match days. As a result, all of the ringleaders are banned from home games – and most away fixtures. However, this has only succeeded in inspiring them to be more inventive with their planning – something proven by the fact that in September 2002, together with members of

Ultra White Pride, they were involved in fighting following Denmark's draw against Norway in Oslo. This is evidence that, for the first time, Danish hooligans are looking to follow the English lead and establish a hooligan following around the national side.

The most surprising thing about the third of the big three hooligan groups in Denmark is that they exist at all. For when FC Copenhagen was founded in 1992, it was difficult to see where their fan-base was going to come from. Of the two clubs who merged, B1903 had practically no following to offer, while the majority of KB's hardcore fans made it clear that there was no way that they were going to support what was almost universally regarded as nothing more than a cynical business exercise that had taken over the club they held so dear and buried all its traditions.

However, a few renegades took the new club to their hearts and they were soon joined by many of Copenhagen's residents who were sick and tired of Brondby IF's domestic dominance. At the end of their first season, the club took a couple of thousand supporters to the title decider at Brondby Stadion. More importantly, within just three seasons, the club had attracted a sizable hooligan element. Inspired by the HH Ultras of SV Hamburg, with whom they had teamed up on a few occasions at matches in the German Bundesliga, they called themselves Copenhagen Ultras.

From the outset, at least to the press and public, the group were far less visible than their fierce rivals Southside United. The main reason for this was that unlike Brondby IF, a club which carried an almost inherent stigma of violence and disorder, FC Copenhagen had a reputation for having a well-educated and wealthy following. To a certain extent, the group not only enjoyed this, they capitalised on it by creating a sense of style, arrogance and élitism around themselves. So successful was this that as the millennium approached, they changed their name to Copenhagen Casuals.

Like their near neighbours, Southside United, the Copenhagen Casuals have also forged ties with hooligan and Ultra groups in other European nations. But their strongest link is with the Frontliners of Swedish club Helsingborg. The fans of both clubs have reportedly fought side by side on numerous occasions, but the relationship was further cemented when Brondby IF persuaded the trainer and a key player to leave Helsingborg's double-winning side of 1999 and sign for them.

While these three are undoubtedly the major players on the Danish hooligan scene, recent years have also seen the emergence of groups at some of the smaller Danish clubs such as Aalborg, Lyngby, Odense and Silkeborg. But there are increasing signs that the Danish authorities are finally starting to take the problem seriously. And the reason for that is simple: the 2000 UEFA Cup final.

There is no doubt that the Danish police were made to look very inefficient by the events surrounding this fixture. For while they were more than familiar with hooliganism and had plenty of experience in containing and controlling rival factions, it had always been on a relatively small scale. Indeed, prior to this fixture they had only ever had one serious incident of mass violence to deal with, and that was the riots that had followed the referendum on the Edinburgh treaty in May 1993. On that occasion, they had fired 113 shots in an effort to bring the crowds under control!

Normally, of course, the game would have passed by without major incident, and the typically Danish way of dealing with things – relaxed and welcoming – would have been perfectly suited to a match between Arsenal and Galatasaray. But in the wake of the murders of the two Leeds fans in Istanbul, serious trouble was inevitable;

yet instead of going on the offensive, the police simply sat back and relied on their normal approach. The results of that tactic were beamed around the world, and the police were quite rightly subjected to huge criticism and ridiculed for their disorganised and pitiful attempts to persuade incensed hooligans on both sides not to hit each other too hard.

To be fair, much of this criticism was taken on-board and the Danish police have definitely learned valuable lessons. In April 2002, as a result of the Middle East conflict, numerous demonstrations were announced in connection with the friendly between Denmark and Israel and there were even threats that Palestinian immigrants would do all they could to get the game called off. To counter this, the police made a fortress out of Parken and managed to keep the demonstrators well away from the ground. One hundred and fifty-three arrests were made and the police regained a lot of credibility and respect. More importantly, this experience has also had an impact on football, as they increasingly focus on the few 'known faces' that make up the Danish hooligan scene.

Quite what effect this will have in the future is uncertain. But there is little doubt that while the Danish hooligan scene does not currently pose the same degree of threat to public order as it does in England, Germany or Italy, the firms certainly pose a threat to any potential rival groups no matter where they come from.

More worryingly for the authorities, if the firms could manage to set aside their differences to join forces when the national side play – and there is no doubt that moves are afoot to do just that, as evidenced by events in Oslo in September 2002 – then it would surely be only a matter of time before the 'Roligan' reputation would face a severe testing. One it might not be able to survive.

CHAPTER ELEVEN
Sweden

When the subject of European football hooliganism is discussed, Sweden isn't one of the countries that would immediately spring to mind. But those in the know are well aware that football violence exists there. Not on the scale of England, Germany or Russia maybe, but it is just as hard and merciless. Indeed, Sweden is home to two of the most notorious hooligan groups in European football: the Black Army and Firman Boys. Both of whom follow AIK Stockholm.

Violence has actually existed alongside Swedish football for many years but it was only when the country hosted the 1992 European Championships that it really came to the public attention. Riots involving mostly English and German supporters not only shocked the Swedish public, but they proved to be inspirational to local hooligans who witnessed organised violence on a scale they had previously only ever imagined. Such was the impact that in the aftermath of the tournament copycat groups began springing up at all of the main Premiership clubs, particularly those in the two main cities, Stockholm and Gothenburg, and in the heavily populated area of Skåne which is home to both Malmö and Helsingborg.

Since those early days, Stockholm has come to be considered the centre of the Swedish hooligan scene and with good reason. The three Premiership teams from the city, AIK, Djurgaarden and Hammarby, are all giants of Swedish football and have strong support. However, only AIK and Djurgaarden have seriously active firms and, of the two, it is AIK who are the more interesting. The exploits of the two firms who follow them could fill a book all of their own.

Key to this is the fact that both groups have worked hard over the years to cultivate an image for themselves. Firman Boys, in particular, regard themselves as being protectors of the club and central to its continued success. Indeed, their website boasts of their being 'The leading hooligans of Sweden' and 'A brotherhood of violent casuals who no one stands on'. To a certain extent, this is supported by the media hype which surrounds them. For example, in 1998, the English newspaper the *Daily Mail* published an entire page about their exploits and, just a year later, when AIK were due in London for a Champions League fixture against Arsenal, the group were again featured in the English press and labelled 'the most dangerous hooligans in Europe'.

While Firman Boys revel in such publicity and do whatever they can to achieve more, it is fair to say that the 'accolades' given to them are well deserved. For they are a very nasty group indeed.

Before the 1992 European Championships, there had been no real need for any kind of firm in Sweden and so the history of Firman Boys is more violent than long. In effect, they are a sub-group of the bigger and more organised Black Army and were formed in the early nineties when it became increasingly fashionable to fight for your team.

Almost uniquely, the group quickly adopted a uniform to identify themselves. This comprised a black bomber jacket turned inside out to display the orange lining. Not so surprisingly, they also adopted the logo (a black triangle with Alex, the film's 'hero', staring out of it) from

Stanley Kubrick's violent film, *A Clockwork Orange.*

While their image was one thing, their reputation for violence was another, and it quickly spread through both Swedish and European football. Before a Cup-Winners' Cup fixture against the Danish side Aarhus, they even set fire to a building and, when AIK qualified for the European Cup in 1993, Firman Boys travelled to Czechoslovakia for their team's fixture against Sparta Prague and caused mayhem. In 1997, Barcelona supporters were the victims when the group laid waste the Olympic village while at home. Anyone who comes to Stockholm is regarded as fair game. The Swedish police have even been forced to fire gunshots to disperse them and save people in danger.

It isn't just at matches that they cause problems. In the past, the group have issued death threats to referees, ex-players and even journalists, while they have reportedly been involved in several incidents at ice hockey games.

The other large firm in the city are DFG who follow Djurgaarden. Like their near neighbours at AIK, they have a reputation for violence and so derby games between the two clubs are usually tense and bloody affairs, and never more so than in May 2001.

With Djurgaarden the visitors, and Firman Boys ready, waiting and willing as always, arrangements were made for a clean fight with no weapons. However, DFG had decided that this time they would really go for it and not only took a mob which for once matched the Firman Boys for numbers, but went heavily tooled-up. After a few hours of hide-and-seek with the police, the two firms arrived at a park in the centre of the city, but for reasons that are still unclear, both somehow had the police behind them. With nothing to keep them apart, they immediately went for it and indulged in a toe-to-toe battle that was so ferocious, the police could only sit back and watch. Having arrived armed with everything from iron bars to plastic bags filled with broken glass, DFG gave Firman Boys a serious beating. Several people were hospitalised and a number arrested, but after the game things were just as bad. A Djurgaarden supporter was seriously assaulted during battles outside the main AIK stand and a man was stabbed at a tube station in the city centre.

While this incident ensured that hostilities between the two firms will continue for some considerable time, it almost pales into insignificance when compared to the other great Swedish club rivalry: AIK and IFK Gothenburg.

Gothenburg is the second biggest city in Sweden and is home to the most successful Swedish club side, IFK. More importantly, the citizens of the city have long harboured a bitterness towards their so-called 'big brothers' who, in response, often refer to Gothenburg as 'Sweden's arsehole'. Inevitably, such friction manifests itself in football, and fixtures between club sides from the two cities almost always involve violence. And if IFK Gothenburg are involved, at the front will always be their firm, Wisemen.

There is no doubt that games between AIK and IFK are the biggest in Swedish football. Exactly the same applies to the two firms, who regard each other with that odd mixture of hatred and respect that typifies hooligan rivalries. Meetings between the two are always tense and dangerous affairs usually involving pre-arranged fights to avoid the attentions of the police. In one instance, before a Swedish cup final between the two teams, some members of Firman Boys even managed to make their threats live on national television.

The police have always struggled to keep a lid on the activities of the two firms, and recent years have seen a number of high profile and extremely violent incidents. In May 2001, AIK travelled to Gothenburg in their hundreds and, once inside the ground, set fire to a huge IFK flag they had stolen from the home stand. The IFK fans went berserk and, after the game, hundreds fought outside the stadium. More recently, in August 2002, a member of Wisemen died of head injuries sustained during a pre-arranged fight between the two groups in a park three miles from Rasunda stadium where a match involving the two teams was due to be played. According to the coroner, the majority of the injuries came about as a result of his head being repeatedly stamped upon. It was Sweden's first ever hooligan-related death.

The inter-city rivalry isn't limited to AIK either. In July 2001, the Djurgaarden firm DFG appeared in central Gothenburg and were directed by Wisemen to a meet outside Scandinavium, a giant hockey stadium in central Gothenburg. Almost immediately, DFG were picked up by a police escort and only half of them made it to the meeting place, but this turned out to be a blessing in disguise for those who failed to make it. Wisemen had set an ambush and led the visitors into an alley where vicious fighting broke out and DFG were hammered. Numerous people were seriously injured, including police officers who struggled to restore order despite using dogs and truncheons. After the game, battles continued in the city until late in the night.

Just a month later, in August 2001, IFK played host to Hammarby at the Gamla Ullevi. Although Hammarby have no real firm to speak of, Wisemen had already been involved in a short battle with some of their fans outside a bar in the centre of the city when, just a quarter of an hour before the game, it exploded again. This time it was right outside the ground and in full view of the media which included Swedish football legend Ralf Edström, who was covering the game live on radio. During the fighting, a Hammarby supporter in his twenties was assaulted with an iron bar and then suffered several stamps and kicks to his head and body. Tragically, such was the ferocity of the fighting that no medical assistance could get to him until riot police arrived, with the result that the supporter suffered major injuries.

It should not, however, be thought that violence is confined to the Swedish Premiership, because that is certainly not the case. The lower divisions have their fair share of trouble, in particular at another Gothenburg-based club, GAIS.

'The Mackerels' as the club is known, has a small but strong mob of violent followers who delight in scaring the life out of fans and stewards in the lower divisions. In 2001, when they were in the second division, they played away in the cup against Kalmar FF, a team whose firm never have been a dazzling success on the hooligan front. GAIS had kicked it off the night before the game when 30 of them fought with locals and the police. Ten of them were arrested but the trouble continued at the game when a smoke grenade was thrown at the Kalmar supporters. The police immediately went in and arrested a group of GAIS supporters who, it turned out, were the same ones that had been arrested the night before.

A few weeks later, GAIS travelled east to Västeraás for another day of fun with the local fans. After first fighting with the police and then with a mob of locals, more trouble erupted in the ground when a group of Skinheads appeared and were battered by the GAIS. After the match, they went for it again. This time attacking the police with bricks.

Aside from violence, the other problem that has been having an impact in Swedish football is racism. One of the reasons for this is that in Sweden immigrants have allied themselves to specific teams, some of whom now have an almost entirely immigrant following. Inevitably, this leads to clashes with those clubs who have a right-wing element and never was this more evident than in the autumn of 2001 when one of the immigrant-supported teams, Syrianska, travelled to Åtvidaberg for the final game of the season. With Syrianska still looking for promotion, the game was naturally classified as high-risk yet, amazingly, not a single policeman was present and, inevitably, it ended in chaos.

After the game, a hundred or so Syrianska supporters, furious at some inept refereeing and the amount of racist abuse pouring from the Åtvidaberg stands, invaded the pitch and fought with local supporters. This fighting continued as the fans left the pitch, with some fans being attacked with crowbars. Thankfully, the police finally arrived and broke it up, but not before a large number of people had ended up in hospital.

That said, the Swedish police have done great work with the racist problem. During the nineties, a large number of immigrants, mostly from Yugoslavia, moved to Sweden and were not well received by everyone. This quickly exploded onto the terraces where racists were openly allowed to express their views free of criticism. Things have changed a lot since then as most Swedes believe in a multicultural nation with a place for everyone. There is also a genuine belief that the country has escaped the recent tide of extreme right-wing opinion that has swept through Europe.

It is also fair to say that the police are finally beginning to make an impact on the hooligans. CCTV cameras tape every spectator's move at Premiership fixtures and the film can be used in trials as evidence. However, there are still many who think that the police are treating the problem too lightly.

At an ordinary match in the Premiership there are between six and ten policemen inside the grounds and even the biggest games are deemed to require between 150 and 200. There also seems to be some naivety when talking about the organised side of the Swedish firms, as the police seem convinced that it is simply about alcohol and drugs rather than football rivalry.

The accusation of naivety can also be levelled at the Swedish media. On the rare occasions they do write about hooliganism, they never carry out any kind of examination but simply accuse the hooligans of being poor, fat junkies, with nothing better to do. I hadn't read a Swedish article about hooliganism worthy of note until some weeks before the World Cup 2002.

The truth – as most people know – is totally different and, until that is recognised, Sweden's hooligans will continue to enjoy the freedom to carry out their activities seemingly at will. How many more deaths will it take before that changes, and action is finally taken?

I am grateful to Joel and David of IFK Gothenburg for their help with the above article.

Part Four

EASTERN EUROPE

On 14 June 2002, I received a phone call from a producer at BBC Radio 2 who asked me if I wanted to comment on the links between Russian hooligans and the infamous English firm the Chelsea Headhunters.

As it happened, at the time I was in the middle of researching the Russian hooligan scene for this book and so, intrigued by what he had said, asked him where he had discovered this new 'information'. He replied that during the riots in Moscow following Russia's World Cup defeat by Japan, some of the fans involved in the fighting had been pictured wearing Chelsea shirts.

When I pointed out to him that hundreds of thousands of people around the globe wear Manchester United shirts and very few of them are either English or hooligans, his response was simply 'but Manchester United don't have any hooligans, Chelsea have lots'.

Aside from providing a fairly powerful example of how dangerously naive certain sections of the media are when it comes to the culture of football, never mind hooliganism, it also highlighted just how little we in the West know about what goes on in Eastern Europe, particularly when it comes to football. Indeed, I've tested a few people on this and very few can even name more than a handful of either Russian or Polish clubs let alone tell you anything about them.

I am certainly no different. I'd even go so far as to say that until I began working on this book, my knowledge of Eastern Europe as a whole extended no further than what remains of the Berlin Wall. In my defence, much of this was as a result of my 18 years in the military and particularly the seven spent living in Germany. The East was, after all, why we were there and, as a result, was directly responsible for the hours I spent on various guard duties or playing at war when I would rather have been at home. In short, if a country wasn't a member of NATO, it was the enemy, and that's all I needed or wanted to know about them.

To a certain extent, and to my eternal shame, that is still the case. Communism may have collapsed and the Berlin Wall may have been demolished but, aside from the odd flying visit, I have yet to spend any serious time in the region and my knowledge of the football is still limited to activities off the pitch rather than on it.

While that is an incredibly blinkered view, it does lead perfectly on to the content of the next part of this book. For it is here that we will take a look at the Eastern European scene and some of the things that are going on within it.

Initially, we will examine Russia and will follow that with a brief look at two of the smaller states, Ukraine and Lithuania. After this, we will explore possibly the most violent hooligan culture in Europe – Poland – and in the next section will focus on arguably the most volatile region on the continent, the Balkans.

It should be remembered, however, that these are just a small number of the nations that make up Eastern Europe and many of the others, as England football fans know only too well, have strong footballing and hooligan traditions.

In Bulgaria, for example, the 1995 cup final between Lokomotiv Sofia and Botev Plovdiv ended with 5000 fans fighting both each other and the police. Eleven people ended up in hospital including one policeman with a fractured skull and another with crushed ribs.

In Albania, also in 1995, referees staged a boycott of games in protest at the amount of violence directed at them from among the crowd. There were also reports of riots inside grounds and an incident where police were forced to fire warning shots in an effort to disperse fighting crowds.

As recently as June 2002, a conference in Macedonia – a country with only six major teams – set up to discuss the growing problem of hooliganism in the country, descended into violence when delegates began arguing over the quality of their respective clubs. And in Bosnia-Herzegovina, a match between Celik Zenica and Borac Banja Luka in August 2002 was marred by crowd violence and ethnic tension that spilled over onto the streets of Sarajevo.

These are just a tiny fraction of the incidents we actually know about. For many years, the cloak of secrecy that enveloped every communist country kept news of riots and deaths not just from the West, but from everyone.

Aside from hooliganism, the other problem that has affected the game in the region is racism. The shameful events surrounding England's trip to Slovakia in October 2002 will live long in the memory, but the tragedy is that the abuse suffered by Emile Heskey and Ashley Cole was just one in a series of similar problems in 2002 which included the horrific abuse aimed at Fulham's black players by fans of Hajduk Split in Zagreb.

The one positive to be taken from the Slovakian experience is that the subsequent furore might have finally forced UEFA to take action against those clubs and nations who continue to allow this type of thing to go on. In this day and age, racism is simply unacceptable no matter where or why it takes place.

The first article in this section was put together using information from a variety of sources including two Russian correspondents who have very close links to particular hooligan groups. They have asked to remain anonymous but I would like to thank them both for the input as I would 'Red-dark blue support' (CSKA Moscow) and Nikola from Belgrade.

The articles on Lithuania and Ukraine were written by Ziogiukas from Kaunus Ultras and White-Blue Hooligans of Dynamo Kiev respectively.

CHAPTER TWELVE
Russia

In 1972, a fan appeared on the terraces of Spartak Moscow wearing a simple knitted scarf in the team's colours of red and white. This, believe it or not, was the very first sign of any kind of fan culture in the former Soviet Union.

Until that point, displaying any kind of open support for your team wasn't only frowned upon, it was actively discouraged. Indeed, at that time, following football was even regarded as a way of proving that you had something of an anarchic streak in you. However, the sight of this single woolly appendage began to change things and, pretty soon, the females of Moscow were busily knitting for all they were worth.

Not surprisingly, not everyone was happy with this, particularly the KGB, who regarded the very idea of supporting anything other than the Mother Country as being anti-Soviet. While they put up with it for a time, by the late 1970s a clampdown of sorts began and some leaders of supporters' clubs were even accused of being a part of a CIA plot! Even wearing a simple badge would see you thrown out of a stadium!

For the fans of the Moscow clubs, this was a difficult time, as the police in the capital were particularly heavy-handed. But they would not be put off, and to avoid the attentions of the authorities, a few even began travelling to away games where they could openly show their support and, at the same time, receive less harassment from the local police, many of whom had never seen football fans like these before.

Despite the clampdown on supporters, the first proper, albeit unofficial, supporters' clubs were established in 1979, with Spartak Moscow leading the way. Formed partly to help overcome the difficulties (and share the fun) of travelling across the largest league in the world, the groups also provided a degree of protection. For in many towns and cities in Russia, Muscovites were less than welcome and would often come under attack from local youths while the police stood by and watched.

Up to that point, most Russians referred to football supporters simply as *bolyelshchiks*, which means literally 'one who is sick for football'. But, increasingly, fans, especially younger fans, were looking towards the game as a way of providing them with some kind of identity. The problem was, having been largely isolated from what was going on in the rest of world, they had been given only fleeting glimpses of fan cultures in other countries when Italian, English and even South American clubs had played on Soviet soil. As a result, although they knew that the Inchas and the Tifosi existed, they had no real idea what they were about. All they knew is that they wanted something that would have a unique meaning for them and that it would have to start with some kind of title.

The word they adopted was Fanat (from the word 'fanatic') and it stuck immediately. This was particularly so with the Spartak supporters, who had already stunned football in the Soviet Union by separating themselves off at games and indulging in singing, chanting and waving home-made flags.

From that point on, at clubs across the Soviet Union, football became a popular way of expressing individuality and, despite the communist regime continuing to make it as difficult as possible, even away travel started to become a relatively frequent occurrence. This was no mean feat when one remembers that with the football league in the Soviet Union at that time covering such vast distances, some of these journeys would involve train trips of two or three days, often under the most difficult of circumstances. Yet the Moscow teams would often take between 300 and 400 supporters with them!

Thankfully, things got easier towards the end of the 1980s when Gorbachev came to power and introduced *Perestroika* (the restructuring of the Soviet state). Suddenly, everything was simpler for the football supporter, and the clubs, having seen how valuable travelling support could prove to be, even began actively encouraging supporters to attend away games.

For the fans, these were great days and, for the Fanats, many remember them as being the greatest. Released from the oppression of the authorities, they were free to do whatever they wanted and, for many, that meant finally being able to embrace and replicate whatever supporting culture they wished. Immediately, all eyes turned to England.

From out of nowhere, English songs, chants and slang began appearing on the terraces but, more importantly, alongside those came the gang mentality that typified the British game. Sadly, one consequence of that was a sharp rise in violence among the fans.

Not that clashes between gangs were anything new. Many towns and cities across the Soviet Union were divided into different neighbourhoods and these would often see gangs fighting over territory. Even football violence was not unknown. The previous 30 years had seen many clashes at the Moscow derbies as well as in such far-flung places as Latvia and Ukraine. Indeed, in 1987 there was one of the largest incidents of crowd trouble in Soviet history, when almost 300 Spartak

Moscow fans travelled to Kiev and fought with Dynamo fans in the city centre.

But this new wave of violence was something else. It was hooliganism in its rawest form. At clubs across the entire region, mobs were formed from nowhere and openly began confronting both each other and the police. Things even got to the stage where the fans travelled abroad and caused trouble. In 1990, a large group of Spartak Moscow hooligans followed the team to Prague but, after causing some disruption in the city centre, they were attacked by Sparta Prague hooligans and given a severe lesson – this incident was actually a cause of some anger to the Spartak fans who swore revenge but had to wait until a Champions League tie in 1999 to settle the score. And then, as quickly as it began, it was all over.

The collapse of the Soviet empire in 1991 also meant the end of the football league structure, with the result that the fledgling fan-culture was stopped dead in its tracks. Suddenly, Russian fans were faced with trips not to exotic places like Tbilisi or Vilnius but provincial towns such as Yarolslavl and Rostov. Not surprisingly, attendances plummeted to such a degree that it was often difficult for the hooligan groups to find anyone to fight with. This decline continued until 1994 when the first signs of a change began to emerge. As ever, they came from within the Moscow clubs.

Before the break-up of the Union, both Spartak and CSKA had been among the most active clubs on the hooligan scene, with their huge support being involved in trouble almost everywhere they went. Now, from among their number emerged two groups: Red-Blue Warriors at CSKA and Flints Crew at Spartak. Although not the only groups in Russian football or indeed at either of the Moscow clubs, the big difference with these two was that they were tight-knit and extremely well organised. More importantly, within months they had rekindled interest in the culture of hooliganism among the nation's football fans.

By the end of that season, groups had appeared at almost every large Russian club, though fights were infrequent, brief and usually involved only a relatively small number of lads. But in the spring of 1995, the return of the hooligans was broadcast in the biggest possible way when CSKA and Spartak met in the Moscow derby and over 200 members of Red-Blue Warriors and Flints Crew battled with each other before the game.

From that point on, not only did the police take a decidedly firm line with the mobs, but to avoid their attentions, the hooligan community became more insular in exactly the same way as had happened in England. They also began to mirror the English scene in other ways, as the first 'Casuals' appeared on the Russian terraces. Clad in a mix of sports clothing from companies such as Nike and Umbro, as well as the more traditional terrace labels of Lacoste, Fred Perry and Ben Sherman, their emergence gave a huge boost to the hooligan groups who now began to feel that their scene was taking on a true identity of its own. Interestingly, the Russian scene also began to see the emergence of a scene akin to the English 'Under 5s'. Called Carlics (dwarfs), these young lads would often be trained in the art of street-fighting by older hooligans from their particular club and quickly forged a reputation for being fearless, especially when it came to fighting with the police, who were almost universally regarded as the main enemy to the terrace culture.

Despite the evolution of the Russian scene, the English influence remained. So much so that in 1996 a group of Flints Crew travelled to England to observe at first hand the activities of their mentors during Euro 96. They are even reported to have been involved in the fighting with the Scots fans in Trafalgar Square – while a small number of Flints Crew were also in Marseille during France 98, and Belgium for Euro 2000. Bizarrely, in an effort to learn all they could about the scene in the UK, they also befriended some of the builders involved with the construction of the British Embassy in Moscow.

By 1997, despite the attentions of the police, the hooligan scene in Russia had become firmly entrenched in the fabric of Russian football. So much so that in August one of the most violent incidents in the short history of the nation's game occurred. Not surprisingly, one of the major clubs involved was Spartak Moscow and the increasingly notorious Flints Crew.

Just weeks after they had come off worse during a huge fight with CSKA's Red-Blue Warriors, Spartak supporters set out to repair their reputation and busily prepared themselves for the visit of another club with whom they had a bitter rivalry, Zenit St. Petersburg.

Their target was one of Zenit's main hooligan groups, Nevsky Front, who had a reputation for being fierce fighters at home, but less than active on their travels.

As approximately 500 of them left the train station at Shchelkovo, they were spotted by Spartak scouts who quickly passed on news of their arrival to the home support. When Nevsky Front were about 2 kilometres from the station, they were suddenly confronted by approximately 200 Spartak fans which included Flints Crew and some of the other Spartak firms such as Young Crew, Mad Butchers and Gladiators. Despite being hugely outnumbered, Spartak's fans steamed in and attacked the Zenit supporters. By the time the police arrived, the battle was in full swing and they were forced to use gunshots to drive the Spartak support back. However, 20 of them broke back through the cordon and continued the assault before being arrested. By the time it was all over, almost 170 Spartak fans had been arrested and many Zenit fans had been seriously injured. The incident sent the media into a frenzy and they quickly christened it 'The Battle of Shchelkovo'.

Just a month later, Spartak and CSKA once again hit the headlines when they met on a hockey field on the morning of yet another derby game. With no police around, the fighting continued for almost 20 minutes, but despite CSKA outnumbering them and being heavily armed with wooden clubs, Spartak drove them back and away.

There were, however, serious injuries on both sides and the subsequent media attention finally forced the authorities into action. The police, who had always been a major problem to football fans in Russia, saw this as the green light to go all-out against the hooligans and began to get increasingly violent towards any supporter who showed even the slightest inclination to step out of line. For big games or derby fixtures, backed up by horses and specially equipped police troops known as Omon, they would control everything going in and out of the surrounding area. Cordons would be formed to escort travelling fans to railway stations or buses, and supporters would be made to remove any scarves, shirts or colours. Similarly, at the first sign of fans gathering together, they would be in to break things up, often using the very worst kind of aggression. Inside grounds, things were even worse. Pitches would be surrounded by hundreds of police and Omon who would do their utmost to control what happened on the terraces. Flares and pyrotechnics were banned and even 'Slamming' – the practice of fans jumping into each other, hugging and then bouncing around after a goal has been scored – was often enough for the police, who would wade in and batter anything that moved, usually with rubber truncheons. More often than not, this would actually cause trouble inside the ground as fans ripped out chairs to use as weapons to protect themselves with.

The police also began to use technology for the first time. Having seized a video of 'The Battle of Shchelkovo' that had been taken by a local resident, they set out to arrest everyone they were able to identify. Although they enjoyed limited success, they became convinced of the value of such a weapon in their fight against the hooligans, and CCTV quickly became a resident feature inside and outside Russian stadiums.

For the hooligan groups, who already harboured a long and traditionally Russian hatred of the police, all of this was bad news. And while fighting didn't stop between the groups themselves, they increasingly began to concentrate their efforts on causing the police as many problems as possible.

Things finally came to a head in 1999. And once again Spartak were at the root of the trouble.

In June, the fans travelled to Ramenskoye just outside Moscow and were met at the stadium by a huge police and Omon presence. Almost immediately, Omon began lashing out and then arresting innocent supporters, much to the anger of the hundreds of Spartak lads who began fighting back in an effort to protect their fellow fans. Within minutes, this fighting had escalated into a full-blown riot and spread to the inside of the stadium where supporters began ripping out seats to use as missiles to throw at the police. Only when the Spartak coach and the team captain came out and appealed for calm did things settle down. But just two months later, it all kicked off again, at exactly the same stadium.

With Spartak again the visitors, the police for once kept a discreet distance but, with the fans still buzzing from their previous visit, it wasn't long before trouble surfaced. Following a Spartak goal, the police poured onto the terraces, but this time the fans fought back. For 15 minutes the battle continued, and was so fierce that for the first time in the history of Russian football, the game had to be suspended. Only when the police withdrew from the stadium did the situation calm down, but by that time many fans on both sides had been injured and the terraces all but wrecked.

For the hooligans, though, it was a major result and sent a clear message to the authorities that enough was enough. However, to reinforce that message, they had one more card to play.

Thanks to an extremely nasty element among its police force, the small town of Novgorod held bad memories for many Russian hooligans, especially Spartak whose younger lads had been brutally beaten during a previous visit in 1997. This time, however, the team travelled still buoyed-up from events in Ramenskoye and, inevitably, trouble erupted. So bad did the fighting get that a policeman died of the injuries he received. The fans were unrepentant, many claiming that the police had got exactly what they deserved after years of dealing out often vicious physical abuse. The authorities, however, did not see it like that and, following similar riots involving CSKA, Zenit Petersburg and Dynamo Moscow supporters, they decided that the only way forward for them was to increase security at games. Some even employed elements of the armed forces to keep the peace inside stadiums. But, for the fans, the point had been proved. They were no longer prepared to accept the treatment that had been handed out to them for years and now the authorities knew it.

By the time the 1999 season came to an end (due to the severity of the Russian winter their season runs from spring to late autumn), an uneasy calm had developed between the two warring factions. However, there were other rivalries for the fans to concern themselves with and, in December, the animosity between CSKA and Spartak exploded again.

On 12 December, 300 members of the CSKA firm Red-Blue Warriors gathered together for their end-of-season party. At about 7 p.m., as things were just getting going, a group of 70 tooled-up Spartak supporters, drawn from all of the major Spartak groups including Flints Crew, Young Crew and Clockwork Orange, suddenly appeared and launched a frenzied attack on the building and everyone standing near the main entrance. For over five minutes the attack continued before the group vanished as quickly as they had arrived, although not before they had left every window smashed in, and a large number of CSKA fans, including some of their top boys, seriously injured.

It has been said that the violence was in revenge for the actions of some 70 CSKA lads who had attacked a small group of Spartak fans who had been waiting for a train to take them to Prague the previous season. But, whatever the reason, it firmly established Spartak at the top of the Russian hooligan ladder and ensured that the rivalry between the two firms was back on the agenda.

The 2000 season was a frustrating one for the hooligan groups, who often found their plans thwarted by the police. However, of increasing concern to everyone was the growing use of weapons, especially knives. Following the death of a Zenit supporter after he was hit with a steel bar during a clash involving 350 hooligans, the leaders of the groups at both CSKA and Spartak met to lay down some ground rules for future conflicts between their two clubs. Chief among these was a ban on weapons but, despite agreeing, it wasn't long before some of the CSKA hooligans went back on this – something Spartak only discovered when the two groups met on the Moscow underground!

The two groups did, however, manage to set aside their differences on one occasion during 2000 although, to be fair, it wasn't the first time this had happened. (Both groups were present, and in numbers, outside the US Embassy in 1999 when the people of Moscow staged a protest against the bombings in Serbia.) The second time it was at least football-related.

For many Russian football fans, the international side has become something of a natural focus particularly when they are playing those near-neighbours who were once a part of the Union. One of those countries is Ukraine, who many Russian hooligans regard as second only to Poland as a national rival. When the two countries first met after the break-up of the Union, the Russian hooligans united and took more than 2000 lads to Kiev where they rioted in the city centre and in the stadium.

Another incident took place in Belarus. Despite being thought of as brothers-in-arms by the majority of the Russian people, when a group of hooligans from various Russian firms travelled to Minsk for an international friendly, they found themselves the target of nationalist and anti-Russian abuse from local fans. Instinctively, they steamed in but, after dealing with the fans, they were confronted by the local riot police, who weren't such easy prey. Despite this, the Russians, led by a hardcore from Moscow, gave a good account of themselves only to discover later on that the whole thing had been caught on CCTV. The subsequent court cases saw a number of them jailed for a considerable time.

It was actually events surrounding the international side that finally managed to drag the burgeoning Russian hooligan scene to the attention of the world's media. In 2002, following Russia's World Cup defeat by Japan, fans all but blitzed parts of Moscow which, in a World Cup bereft of any violence, attracted huge amounts of coverage around the globe. It received more negative publicity in September 2002 when brawls broke out before a Euro 2004 qualifier with Northern Ireland in Moscow that resulted in nine people being put in hospital.

On the domestic front, the Russian scene has carried on along a fairly predictable path. Violence continues to increase, as does the amount of police time dedicated to eradicating it. And, although not the only clubs to have hooligan followings by any means, CSKA and Spartak have continued to lead the way, with Flints Crew in particular being at the forefront of developments. Derby games in the capital will often see groups of up to 500 looking for each other and, while Stone Island and Burberry haven't reached Russia as yet, it's surely only a matter of time. Interestingly, both groups have also taken to using the media to publicise their activities. CSKA's Red-Blue Warriors have led the way here, and there are even a number of fanzines dealing exclusively with hooligan-related matters, on open sale.

Quite what happens next is anyone's guess. But with the scene already one of the most violent in Europe, the big fear for many is that the Russian hooligans will one day manage to travel abroad *en masse*. Many of them talk openly of what will happen should they ever meet their big and true rivals, Poland, but others look towards England as the real test of how far they have come.

The truth is, whatever happens, it's certainly going to be interesting.

CHAPTER THIRTEEN
Ukraine

Like many post-Soviet nations, the history of Ukrainian football culture really began only as communism started to lose its stranglehold on Eastern Europe in the late 1980s and early 1990s.

That is not to say that the supporters were well behaved before that – far from it, in fact. Rivalries, particularly with the large Russian clubs, were often extremely vicious. In September 1987, for example, Dynamo Kiev fans were involved in one of the USSR's most violent civil disturbances when 500 of them attacked a 300-strong mob of Spartak Moscow fans at Kiev railway station.

Things began to change in 1991 once Ukraine had achieved independence. Initially, however, things did not go so well for the Ukrainian fans for, once their teams' regular meetings with the powerful Russian clubs – and their hooligan firms – came to a halt, interest in the game began to wane. This had an obvious effect on the hooligan gangs, who suddenly found their numbers falling.

This continued for a number of years, but as rivalries developed within the newly formed Ukrainian league, the number of fans finally levelled out. Thankfully, they soon began to increase and from among them there developed a specific footballing culture. Initially this revolved around supporting their team, drinking and the simple enjoyment of being with a group of lads who travel to football home and away. It also involved a large degree of politics that ranged from extreme right-wing to extreme left. But for the most part, the majority of fans remained focused on the concept of Ukrainian nationalism.

By the late 1990s incidents of football violence began to increase, and the Ukrainian fans began looking further afield for their influences. In particular, they focused their attentions on England. The reason for this was simple.

Ukrainian hooligans had always recognised that Europe was home to a number of different supporting cultures, ranging from the terrace fanaticism of the Italian game to the violent madness of the Polish leagues. However, since the late 1980s they had regarded England as the home of football violence and now they began to consciously mirror the Casual culture.

Suddenly, the terraces were full of lads dressing in various labels including Ben Sherman, Lacoste, Fred Perry and the ubiquitous Stone Island (although, bizarrely, Umbro has been considered the top brand since Soviet times). At the same time, they began showing a less expressive and almost apathetic support for the team; instead, they started to pay more attention to the organisation of their respective groups and, in particular, their match-day 'activities'. This was something that, by their own admission, had always been one of the weaker aspects of the Ukrainian scene.

Indeed, for years the police and militia had battled to control the hooligans and often this had involved some extremely heavy-handed tactics. However, as the 2000–01 season approached and the 'English' style of hooliganism began to take a strong grip, the police suddenly began to find themselves coming under attack from fans who had become increasingly angry at this treatment.

In March 2001, the first sign that real problems were coming was when civil unrest broke out in Kiev. During street rioting, known hooligans from Dynamo openly stood beside groups opposed to the regime of President Kuchma and fought against the police and militia. As a result, many were arrested and jailed. But just days later, the police had more problems when, for the very first time, 120 lads from firms across Ukraine joined together as a single mob to support the national team when they played Belarus. During pitched battles involving a group of over 80 Belarus supporters, a number of fans from both sides were injured.

As the police struggled to work out what to do next, things finally came to a head when a large group of Kiev fans attacked the militia's special forces during an away match in Poltava.

For the authorities this was enough, and both the Ministry of Internal Affairs and the Ukrainian Security Service (ex-KGB) formed special departments to curb the hooligans' activities. Several court cases were immediately initiated and a number of hooligan ringleaders jailed. This had an immediate effect, but it did not stop the problems entirely.

In August 2001, almost 100 hooligans from Kiev and Odessa fought a pitched battle before their game in Kiev. Although nothing spectacular in terms of numbers or the violence involved, what marked this incident out as special was that it was the very first at which both mobs had agreed in advance to use no weapons.

This caught the attention of the mass media in Ukraine, who suddenly began to give increased coverage to the hooligan problem and, in particular, the activities of the firms. The inevitable result of this attention was that the number of incidents increased as did the number of people involved, all drawn into it by the publicity their actions received.

But, in April 2002, something happened which shocked Ukrainian football to the core. After a routine home fixture, a group of extreme right-wing Kiev supporters staged an attack on the city's central synagogue as a protest against Jewish influence and culture. While terrible enough in itself, what really stunned everyone was that a number of the Kiev fans involved were so-called 'dwarfs' – young fans usually aged between 15 and 16 years old. The media were outraged and demanded action from the police who, in turn, promised to bring those involved to court and hand out severe sentences to any convicted.

For Ukrainian football fans, particularly those involved with the hooligan firms, the subsequent clampdown had a major, albeit short-lived, impact. For once the court cases arising out of it were over and done with, things quickly returned to normal and are now actually worse than they were before it happened.

CHAPTER FOURTEEN
Lithuania

As you can imagine, Lithuania's hooligan problems are hardly at a level that will stand comparison with many of Europe's more illustrious football nations.

Yet it is fair to say that while the scene might be small – encompassing as it does fewer than ten active supporter groups of which the best is widely recognised to be the Zalgiris Vilnius mob Pietu 4 – there are two aspects of it that are extremely interesting.

The first is that Lithuania is one of the few countries in Europe where just about all of the groups not only get along, they actually come together to support each other in potential conflicts. Primarily, these involve fights with either the local population or fans of clubs from Poland, Russia, the Czech and Slovak Republics and Germany who, thanks to historical differences between the respective countries, can be assured that any welcome they receive in Lithuania will be less than friendly. Indeed, when Zalgiris Vilnius met Polish side FC Ruch Chorzow during the 2001 UEFA Cup, hooligans from three clubs mobbed up to fight with the visiting Poles. They were even supplemented by a large gang of local Skinheads just for good measure!

The other almost unique feature of Lithuanian football culture is that while there may not be any especially violent rivalries between the nation's football supporters, there are plenty between football and basketball clubs. In fact, one of the largest ever incidents of crowd violence in the country involved a ruck between two mobs from different sports!

When Senoji Gvardija – the Ultra group of Lithuanian champions FBK Kaunas – stepped off a bus, having travelled to watch their team play Zalgiris Vilnius, they were met by the leader of the local firm and told that a group of lads from the city's basketball team Lietuvos Rytas had been mouthing off about them.

Immediately, Senoji Gvardija went off looking for their new-found enemy and, having finally tracked them down, gave them a good kicking. However, to put this into context, not only were just 40 people involved in total, it was Senoji Gvardija's only real fight of the season.

Another source of problems for the Ultra groups in Lithuania are those home supporters who simply follow football but dislike any travelling fans who arrive at their ground. One example of this occurred in May of 2002 when 59 Ultras from the Zalgiris Vilnius group Pietu 4 travelled to watch their side play Atlantas Klaipeda. Once inside the stadium, they soon came under attack from a group of 200 local supporters but, amazingly, found themselves being helped out by a small group of Vakaru Frontas hooligans from the home team!

In common with a number of East European leagues, one of the things that Lithuanian football does have a reputation for is politics, for they are most definitely right-wing and that extends way beyond the supporters. This is so much the case that in 1997, at a match between Zalgiris Vilnius and Israeli club HaPoel, one Lithuanian FA official is reported to have remarked to two Jewish employees: 'It's a shame the Germans didn't wipe you out.'

CHAPTER FIFTEEN
Poland

Ask any European football fan to list the most violent supporters on the continent and they will invariably name the Polish somewhere in the top two or three. Similarly, Poland is almost universally considered to be one of the most dangerous countries to visit with your team, and with good reason, as the excellent article that follows explains.

England fans, of course, have experienced this at first hand. Indeed, the trouble surrounding the game in Warsaw in 1999 has been the source of much debate over the years due to a number of the Polish hooligans in Siska Park – the scene of possibly the most violent encounter – who used knives during the fighting. This was initially denied by the Polish hooligan groups until various photographs of their lads waving blades around began appearing on the Internet.

However, this was just one of at least four serious encounters between the two sets of fans around that game over a period of two days, which culminated in a battle inside the stadium. It has also been claimed on many occasions that there was a group of Germans hooligans present who had come to Warsaw to take on the English.

Although the Poles' claim that they defeated the English has been hotly denied, what the various confrontations did do was to cement their reputation as being both extremely violent and one of the few nations whose hooligans were happy to take the fight to the English. However, as we shall see, the friction between the various hooligan mobs caused immense problems during international games, and so eventually saw the collapse of the various coalitions that had been set up. To me, this makes the Polish scene one of the most interesting in Europe because, in just about every other European nation, rivalries are either set aside when following the national team or the groups involved keep a distance from each other. This is certainly not the case in Poland where, uniquely, they now regard international games as just another platform for attacking each other.

There is, however, another aspect of the Polish game that is more common. Indeed, it is something that is becoming of increasing concern to the authorities across Europe: racism. There is no doubt that together with fascism, it has become deeply entrenched on the terraces of Poland, so much so that some of the banners sported by hooligan groups at games openly carry Nazi symbols.

Much of this can be attributed to the activities of the fascist party, the National Revival of Poland (NOP). They have enjoyed huge success when recruiting on the Polish terraces and have in the past even organised hooligan groups into what they call 'national revolutionary cells' because the entire football subculture is so strongly violence-oriented.

It isn't only the fans who exhibit this problem. It is well documented that at certain clubs the players have put pressure on the management not to sign or play black players. When Emanuel Olisadebe became the first black player to turn out for Poland, the decision was roundly condemned in some sections of the Polish media.

Ironically, Olisadebe went on to become something of a torchbearer for the anti-fascist movement in Poland for, not only did he score three goals in his first two international outings, but he has also been at the forefront of the 'Let's Kick Racism Out of the Stadium' campaign that was launched by the anti-fascist 'Never Again' Association.

However, it is fair to say that the various anti-fascist organisations have some way to go in Poland. This problem is certainly something both UEFA and FIFA are keeping a wary eye on.

What follows is a closer examination of the scene in Poland as written by Piotr Jaworski, editor of *To My Kibice*, the official magazine of the Polish Ultra and hooligan scene.

The first Polish hooligan gangs appeared at Legia Warsaw and LKS Lodz at the beginning of the 1970s and, within ten years, over 20 had been formed at clubs including Polonia Bytom, Wisla Cracow, Lechia Gdansk, Slask Wroclaw, Ruch Chorzow and Pogon Szczecin. However, unlike in other countries where gangs were formed to provide support for the teams and to give a degree of protection on away trips, these gangs were almost universally created with another aim in mind.

At that time, the police never travelled with supporters on trains and so, often, groups would step onto a platform in another town or city to be met by local fans looking for trouble. This meant that every away game was a potential problem, but rather than stop travelling or lobby the police for protection, the fans decided to go the other way and take up the challenges offered. The result was that almost every trip saw some degree of violence.

This approach continues even today, for the feeling among Polish supporters is that real hooligans are those who regard their club as being everything to them and for which they will do anything. Equally, hooligans only become 'real' when they start travelling to away games, and the pecking order at almost every hooligan group is decided by how many away games people have travelled to. Some hardcore hooligans are known to have travelled to over 300 away games during their careers.

This mentality meant that by the late 1970s, fights between fans had become regular occurrences, but it was never regarded as a problem by either the authorities or the public who, as a result of the censorship laws in place at the time, which stopped information about hooliganism from being released, remained largely ignorant of what was going on. This began to change in 1980 after the first major riot erupted at a football stadium in Poland. The occasion was the Polish cup final between Legia Warsaw and Lech Poznan in Czestochowa city.

Expecting nothing out of the ordinary, the police were shocked when 7000 Poznan supporters and 2000 from Warsaw began fighting in the stadium and on the streets using knives, stones and clubs. Unable to cope, the police summoned help that quickly arrived from Katowice in the form of the special riot police called ZOMO – who throughout the 1970s and 1980s were instrumental in suppressing civil unrest. They dealt with the hooligans in their typically brutal manner which, by the time it was all over, left more than 100 supporters seriously injured and at least one Warsaw fan dead. Amazingly, it was a decade before news of this appeared in the media but only a matter of weeks before it had filtered through to other hooligan groups via word of mouth.

The trouble at this game sparked off a hatred that is still one of the biggest in Polish football, but it also put Legia at the top of the hooligan ladder and, over the next few seasons, they became known as a group who would show up at even the most dangerous of stadiums, ready and willing to fight anyone who stood in front of them, including the police and even ZOMO.

Yet despite the increasing amounts of trouble on the terraces, the public were still largely ignorant of the hooligan problem. So much so that a year after the trouble at Legia, they were stunned when Polish television broadcast a live game between Widzew Lodz and Legia Warsaw and trouble kicked off right before their eyes.

Outnumbered by the home fans, the Legia supporters soon found themselves under attack and, eventually, had to run onto the pitch to escape. Within seconds, the caption 'We apologise for this interruption' had appeared on the previously animated screen, but it was too late. The watching nation had witnessed its first football-related violence and it wanted to know what was going on. The trouble was that the media wasn't allowed to tell it. This situation continued even after the running battles involving Liverpool and Juventus fans at Heysel in 1985 were broadcast live on Polish television.

However, in 1986, with the hooligan debate raging across most of Europe, Polish football was finally dragged into the media spotlight by an event that sent shock waves through the game: the murder of a teenage fan.

His death came about simply because he climbed onto a train wearing a jacket with an LKS Lodz badge on it. Unfortunately, in his compartment were a group of Legia Warsaw fans who, after a struggle, threw him from the train. He died of his injuries. Not surprisingly, the LKS fans went mental – even today, they will sometimes sing 'Mariusz, we will avenge your murder. We will kill Legia. We'll burn their stadium down and massacre them' – but the media were equally outraged and finally began to print the truth about what was going on, albeit in very small doses. Indeed, it was only in the 1990s that they were finally allowed to print the type of exposé we have become familiar with, and this was largely as a consequence of another football-related murder which took place at the Poland versus England game in 1993.

However, during the 1980s, specific rivalries began to develop as the groups became more organised. One of the most interesting can be found in the city of Lodz where, from the 1970s LKS had been the dominant club and its fans the most violent. But as the young fans who had begun following Widzew Lodz in the 1970s grew up, their natural hatred of their local rivals saw them form a group of their own which, by the late 1980s, was as strong if not stronger than their near neighbours. This led to a series of battles between the two sets of fans that continues to this day, but one of the more interesting aspects to come out of this was the growth of the 'hunting' phenomenon. This involved the theft of scarves and flags from rival fans at every possible opportunity and often rival groups would ambush travelling supporters at bus and train stations. The object of the exercise was to exhibit these 'trophies' on the fences at derby games to wind up the opposing fans. Interestingly, this practice still continues, which is why it can be dangerous to wear any kind of club memorabilia when walking around the streets of Poland.

A similar situation to the one in Lodz arose in Cracow where, from the end of the 1980s, fans of the third division side Cracovia Cracow grew into what is widely regarded as the single most violent mob in Polish football. Often, they will fight using knives and have even been known to attack a rival group using axes! Equally surprising is that while they have remained a third division team, their local rivals, Wisla

Cracow, were champions of Poland in 1999 and 2001 – something which the Cracovia hooligans actually regard as a bonus because it means that the bigger clubs such as Legia and Warsaw regularly arrive in Cracow and provide opposition for them.

Throughout the 1990s, the Polish game continued to experience terrible problems and, if anything, things were getting more violent by the season. Even England fans were shocked at the level of violence when they came under a sustained attack in Katowice on the night of a World Cup qualifier in 1993.

By 1995, the dominant hooligans on the Polish scene came from Lech Poznan. Their group, Brygada Banici, had a reputation for fearless fighting but their leaders also saw that, potentially, they could remain at the forefront of hooliganism in the country for the foreseeable future. To that end, they formed a coalition with hooligans from two other clubs, Arka Gdynia and Cracovia Cracow, and labelled it ALC after their respective teams. Together, they proved to be all but unbeatable and, for the next five years, dominated the terraces of Poland. However, things were slowly beginning to change.

For years, the media had struggled with the culture of violence surrounding the Polish game and on 19 April 1997, it exploded again when a huge riot broke out at a game between Legia Warsaw and Polonia Warsaw. The pictures were broadcast around the world and suddenly the media went to town demanding answers. The police blamed the fans and the football authorities; the fans blamed the police; and the authorities blamed the police, the fans and the regulations.

The underlying causes of football violence became a subject of fierce debate and, not surprisingly, the academic world had plenty to say. They laid the blame fairly and squarely on the simple fact that Poland hadn't had a war for over 50 years!

For the hooligans, this was a great time. Now they weren't just hated by their rivals, they were hated by everyone. For the authorities, however, worse was to come.

Football isn't the only sport to be affected by hooliganism in Poland, as has been the case for some considerable time. Basketball, hockey and even speedway teams have hooligan groups attached to them, although often these are the same lads who follow football teams. What this means is that occasionally rivalries will cross over into other sports, which not only makes it difficult for the police, but means that, potentially, incidents could be carried on for days, weeks or even months. That potential was realised in January 1998.

After a basketball match in the city of Slupsk in North Poland, a group of fans were crossing a street when the police began berating them because the crossing light was at red. During the argument, a skirmish broke out during which a 13-year-old boy was hit on the head by a police baton. Tragically, he died of his injuries.

Fans from the basketball club Czarni Slupsk and the local football team Gryf Slupsk immediately came together and, along with members of the local community who were outraged at what had happened, began a series of attacks on the local police. The next day, hooligans from clubs and sports across Poland travelled to Slupsk to protest in the city centre against the police. Inevitably, rioting broke out which resulted in cars and buildings being set on fire. On the day of the funeral, more fighting broke out as sports fans from all over the country converged on the city for a second time.

From that point on, the authorities staged a clampdown. Football stadiums were closed and the media, free of the shackles of censorship, began writing a series of scathing articles about the hooligan scene, accusing the fans of being no better than animals. Alongside that, the police went on the offensive, staging a series of high-profile anti-hooligan raids that resulted in a large number of arrests. Discussions also began about the introduction of ID cards for supporters as a way of clamping down on trouble inside grounds. But to combat that, all the fans did was to take the trouble outside, into the surrounding streets and local forests. Ultimately, the effect on the hooligans was zero.

Later that year, in October, the Polish game suffered another major setback as a result of hooligan activity. During a UEFA Cup tie against Italian side AC Parma, a fan of Wisla Cracow – who were at the time leading the first division and were regarded as the great hope for the Polish game – threw a knife at the Italian player, Dino Baggio, which struck him on the head. Incredibly, one of the Wisla players picked up the knife and threw it off the pitch – hc later admitted he was trying to avoid the game being stopped which earned him a ban from the second leg – but it was too late. UEFA awarded the club a year's ban from any European competition.

Once again, the authorities began looking at ways of tackling the problem but with little or no success. Even Polish radio had a try when station PR1 launched a campaign called 'The Safe Stadium' at a game between Widzew Lodz and Legia Warsaw. Their idea was to create an atmosphere of fun rather than of tension, but their plan backfired when fans took the T-shirts they were handed as they entered the stadium up onto the terrace and set fire to them. They then went on the rampage, ripping the stadium apart before looting a storeroom and using the contents to attack the police.

The authorities were dismayed, but it was becoming clear that there was little they could do to control the hooligans. However, even as they struggled to work out what to do next, the hooligans were involved in a power struggle of their own. This time it involved not the domestic league, but the international side.

The collapse of communism in the early 1990s meant the opening of Poland's borders and, for the first time, fans had been able to travel to support the national team. The first trip for the fans was to Holland in 1992 but, having travelled to Rotterdam, hooligans from Wisla Cracow soon found themselves under attack not from Dutch fans but from a group of their local rivals Cracovia Cracow. After the game, hooligans from other Polish clubs including Slask Wroclaw and Lechia Gdansk backed up the Wisla fans, who staged a counter-attack on the Cracovia hooligans, who were forced to back off.

Sadly, this in-fighting between groups quickly became a characteristic of international away trips with the Poland team. When Poland travelled to San Marino in 1993, two coachloads of Wisla fans waited for Cracovia fans intending to attack them, only to discover that the police had learned of their plans and had turned the Cracovia fans back when they arrived at the Polish border. And it wasn't only on away trips that trouble broke out. When England travelled to Poland in 1993 – a game that saw a great deal of trouble – a fan from Pogon Szczecin was killed when the bus he was on was attacked by hooligans from Cracovia.

Increasingly concerned by what was going on, in February 1995 the leaders of all the major Polish hooligan groups decided to do something about it and met for an indoor football tournament in Gdynia. The tournament, which had been organised by the leader of the Arka Gdynia hooligans, resolved some of the differences between the rival groups, but the key agreement was that all rivalries would be put aside when the national team were playing. However, the one team not at the tournament were Cracovia and they not only refused to agree to this but, when Poland travelled to France later that same year, they actually attacked a group of Legia and Pogon hooligans. To make matters worse, they were helped out by a group of hooligans from Arka Gdynia, which meant that the agreement was over almost as soon as it had begun.

Within months, hooligans from Lech Poznan had joined with Arka Gdynia and Cracovia Cracow and formed the previously mentioned ALC. This led to all-out war, with hooligans from every other Polish club uniting in their battle against this alliance.

It is generally accepted that the ALC won this war and, in 1999, they were even joined by hooligans from other clubs including Ruch Chorzow, GKS Tychy, GKS Jastrzebie and Zaglebie Lubin to form an alliance called Opposition. But to counter this, hooligans from another 11 clubs – Legia, Pogon, Zaglebie Sosnowiec, Slask, Wisla, Lechia, Widzew Lodz, Baltyk Gdynia, Jagiellonia Bialystok, Stomil Olsztyn and Motor Lublin – formed an alliance of their own called Coalition. However, after a few confrontations, Coalition fell apart as a result of an ongoing feud between Teddy Boys from Legia Warsaw and Mlode Orly of Lechia Gdansk. It was this feud that saw the two groups trying to fight each other when Poland played at Wembley in March 1999.

The ongoing rivalry between the hooligans' groups did not stop them causing problems for teams that travelled to play in Poland. The most famous example involved England in 1999 when fans from Legia, Gdansk and Cracow attacked a large group of English hooligans in Saski Park when they came to Warsaw.

Today, all of the alliances are over, and the only groups who come together when the national team play are those who have long-standing friendships such as Legia Warsaw and Pogon Szczecin. However, for most hooligan groups, interest in international matches is low and about 80 per cent of the fans are just normal football fans.

Quite what happens next is something of a mystery. Hooliganism has become firmly entrenched in Polish sport to the extent that it even has a number of magazines dedicated to it – titles such as *Football Bandits, Psychofanatic* and even *Fanatic and Hooligans* are on open sale and sell in significant numbers.

But what is clear is that the power struggle that has gone on inside the Polish Football Association (PZPN) for years now is not helping things. Until people in authority know who is in charge of what, the hooligan problem is almost certain to continue unchecked.

Part Five

THE BALKANS

Of all the regions of Europe that the hooligan and Ultra situation exists in, the Balkans is probably the most complex. For while rivalry between teams and even firms is one thing, conflict between religions and ethnic groups is something entirely different. Sad to say, in the Balkans, they met head on and eventually exploded on the terraces of the former Yugoslavia.

The origins of the most recent conflict date back to the end of the Second World War, when Yugoslavia was forged together by the communist party in the wake of Germany's defeat and a brutal civil war that raged across the region from 1941–45.

The new post-war country was multicultural in every sense, but although any talk of nationalism was banned by the government, it continued to simmer underneath the surface. When the communist leader Tito died in 1980, historical differences between the various cultures, particularly the Serbs and the Croats, began to emerge.

In July 1991, after years of political and civil unrest, both Slovenia and Croatia declared themselves independent from Yugoslavia. The Serb-dominated Yugoslav People's Army (JNA) was sent to both republics in an effort to disarm their defensive forces and secure the borders. But after being repelled by Slovenia, the JNA became bogged down in an increasingly violent struggle with the Croatian Army, a struggle that quickly developed into all-out war.

Inevitably, this conflict engulfed the region and in 1992 it spread to Bosnia when the Muslim-dominated government also declared itself independent from Belgrade.

By 1995, many thousands had been killed, millions displaced and an entire country decimated. The result was that instead of a single nation, there were now six republics and two provinces.

However, while a war in the very heart of Europe had sent shockwaves around the world, what many people failed to realise was that the tensions between the various ethnic groups had simmered on the terraces of the major Yugoslavian football clubs for years. It is also fair to say that, from the outset, the bulk of the front-line forces came from among the region's numerous hooligan groups. As proof of this, very few of the main faces from Dinamo Zagreb's Bad Blue Boys returned from the fighting while Arkan, the notorious leader of the Serb Volunteer Guard, had been a senior figure on the terraces at Red Star Belgrade for many years before the war and drew his troops almost exclusively from members of their firm Delije. It is even alleged that during the war, troops from both sides hunted down and murdered key members of rival hooligan groups for no other reason than to settle old scores. Such information provides a terrible indication of just how important a part football and the culture that surrounds it can become in some people's lives. More importantly, it puts some of the things that happen in other countries into proper perspective.

However, it must be stressed that while nationalism found a natural home on the terraces, there had never been much love lost between club sides no matter what the ethnic make-up of their support. Before the war, the Yugoslavian league was one of the strongest in Europe and the so-called 'big four' clubs – Red Star Belgrade,

Partizan Belgrade, Hajduk Split and Dinamo Zagreb – hated each other with a passion. So deep was this hatred that it often involved incidents that quite simply leave you shaking your head in disbelief. Possibly the worst involved a group of Partizan fans who kidnapped one of the top boys from the Hajduk Split group Torcida and repeatedly anally raped him.

For these rival groups, almost every game involved a battle of some kind and, while all of the individuals concerned were more than happy to fight, others began to record events as they happened. This practice – which continues to this day, although video cameras are now the norm – spawned a cottage industry as fans across Europe began to trade in hooligan paraphernalia. It even saw the publication of a magazine *Ciao Tifo*, which ran from 1989 to 1991. So popular was it that the final edition sold 70,000 copies!

The demise of Yugoslavia has changed everything forever but, as we shall see, the culture surrounding the game in the region remains as interesting, and as violent, as ever.

What follows are four articles which go some way towards explaining the way in which hooliganism has developed in the region. We start with an examination of the two most important of the new nations – at least in a footballing sense – Croatia and Serbia-Montenegro. The first was written anonymously and the second by Zgro from Novi Sad. Inevitably, they are slanted towards their particular clubs and it is not hard to see that references to former rivals are clouded in a degree of hatred, but they make for fascinating reading. These are followed by an examination of the football scene in Slovenia written by Peter Giber and Lovro Skrinjaric and finally an article exploring Greek football and the activities of the supporters who follow it.

CHAPTER SIXTEEN
Croatia

When examining the culture of Croatian football, there are two major topics of significance to be considered.

The first is that until 1991 Croatia was part of Yugoslavia and the second is that up until that point, on average, only four or five clubs from the region appeared in the first division. The majority languished in divisions two and three.

Despite that, the region boasts one of the first organised supporter groups in European football. On 28 October 1950, during a game against their hated opponents Red Star Belgrade, fans of FC Hajduk Split gave themselves the nickname Torcida (from the Portuguese 'torsida' which means 'frantic support'). Interestingly, the Torcida did not immediately spawn a stream of imitations but it is fair to say that by the 1970s, with the Hajduk Split supporters travelling widely around Yugoslavia, fans of other clubs, including those from Croatia, began to become more organised. This process eventually led to the formation of one of the most famous hooligan groups in European football, the Bad Blue Boys of Dinamo Zagreb – allegedly named after the famous 1983 Sean Penn movie, *Bad Boys*.

But the traditional and historical differences that were eventually to lead to the end of Yugoslavia were already having a huge influence on football. It became normal practice for both the Torcida and the Bad Blue Boys to have their numbers swelled by supporters of Croatian clubs from the lower divisions whenever any of the bigger Serbian clubs were in opposition and, by the end of the 1980s this intensified, particularly when the opposition was either of the two teams from Belgrade, namely Partizan or Red Star.

Although it had always been dangerous for Croatian supporters to travel to Belgrade, things got worse from the 1987–88 season. As the communist system collapsed across Europe and the Serbian people began looking towards a Serb state, it became routine for elements of both the Torcida and Bad Blue Boys to travel with the other to boost their numbers. This practice, to be fair, was also practised on occasions by both Red Star and Partizan.

One of the main reasons for this was the Belgrade police, who had begun to take alarming exception to the sight of Croatian banners and flags in their city. Since this was also accompanied by the use of flares and smoke bombs to create atmosphere, it eventually got to the stage where the authorities began to clamp down. And, increasingly, those interventions became brutal, especially when the Bad Blue Boys – who had long been considered as the strongest of the right-wing Croatian groups – were involved.

For the fans, European competition provided a welcome distraction from the politics of home; particularly away trips, which were always accompanied by huge displays of the now traditional flags and flares. Occasionally, however, their passion spilled over into violence. In 1987, during a game against Olympique Marseille, elements of the Torcida sneaked among the Marseille support and set off a tear-gas canister which caused a massive stampede inside the ground. Incredibly, no one was seriously injured; however, the actions of the crowd forced the abandonment of the game and, as a result, UEFA banned Hajduk Split from the European Cup.

But problems at home were far more pressing. Relationships between Serbia and both Croatians and Muslims were deteriorating at an alarming rate and the country was seemingly heading for an inevitable break-up.

In late 1989, Dinamo Zagreb travelled to Banja Luka city stadium and for the first time, even in Yugoslavia, the supporters were attacked and eventually driven out of the stadium by the police for displaying Croatian symbols. Two weeks later, in Novi Sad, only the intervention of the Dinamo players and officials prevented exactly the same thing from happening.

However, on 13 May 1990, the situation in the region took a turn for the worse with the first of two incidents which have become infamous in European hooligan history for sparking off an even greater and far more dangerous confrontation.

Red Star Belgrade and its fans arrived in Zagreb and took station in the stadium. Their fans soon launched an attack on the home support but, rather than target the area of the ground where the Bad Blue Boys were situated, they ripped down a fence and attacked normal supporters. The rest of the ground erupted into violence that quickly spilled out into the surrounding street as two sides of the stadium were set on fire, forcing the game to be abandoned. By the time order was restored, scores of policemen and fans were in hospital, while the damage to property was immense.

Within a matter of months, during a game against Partizan Belgrade, the Torcida of Hajduk Split sent another message to the Serbian people when their fans invaded the pitch and burnt the Yugoslavian flag in the centre circle.

Soon after that, the country exploded into war and, in 1991, the old Yugoslavia ceased to exist.

Having provided many of the high-profile confrontations between the two peoples, it should come as no surprise to learn that many football lads became involved in the fighting. Tragically, some never returned, including a number of the top faces from both the Bad Blue Boys and Torcida as well as from other groups including Kohorta of Osijek and Armada of Rijeka. These brave young men fought together against the Serb aggression and, after the war, statues and monuments were erected in their honour at many stadiums across the country.

With the war finished and Croatia now a separate republic football returned, but it was totally different. With many of the top faces gone, the terraces were taken over by teenagers who started to reconstruct the fans' movement. However, with many of the small teams now promoted up to the new first division of the Croatian league, a lot of the Dinamo and Hajduk Split fans from smaller towns began to support their local teams. This meant that many smaller hooligan and Ultra groups suddenly became larger while some new ones were formed. But the main groups were still Bad Blue Boys and Torcida, who could each mobilise well in excess of 5,000 for bigger games. And with so many men, it did not take long before they also began to take an interest in the government.

This started when the leader of the HDZ [the Croatian Democratic Union], who also happened to be the President of the Republic, decided that since Dinamo had always been considered a communist name, it had no place in his country. He exerted pressure on the board of the club who, without any consultation with the fans, changed the name from Dinamo Zagreb to FC Hask Gradjanski. The reason for this name was that before the Second World War, FC Hask and FC Gradjanski were the two biggest teams in Zagreb, but they had been banned by the communists for being too strongly Croatian-orientated.

The Bad Blue Boys and all other Zagreb fans were outraged. Dinamo is a sacred name to them and they demanded that it be returned. However, the club refused. Instead, in 1993, they changed the name again, this time to Croatia Zagreb.

At the first game under the new name, the fans staged a massive protest, but this was broken up by the riot police who, having been ordered to confiscate anything displaying either the name or symbol of Dinamo, simply waded in with batons and put many people into hospital. Not one word of this made it into the media as the government put pressure on journalists not to cover the story.

On the football side, Hajduk Split had become the dominant team in Croatian football and the Torcida were having a much better time of it. They would bring between 2000 and 10,000 to Zagreb and were often protected by many hundreds of police. They also took large numbers on European excursions to such places as Budapest, Lisbon, Amsterdam and Sofia.

In 1996, one of the HDZ party's main men became president of Croatia Zagreb and took the club back to its number one position in Croatian football. However, he also decided to deal with the Bad Blue Boys and the police pressure on them became all but impossible, so much so that many decided to boycott all home games. Away games, however, saw massive numbers turning out, especially during European competition. And, on more than one occasion trouble erupted, particularly when either police or locals tried to steal their flags, which were regarded as sacred, and symbolic of both their history and their struggle.

In October 1997, the club and the fans travelled to Zurich to play Grasshoppers in the UEFA Cup. On the pitch the team were rampant, winning the game 5–0, but off it things were bad. Eight thousand Zagreb fans made the trip and afterwards caused over $150,000 worth of damage to the city. There were also reports that the fans were terribly racist, spitting on black people in the streets and on trams. Yet there were only three arrests, one of which was a Swiss girl. Not long after that, more trouble in Auxerre saw UEFA hand the club a one-year ban from all European competition.

In 1998, the Bad Blue Boys decided to return to home games, but with the ban on anything referring to Dinamo still in force, the fans took to sneaking banners and flags into the ground which led to increasing trouble as the police tried to confiscate them. Things came to a head at the home fixture against Hajduk Split. As the police tried to seize banners, chairs were ripped up and the police attacked. In the resultant trouble, a number of Hajduk Split fans were stabbed and much of the blame was directed at the police for causing all of the initial problems. From that point on, they took a softer line against the Zagreb fans and their flags.

In 2000, when the HDZ lost their majority in parliament, one of the first actions of the new government was to return the name of Dinamo to the fans. The protests turned to celebrations but the rivalry between the Bad Blue Boys and the Torcida has continued as strong as ever. Serious incidents have taken place at every meeting between the two teams since 1998 and, worryingly for the authorities, that trouble has also spread to other clubs including Rijeka, with signs that things look set to get worse.

The big concern is that with the Croatian clubs taking a more active role in European competition, it can only be a matter of time before more incidents take place involving foreign sides. And if that happens, there is no doubt that UEFA will come down hard on both the clubs and the fans.

CHAPTER SEVENTEEN
Serbia and Montenegro

Not surprisingly, the history of football hooliganism involving Serbian teams dates back to long before the Serbian nation actually existed. The fans of both Red Star Belgrade and Partizan Belgrade were a source of major trouble for the authorities in the former Yugoslavia and continue to be so whenever they are involved in European football. Indeed, the supporters' group at Partizan can trace their history right back to 1945.

However, although the fans of both clubs have a long history of violence both at club and European level – including at the 1966 European Cup final in Brussels when Partizan fans were involved in numerous pitch invasions and disturbances during their 2–1 defeat by Real Madrid – it was only in the 1980s that the hooligan scene really became significant. That was almost entirely due to the formation of the two most important supporter groups in Serbian football: Partizan's Gravediggers and Delije at Red Star.

The name Gravediggers came about in 1959 when the club, who had up to that point played in red and blue – under the communist regime at that time it was forbidden for any club to wear any colours but red, white or blue – played in a tournament in South Africa and not only won, but in the final they beat one of the most successful European club sides of the period, Juventus. The Italian club's owner, Senor Agnelli, was so impressed with

Partizan that he presented them with two sets of his club's strip, with the result that the Yugoslavian club decided to adopt the famous black and white stripes.

Almost immediately, as the only club in the league to wear black, rival fans christened them Gravediggers and the name was quickly adopted by the Partizan fans as a collective term for themselves. They also came up with a motto: 'Bury our rivals'. Within a few years, the group had become resident in the southern end of the ground – where it remains to this day – and had developed a reputation for displaying banners and flags, while some had even begun to travel to away games, something that up until then had been all but unheard of.

For decades, Gravediggers became the name associated with Partizan fans but it is, as I have mentioned, very much a collective term, for there were actually many separate groups of fans who came from all different parts of Belgrade. These included Commando, Sexton's Lions, Black Rats, Marines, Untouchables and Undertakers.

Since the creation of the Serbian nation, the Gravediggers have remained one of the few constants in what has been a tumultuous period and, in 1992, they even organised a legitimate fan club to provide tickets, travel and merchandise as well as the planning of match-day activities within the ground.

However, in 1999, after a Red Star fan was killed when he was hit by a flare fired from among the Partizan fans, police arrested the leaders of the group and it was immediately banned. This led to the creation of two new fan groups, the first being the official fanclub entitled Grobari 1970 (grobari actually means 'gravediggers' in Serbian) and the second, an independent group called South Front. It has to be said that relations between the two are not always good and have led to trouble on more than one occasion. Much of the friction revolves around the age differences between the two groups – Grobari

1970 are generally aged between 25 and 35 years old, while South Front are mainly younger lads. Another source of contention is the fact that the leaders of Grobari 1970 are actually paid by the club to travel to away games to support the team.

Like their near neighbours, Red Star supporters are also known universally by a collective term which in their case is Delije which literally translates as 'heroes'. Their origins are equally interesting.

The population of Belgrade had always had an anti-communist streak and, for many years, the city had been a hotbed of nationalism. Nowhere was this more evident than on the terraces of Red Star, and from among their number emerged two significant groups of fans: Ultras, who followed the Italian way of supporting their team; and Red Devils who were more 'English' in their approach in that their match days revolved around drinking and fighting. These two were soon joined by a third group, Zulu Warriors, but as nationalism took an ever stronger hold on the Serbian people, the supporters united under one banner and, on 6 January 1989, Delije were formed.

Despite the fact that the political leanings of the group were extreme, the group's stated ideal was that for each and every one of them, Red Star was the most important thing in the world and their greatest enemies were not Croatians or Muslims but Partizan supporters. They even passed a rule that no other club name should be mentioned inside the ground, a rule that is still in force, and adhered to, today.

Inevitably, relationships between the two groups have a history of violence, but it is important to understand that prior to the break-up of Yugoslavia rivalries went far further afield, and ran far deeper.

One of the first major incidents to receive widespread media attention took place in the town of Vinkovci in 1983. The locals, being Croatian, took exception to the presence of thousands of Serbian Partizan fans and a small battle broke out between the two groups. At one point it became so bad that local women were pouring boiling water from their balconies down on to the fans below.

Two years later, when en route to Sarajevo, Partizan first demolished the train they were on and then the train station it had stopped at. This caused several hours of delays.

By 1988, with nationalism a significant feature in Yugoslavia, violence was a regular feature at almost every major game and it was also spreading to the European scene, particularly when Red Star were involved.

In November 1988, police raided a flat and seized more than 100 flares before a UEFA Cup match against AC Milan. Just days later, Partizan fans fired so many flares at the pitch during their UEFA Cup tie against Roma that the athletics track caught fire, delaying the game for 40 minutes. Just to add insult to injury, in the second half the Roma captain was hit on the head with a Zippo lighter: UEFA fined the club and forced them to play their next European tie 300 miles from Belgrade.

By now, the hooligan scene had become firmly entrenched in Yugoslavian football and umbrella groups had surfaced at a number of other Serbian clubs. These included United Force at a third Belgrade-based team, Rad FC, and Red Firm at Vojvodina FC from Novi Sad. Both these groups were involved in serious disorder when their teams played Dinamo Zagreb but, with so much else going on in the political background, it was all the police could do to contain what was going on.

One of the most serious incidents at that time involved two of the biggest clubs, Partizan and Red Star. When a last-minute goal secured victory for Red Star, at least 200 of their fans jumped over the fence and on to the pitch to celebrate. As the final whistle blew, Partizan fans steamed onto the pitch and a huge battle broke out during which 17 policemen and 25 stewards were injured. The fighting continued long after the match.

In 1989, things got even worse. There were incidents at every away match featuring Partizan, Red Star, Hajduk and Dinamo but, increasingly, nationalism was the key factor. In Novi Sad, Sarajevo fans, who were at that time something like 80 per cent Muslim, attacked the home fans and the police after being taunted with the chant 'From Sarajevo to Iran there will be Muslims' graveyard'.

But if 1989 was bad for Yugoslavian football, 1990 was worse. Much worse. And once again, nationalism was the major factor.

On 13 May, Red Star travelled to Dinamo Zagreb and caused mayhem. Fuelled by their hatred of the Croatians, the Red Star fans attacked the home fans from the upper section of the terracing, but as the Dinamo group Bad Blue Boys tried to get at them by tearing down the fencing keeping them apart, the police attacked using tear gas and batons. Such was the ferocity of the fighting that not only was the game abandoned before it had ever begun, but by the time things had been brought under control, the stadium was ablaze.

Despite the problems surrounding them and their nation, Red Star had actually developed a successful side and even managed to qualify for the 1990–91 season's European Cup final. However, this did not go down well with the Partizan fans and, when their team visited their near neighbours shortly before the final, 4000 of them travelled to make their feelings known. In the first half, they ripped down some scaffolding and attacked the police as well as staging a number of pitch invasions that forced frequent stops in the game. In the second half, a section of the 60,000 home fans responded by breaking into the Partizan enclosure and serious disorder broke out which only stopped when the police forced the Gravediggers out of the ground and out of the area.

For UEFA, the situation in Yugoslavia was already of great concern, but now their fears for the European Cup final were becoming greater by the day. During their qualification for the final, Red Star fans had caused problems in Zurich and Glasgow and had run riot in Dresden where they had fought with the German police and local neo-Nazis for almost four hours. God only knew what would happen in Bari.

In the event, thousands of Red Star fans travelled for the game – some even went on bicycles – which went off reasonably peacefully other than for a few Olympique Marseille fans who had banners, flags and scarves stolen. The absence of trouble was almost certainly due to the fact that Red Star won the game, which made the night one of the greatest in Yugoslavian football history. Not that Partizan fans see it like that!

But just as things were looking good for Yugoslavian football, at least on the pitch – Red Star went on to win the 1991 World Club Championship in Tokyo – off the pitch things were going from bad to worse as war threatened. UEFA immediately imposed a ban on clubs travelling to the region and Red Star were forced to play their 'home' fixtures in neighbouring countries. Yet despite this, wherever they played and notwithstanding the problems at home, Delije were always present in numbers. They even battled with fans of Panathinaikos in Greece.

But it couldn't last and when war finally broke out, the country fell apart. By the time it was over, a separate country had emerged and, in 1992, when football began again, there were no more clubs from Croatia, Bosnia or Slovenia in their league.

It is, however, important to note the role that lads from the Serbian clubs played in the war because almost all of them were involved at some point. The most important of these was known as Arkan. Before the conflict broke out, he was actually one of the most respected faces at Red Star and, during the war, his voluntary guard, which comprised almost exclusively lads from Delije, became one of the most feared paramilitary groups that took part in the conflict. It is even said that they hunted down, captured and killed some Croatians who were known to them from football.

Sadly, as is the way with war, many of those who went to fight never returned and they will always be in our hearts. But the fighting did nothing to defuse the friction between the fans of Partizan and Red Star, and the first two derby games after the split of Yugoslavia were crazy. In March 1992, a Red Star fan was killed after being hit around the head with a baseball bat and, in October, Partizan fans threw tear gas grenades into the Red Star end forcing the game to be suspended for 20 minutes.

However, after that, due in no small part to the NATO sanctions, things were very quiet as only diehard fans went to football. The one exception was the one hundredth derby match between Red Star and Partizan that was played on 6 May 1995. With the ground full for the first time since the war, trouble was inevitable, and a huge battle broke out which required a massive effort from the police to break it up.

By the time the 1996–97 season came around, things had begun to return to normal. The newly formed Serbian league had seen a lot of new clubs put into the first division and among these were some small yet violent groups including Red Devils of Radnicki Kragujevac FC and Despots of Sartid FC. It also saw the emergence of another group allied to Red Star: Belgrade Boys.

Although still under the umbrella of Delije, Belgrade Boys brought a new style of violence to Serbian football that in many ways is similar to the English style of hooliganism. Ambushes are a favourite tactic and, in one instance, they even hit a train full of Partizan's Grobari 1970 as they arrived for a derby game. But their most famous attack came when they attacked a group of United Force from FC Rad. Over 400 hooligans ended up fighting and three were seriously stabbed.

The very next season, Partizan were back in the news when their fans travelled to Radnicki FC and were involved in vicious fighting with the Red Devils. Partizan fans tore down a fence and fought the police in an effort to get at the home fans who, in response, invaded the pitch and attacked the Partizan players, forcing the match to be delayed for 30 minutes. In the lower leagues, trouble also broke out between fans of Balkan, Vozdovac, Zvezdara and Pancevo while Novi Sad saw numerous incidents in the first few months of the season.

In early 1999, after numerous warnings, NATO began bombing Serbia in an effort to remove the Milosevic regime from power. Despite this, just three days before the bombing began, Red Star and Partizan met in a local derby and, not so surprisingly, it was a match surrounded by violence. Four hours before the match, a group of approximately 250 Delije attacked some 400 Partizan supporters with iron bars, bats, stones, bottles, fireworks and even rockets. Later that day, Partizan responded by ripping up seats and attacking the police. By the time everything had settled, over 60 people had been arrested and 16 were seriously injured of which one was in a coma after being stabbed and another a policeman who had nearly had his throat cut with a plastic chair.

In October that year, after NATO had stopped its bombing campaign, the fans clashed again. This time a 17-year-old Red Star fan was killed when he was hit in the head by a flare. This violence resulted in the arrest of over 100 Partizan fans and the jailing of ten of the hooligan group's ringleaders.

But if this police action was designed to send a message

to the hooligans of both clubs, once again it failed. When they met again a year later, play was held up after only two minutes when ten Partizan fans invaded the pitch closely followed by large numbers of Red Star fans. During the subsequent fighting, Partizan players and the police were attacked before both sets of fans spent 30 minutes tearing out seats and throwing them at each other. It was a pattern that continued at matches up and down the country with seemingly little interference from the authorities. However, events in 2001 were finally to provoke some action.

Incredibly, with Milosevic finally removed from power, the police had taken a softer line against violence at football with the result that it had begun to spread to other sports. But their approach also resulted in two of the biggest street battles ever seen in the country. Not surprisingly, Partizan and Red Star were involved in both.

On 14 April 2001, Red Star fans attacked the Partizan firm in front of the Partizan ground just before kick-off. The fighting lasted for over 40 minutes and the police were powerless to stop it. By the time the Partizan fans had driven the Red Star hooligans away, 20 people had been hospitalised and four policemen seriously injured. A total of 46 fans from both clubs were arrested, but not before Red Star supporters had ripped out almost 2000 seats from the away end.

A month later, at the Serbian cup final, hooligans from Red Star, all armed with baseball bats, attacked the police an hour and a half before kick-off in an effort to get at the Partizan support. Twenty-eight policemen were injured but, before the dust could settle, Partizan staged a counter-attack, injuring another four policemen and 11 supporters. In all, 28 were arrested, but more importantly it finally spurred the Serbian government into action. For the first time, they began putting together anti-hooligan legislation, although with hooliganism so strongly embedded in football, and increasingly spreading to basketball, it is difficult to know quite how they will ever be able to stop it. In fact, if anything, things have been getting worse in 2002.

The one area of Serbian football not affected by violence is the national side. The reason, quite simply, is that no one cares about it. This is due to the fact that we are known as Serbia and Montenegro and our flag and national anthem are still the same as the old Yugoslavia when we were together with Bosnians, Croatians and Muslims. Maybe that will change when we are simply Serbia and have our own flag and anthem.

If it does, then world football had better watch out!

CHAPTER EIGHTEEN
Slovenia

Slovenia is a relatively small republic bordered by Austria to the north, Hungary to the northeast, Italy to the west and Croatia to the south.

Like many constituent nations of the former Yugoslavia, the Ultra scene was slow to develop primarily because, while the authorities were unable to control the larger supporter groups such as Torcida and Bad Blue Boys from Croatia, they wasted no time in flexing their muscles at the smaller clubs such as Koper and Novo Mesto and clamping down on anything which might pose any kind of threat to authority.

Things began to change in the 1980s, when a desire, first for greater autonomy and then for outright independence, swept across the country. As communism crumbled throughout Eastern Europe, people-power took on a greater significance in Slovenia. So in 1990, following the first multi-party elections in Yugoslavia since the Second World War, nearly 90 per cent of Slovenia's population voted for independence, which finally came in 1991.

By this time, the first signs of a significant supporter culture had begun to emerge. The original groups had actually been formed in 1987 with names such as Green Dragons, Tifozi, Viole, Trotters, Black Gringos, Celjski Grofje and Terror Boys. However, not all of these groups were violent and the numbers were initially relatively small.

By the time independence arrived, those numbers had swelled significantly. The largest and most organised of the groups, Green Dragons, who follow Ljubljana, were and remain a largely peaceful organisation but another, Viole, who follow Maribor, quickly forged a reputation for fearless fighting both at home and away. In one particular incident, following a 2–0 defeat to Ljubljana, they attacked Green Dragons using small blocks of granite as missiles.

Although less organised and generally younger than the hooligans from Ljubljana, Viole were soon firmly established as the number one hooligan group in Slovenia and, while their membership continued to grow, for others, things were beginning to change.

By the mid 1990s, the number of lads at almost every group in the country had begun to tail off. Even the Green Dragons peaked and things quickly got to the state that only Viole would travel to away games in significant numbers. With no one seemingly willing or able to take them on, they were forced to resort to measuring their power by staging pitch invasions and stealing flags and banners from the home fans which were then burnt when they returned to their own section of the stadium.

Quite why this happened is a source of much debate among football fans in Slovenia. The most likely reason is the quality of the football, which is, by its own admission, akin to the level of the German third division. It is also fair to say that the police have had a major impact on the activities of the hooligans, who have come to regard the police as the biggest hooligan firm in Slovenia. They are known universally as the 'Terminator Cops' and, despite the falling crowds, still attend every game in significant numbers, with tear gas and body armour to hand. The little crowd trouble that does take place is extinguished quickly and often violently.

The cumulative effect of this is that after a single decade, the Slovenian hooligan scene is all but dead. Many groups have ceased to exist altogether and even the larger of the remaining two struggle to pull together 600 lads between them.

There are, however, two bright lights on the horizon for Slovenian football. The first is the Champions League, which has seen NK Maribor playing in front of a packed stadium for the first time in years, and also the success of the national team who qualified for the 2002 World Cup.

For such a small nation, this was a huge achievement, and there is little doubt that the national side have become the focus of football fans across Slovenia. Whether or not this will ever see a return of major crowd trouble to the country remains to be seen but, in a region where football is so important to so many people, it would not come as any surprise at all.

CHAPTER NINETEEN
Greece

Anyone who knows anything about football in Greece will be aware of two things. The first is that Greeks are fanatical about the game and the second is that some of the inter-club rivalries are among the most intense, and violent, in Europe.

There are two main reasons for this. The first is that while the Greeks might be some of the friendliest and most hospitable people to be found anywhere, their temperament includes an element of what is known as *Tsabouka* or 'warrior-behaviour'. Usually, they are able to keep this subdued but, like many other people around the world, football brings out the worst in them. This is especially true when we take into account the second factor: the rivalries. These run very deep in the hearts of Greek football fans.

The most important of these rivalries is between the three Athens-based teams: Panathinaikos, Olympiakos and AEK, and all have their roots in the geographical and social make-up of the city. For example, Olympiakos' core support comes from Piraeus (the area including the port of Athens) and the working-class areas of Nikeia and Egaleo, while Panathinaikos fans tend to come from the more affluent areas of the city such as Perissos, Kifisia and the city centre. The final group, AEK, traditionally draw their fans from within the ethnic Greek community who were expelled from Turkey in the 1920s. They are based in Nea Filadelfia and north Athens. Such is the hate between these three that they will never fight together and so none of them follow the national side.

The hooligan groups attached to these clubs traditionally take their names from the number of the gate where they enter their particular section of the terrace. This practice began in the mid 1970s with the result that the main groups are now Gate 7 of Olympiakos, Gate 13 of Panathinaikos and Original 21 of AEK. Each is very well organised and has official offices in the city, while Gate 7 even has its own TV show on a channel coincidentally owned by the same man who owns the club! The groups have also been known to receive support from their clubs, with free tickets and free travel to away games being provided. There have even been stories that, to keep them happy, the clubs pay any fines received by members of the respective groups!

But even though the groups from Athens are very strong, everyone admits that the most notorious group in Greece are Gate 4 from PAOK Salonica. When they travel to Athens, all of the groups from the three clubs in the capital will try to attack them. In fact things have become so bad that during the 1999–2000 season, the police actually banned any Salonica fans from travelling.

Aside from the football rivalry, one of the main reasons for this hate is that Athens has a large number of powerful anarchist groups that are very strong in Greece and the hooligans from Salonica have many links with extreme right-wing organisations.

Over the years, since hooliganism began in Greece in the middle of the 1970s, there have been some bloody clashes between fans and sometimes these have even resulted in fatalities. One of the first and most serious of these football-related deaths happened in February 1981 when Olympiakos played AEK. After a big fight broke out among Gate 7, frightened fans stampeded as they tried to get away and 21 people were killed in the crush that followed.

The next death happened in 1986 and, as always, it was totally avoidable. With PAOK Salonica playing in Athens, groups of AEK, Olympiakos and Panathinaikos supporters were waiting to attack a contingent of Gate 4 who had made the trip. However, before the PAOK fans arrived, fighting broke out between the Olympiakos and AEK groups when each mistakenly thought the other was Gate 4. After a bloody fight, one AEK fan was stabbed and later died of his injuries.

After that incident, things actually got so bad between Olympiakos and AEK that they were ordered to play all derby games on the island of Rhodes until things calmed down. However, the long-term effect was clearly negligible as, in 1989, the fans clashed twice within six months. The first resulted in 5000 seats being ripped out and 51 people injured, while the second resulted in a huge riot during which 40 supporters and five policemen were injured and a number of police vehicles destroyed by fire.

Indeed, over the years the police seem to have come off worst in the majority of incidents involving Greek clubs. Furthermore, referees and even players have also been victims.

One of the worst examples of this took place in November 2000 at one of the Athens derby games between Panathinaikos and Olympiakos. When the two sets of fans clashed before the game, riot police went in to disperse them. However, they soon found themselves under attack from between 400 and 500 hooligans from both sides, and were forced to use tear gas to protect themselves.

Eventually, the police regrouped and, aided by reinforcements, managed to force the hooligan groups into their respective sections of the ground. But once they were inside, the Panathinaikos hooligans, particularly those involved with Gate 13, turned their attention to the police already on the terraces with the result that they had to leave the ground for their own safety.

Meanwhile, at the other end of the ground, the Olympiakos fans began ripping out seats and throwing them onto the pitch and at the Panathinaikos supporters in the section adjacent to them. Within minutes, both sets of fans were exchanging missiles, including flares, stones, coins and, of course, seats. By the time the police had managed to control the situation, three officers had been seriously hurt, two players injured and around 2100 seats ripped out. Just four people were arrested.

A month later, at another Athens derby, this time between AEK and Olympiakos, the AEK fans began bombarding the pitch and the Olympiakos players with missiles after two of their own side had been sent off. Later in the game, following an Olympiakos goal, three AEK fans pretended they had been seriously injured which forced play to be stopped. However, as police and ambulance men tried to reach them, hooligans from Skepasti – the stand where the most fanatical fans are situated – forced open a gate leading onto the pitch and tried to storm through. Thankfully, a heavy police presence was already in the ground and they managed to keep them on the terraces. But from that point on, a steady stream of stones, metal bars, flares, torches and even a Molotov cocktail were hurled at the broken gate in an effort to get through. So bad did it become that the referee was forced to abandon the game and it took 30 riot policemen to escort him from the pitch; he and his linesmen were kept in their dressing room for two hours until the streets surrounding the stadium had been cleared.

Yet another incredible incident occurred in 2001 when AEK were travelling to Crete for an away game. Having announced that they were going to take a ferry from the port of Piraeus – traditionally an area which is home to Olympiakos fans – they were attacked at a train station by a group of the Olympiakos hooligans from Gate 7 using baseball bats, iron bars and flares.

These are only a brief selection from among a large number of incidents which range from simple fights among fans, to Olympiakos followers firebombing coaches of AEK supporters, to Kalamata supporters rioting after a home defeat by Crete. This riot occurred when the fans tried to get into the changing rooms to attack the players, who were forced to barricade themselves in until the police could rescue them.

The frequency with which trouble of this severity was occurring inevitably attracted the attention of UEFA, who began voicing their disquiet about the apparent lack of effort being directed towards dealing with it. Yet incredibly, in May 2001, the Greek Football Federation [GFF] announced that they were going to mount a joint bid with Turkey to stage the 2008 European Championships! UEFA issued a polite response but their unease was clear, especially since OFI Crete had only just been ordered to play their home games in Rhodes after visiting players had been assaulted during a match against Panahaiki in Heraklion.

Amazingly, in reply to UEFA's concern, the GFF simply pointed to the fact that rivalries between the clubs are so severe that none of the hooligans really cares about the national team so is unlikely to be interested in attending international games!

Less than a month after the bid had been officially submitted, a cup fixture between Nicosia's APOEL and Nea Salamina ended in turmoil when 700 APOEL fans rioted after their team were knocked out of the Cyprus cup.

UEFA were furious yet much worse was to come. In March 2002, the Athens derby between Panathinaikos and Olympiakos saw scenes which were judged extreme even by the standards of Greek football.

Always a high-risk fixture, over 2500 police were involved with security for the game, which began to boil over when visiting fans first began throwing missiles at the home fans and then set fire to their part of the stadium. However, the game exploded when a penalty was awarded to Olympiakos in injury time and they scored to tie the game. Immediately, the home fans came pouring on to the pitch and assaulted the visiting players as well as beating the referee almost unconscious. As he was being taken away, bleeding profusely, he was attacked again – this time by a furious Panathinaikos coaching staff. Even the ambulance taking him to hospital was hit by a firebomb as it left the stadium.

As the fans streamed out of the ground and began fighting with each other, the police struggled to contain the situation, which quickly escalated into a riot. Things got so bad that they were eventually forced to fire live rounds as a warning to the fans who eventually drifted away. Commenting later on the trouble, the Panathinaikos chairman refused to condemn the fans and claimed 'there is a limit to how much bad refereeing that they can take!' The next day, UEFA were calling for an urgent inquiry, even as all of the 40 fans who had been arrested were being released without charge.

Sadly, things have improved little, if at all, since then. Of increasing concern to both FIFA and UEFA is the fact that almost every European cup tie held in Greece sees some degree of trouble. Despite this, the Greek authorities seem to have little concern about the hooligan problem that continues to erupt into violence almost every match day.

For the hooligans, this simply adds to the excitement because violence, and the culture that surrounds it, is something they regard as a necessary part of football.

And at the core of that culture is the humiliation of hated rivals but, sometimes, even that is taken to extremes.

The most graphic example of this involved Olympiakos and, in particular, one of their provincial fan clubs from Volos. For months, coaches carrying fans home from games had been attacked at a specific crossroads by someone throwing Molotov cocktails. The police seemed unconcerned and so the fans decided to do something about it themselves.

Following a Champions League game against Manchester United, a coach stopped at the usual spot and, inevitably, a petrol bomb hit it. However, this coach contained a group of hooligans from Volos and following it were a number of cars containing yet more lads. Having spotted that the firebomb had been thrown by a motor-cyclist, they dived out and steamed after him. Before the biker could escape, they stuck an iron bar into his wheel and he crashed.

Having got hold of him and identified him as a hooligan from arch-rivals Panathinaikos, they dragged him off and headed for Volos. En route, he was beaten, burned with cigarettes, urinated on and eventually anally raped using a stick. He was then stripped off and dumped naked on a mountain in the middle of nowhere. From then on, no Olympiakos–Panathinaikos derby was complete without chants about this incident.

This degree of hatred might seem unreal to football fans outside the Balkans but, in Greece, as in Serbia and Croatia, it is the normal way of things. There can be little doubt that this was a major factor in the failure of the 2008 European Championships bid and, until things change, quite what chance the Greeks have of ever staging a major football tournament remains unclear.

Part Six

TURKEY

O f all the sections in this book, I have to say that this was the one I was least looking forward to working on. This was not because of the difficulty of the research – it was actually one of the easier ones – but because of the tragic events of 5 April 2000.

I didn't know Kevin Speight or Chris Loftus but I do know some good lads at Leeds, one of whom was actually inside the Han Bar when the attack took place. As a consequence, what happened on that fateful night affected me personally. Indeed, I am still angry that so little was done by British officialdom to condemn the Turkish authorities for what happened and, to this day, whenever I get the opportunity, I make sure that those in power are reminded that the process of law and order still has a long way to go before those families see justice.

But what the murder of those two lads also did was to jaundice me against not only Turkish football, but Turkey as a nation. When you're trying to provide a balanced and impartial opinion of something, that can be a major problem! It was one I was not looking forward to trying to overcome.

Thankfully, I was aided by three people. The first, the lad who'd been in the Han Bar, had contacted me within days of his returning home and, when he heard that I was planning to do this book, offered to write a first-hand account of what he had experienced. As you will see, it is a powerful piece of writing for which I am indebted.

The other two people, Rasit and Lion, are Galatasaray fans. Lion in particular has been a huge help with this section and between the two of them, not only did they restore my opinion of Turkish football fans, they also put together the article below which, not surprisingly, gives a slightly different perspective on what happened.

It is not my intention to comment on either of these two pieces as I think it better that you, the reader, make up your own mind. However, it is important to realise that Galatasaray, while a huge and successful club with massive support, are not Turkish football.

It is also fair to say that there are many football fans across Europe who would give almost anything to watch their team play in the kind of electrified atmosphere which Turkish fans create week in and week out. Fanatical is almost an understatement.

However, where you have passion of that level, you will inevitably have trouble, which is something English supporters, and indeed players, have experienced on plenty of occasions. Manchester United and Chelsea are just two of the clubs able to testify to the level of hostility Leeds United witnessed at first hand.

Another problem linked with Turkish hooliganism is the issue of immigrant communities in other European countries. Never was this more evident than at the 2000 UEFA Cup final between Arsenal and Galatasaray in Copenhagen where, during two days of often ferocious fighting between rival fans, more than 40 Turkish locals were arrested. Only weeks later, Euro 2000 provided another example when Turkish fans, including a sizable number living in Belgium, fought running battles with police on the streets of Brussels.

Yet despite these and many other incidents both domestically and abroad, UEFA continually avoided taking any major punitive action against the clubs or the Turkish FA. In the wake of the Leeds tragedy, this attracted frequent accusations that football's governing bodies were being overly lenient with the Turkish game.

Finally, following a battle with Paris St Germain supporters inside the Parc de Paris that forced the referee to suspend play for 26 minutes, even UEFA had had enough and handed Galatasaray a $28,500 fine. At around the same time, the Turkish club were also hit with a further fine of $70,000 as punishment for trouble that had erupted during the Champions League quarter-final match against Real Madrid. More importantly, UEFA ordered the Ali Sami Yen stadium closed for all international matches because of fears over crowd safety and insufficient protection for players and officials.

Not long after this ban was lifted, violence flared on the streets of Istanbul again when Bulgarian side Levski Sofia travelled to Turkey. Although, to be fair, much of the trouble was caused by visiting fans who went on the rampage.

On the domestic front, the amount of trouble is simply staggering. In recent years there have been incidents at almost every Turkish ground from the top clubs through to the amateur leagues. Aside from the frequent battles between fans and the police, stadiums have been ripped apart by rival fans and there have been numerous missile attacks on supporters and players including, on one occasion, a knife being thrown onto the pitch by Fenerbahçe hooligans. More seriously, alongside the all too regular knife wounds, a Besiktas supporter was stabbed to death while sitting in a cafe watching a game on television. Equally horrifically, there was even an incident where a policeman, having been stabbed in the chest and the hand as he searched fans entering a match between Avcilar and Kagithane Hurriyet Gucu, pulled out his gun and fired into the crowd, injuring two people.

But the most bizarre incident I have found, and one that shows more than any other just how far Turkish football fans can take inter-club rivalry, happened on the opening day of the 2002–03 season.

In April 2000, just one day before the murders of Chris Loftus and Kevin Speight, one of Fenerbahçe's most outspoken fans was kidnapped by three Galatasaray supporters. Having bundled him into a car, they took him to a local picnic area and, using razor blades, sliced off his left ear, telling him to 'feed this to the Fenerbahçe pigs'.

Two years later, the same guy, to exact revenge, broke into Galatasaray's Ali Sami Yen stadium on the night before the opening game of their league campaign and hid in an advertising hoarding.

The next day, as the Galatasaray and Samsunspor players were on the pitch warming up in front of a packed stadium, he emerged wearing full Fenerbahçe training kit, ran to the middle of the pitch and planted a Fenerbahçe flag on the spot.

Not surprisingly, the home fans were less than happy but, as he was approached by one of the Gala midfielders looking to remove him, he whipped out a large knife which he used to keep the player, and then various policemen, at bay for some considerable time before being apprehended.

Amazingly, the continuing problems of violence in and around their football grounds did not deter the Turkish FA from putting in a bid to host the 2008 European Championships. Even more incredibly, it was part of a joint bid with Greece. To say that these two countries harbour a long and intense hatred of each other is putting it lightly, but the fact that Greece is also home to a major hooligan problem, meant that their efforts, however well intentioned, were inevitably doomed to failure.

Of more immediate concern, especially to England fans, is the presence of Turkey in our qualifying group for Euro 2004. For, as luck would have it, England's final game will be away in Istanbul.

This was the worst possible news for the authorities because, with that game potentially deciding the outcome of the group, it is certain that thousands will want to make the trip and that is going to provide a major security headache.

Given recent history, and the fact that revenge will be uppermost in the minds of many, it is one they may well struggle to control.

CHAPTER TWENTY
The Gala View

There is one marked difference between football violence in Turkey and other European countries. Unlike the French, Dutch, German and Italians, we don't have any admiration for English hooligans.

You will never see calling cards, casuals or Union Jack flags inside a Turkish stadium nor will you hear cute nicknames for firms or English songs. The other thing you will never hear of in Turkey are alliances between our supporters and foreign firms. Our groups are very loosely organised anyway but we don't want or need them (and I suspect they would feel the same).

What we have in Turkey is a sport like no other. And for us, sport *is* football. Our fans are among the most passionate and fanatical in the world and, at my club, Galatasaray, we believe that we have a vital role to play in the success of our team. That's why we do our best to try to create an electric atmosphere that is both supportive of our boys and intimidating to our opponents.

If you've ever seen pictures of a big match at Ali Sami Yen, you'll see 30,000 people standing for the full 90 minutes and often those fans will have arrived up to five hours before the matches start to work themselves into a frenzy of support. They will wave huge yellow and red flags as if on a battlefield and the singing will not stop (except when a goal is scored against us). Red flares are also set off to create a fiery and smokefilled setting which really is a beautiful thing and something a lot of clubs should actually be jealous of.

Of course, a lot is made of the 'Welcome to Hell' banners and the fact that the Ali Sami Yen stadium is nicknamed 'Hell', but what they do not realise is that it is all done tongue-in-cheek. It is designed to put fear into our opponents and put the visiting team off their game and, in my opinion, there's nothing wrong with that.

That is not to say that we do not have our hooligans, because we do. Especially at the 'big four' clubs: Galatasaray, Fenerbahçe, Besiktas and Trabzonspor.

Games involving these clubs have a history of violence that everyone is so used to now that unless something serious happens, it is not even reported in the newspapers or included in the police records.

In Turkey the hooligans get ready for the games as if they are going to war. They never go around unarmed, no way! They usually have with them either a döner knife, a pocketknife, a butterfly blade or some other kind of cutting weapon. Before the last Trabzonspor versus Fenerbahçe game, the police even found one fan carrying a samurai sword and, before the Goztepe versus Fenerbahçe fixture last season, Goztepe fans were stripped of a number of weapons including, in one case, a pickaxe.

Often, security at these fixtures will involve over 2000 Cevik Kuvvet (we call them Robocops) and all the fans will be checked before they are allowed into the stadium. Anything that can be thrown – coins, lighters, keys, etc. – is confiscated, but it is still always very dangerous, especially during the derbies, for the opposition team's players to come to the edge of the pitch to take a throw-in or a corner.

Attacking the stands of the opposition team and pushing them back is what makes a 'victory' for Turkish hooligans. During these battles, getting injured with a knife and throwing stones at the buses that carry the rival fans, and their team, is almost a tradition.

Outside of grounds there is also a lot of violence when the big four play and especially when Galatasaray and Fenerbahçe meet. That is a very real hatred and one that will never fade.

On the nights of European football, things are different because all of the fans' attentions are on our teams and not rival fans. It is important to understand that for Muslims a guest is a gift from God and should be treated as such, and anyone who has ever visited Turkey will know of the famous Turkish hospitality.

For genuine football fans who come to Turkey just to watch their team, that means that they will be able to enjoy many things including the Istanbul Bosphorus and the Turkish national drink Raki. They will also be able to have their pictures taken in the stadium and in the many historical places and will leave Turkey with very positive and peaceful memories.

But if you come looking for trouble, you will find it here for sure. Turks are fiercely patriotic and we do not take kindly to any disrespect shown to the symbols of our nation. Nor do we accept any insulting comments concerning Allah (God), the founder of the Turkish Republic Atatürk, or about anybody's mother. Those things will all put you in serious danger.

There are other things that are not acceptable here and one of those is drinking to excess. Most Turks, like Englishmen, enjoy a night out drinking with the lads but, while drinking is acceptable (Turkey is 98 per cent Muslim but is a very secular country), drunken behaviour is not. 'Please, do not lose yourself' is a common warning to visitors, especially those trying Raki for the first time, but what might be acceptable behaviour for English fans visiting, say, Munich or Madrid, will not be allowed in Istanbul.

This was really the cause of the very sorrowful event of 5 April 2000. All I really know about the two men is that they had families and, while I do not want to disrespect the dead, after the murders (for that is what they were after all) the Turkish press made much of the drunken yelling, verbal abuse of Turkish women, public urination, disrespect to the Turkish flag and the arrogant tearing up of Turkish banknotes that had gone on among the Leeds United fans. As a group, they could not have been any more insulting and, while most newspapers did not explicitly say, 'Loftus and Speight got what they deserved' the implication was there and the blame was almost exclusively placed on the behaviour of the English fans, hooligans or not.

Obviously the English did not see it like that and, among other things, there was a lot made in England of the fact that the Turkish fans had used weapons and were somehow not 'playing by the rules'. This is simply bullshit. First of all, the use of knives and other weapons is hardly unheard of among English hooligans and, secondly, whatever the situation, Turkish supporters are under no obligation to follow the 'English rules' of football violence.

There happens to be a large element of Turks who use a knife in a fight. That's the way it is and, if English football hooligans are so respectful of 'rules', they should make the slightest effort to observe or at least learn the 'rules' of the country they are visiting. Either that, or do not come.

But as I have said, football fans, true fans, will always be welcome in Turkey. This was proved when Liverpool, the most popular English team in Turkey, played Gala in the Champions League in February 2002.

After what had happened with Leeds, there were naturally some worries about violence, but the clubs did nothing to promote peace between the fans. Instead, it was left to the supporters' groups, including UltrAslan from Gala and the Liverpool supporters' club, to sort things out. About a month before the game, they contacted each other via the Internet and started a dialogue between the English and Turkish fans. Everyone talked about football, realising that they have the same passion for their teams and are not the monsters they both thought each other were. And the match went off incredibly peacefully.

CHAPTER TWENTY-ONE
The Leeds View

Firstly there are a few things I'd like you to know. This account of what happened on that awful night in April 2000 isn't based on ill-informed documentaries nor has it been compiled from semi-fictional newspaper accounts dreamt up by incompetent journalists desperate to heap the blame on supporters of Leeds United. This is the truth. I can say that with total conviction because I was there. And as such I'm one of only 30 or so people who are qualified to provide it.

Secondly, I'd like to thank Dougie for giving me, and others who were there that night, the opportunity to have that truth published. Not just because it will put some money into the fund set up for the families of Kevin Speight and Chris Loftus but because I feel that it is important that they, and their friends, finally discover what really happened in and around the Han Bar in Taksim Square, Istanbul.

I also think that it's important that you know that I am not a 'football hooligan'. I don't have any convictions and have never been arrested either at or away from football. I have, however, been following Leeds United since the late 1970s and have been a regular at away games since the early 1980s.

As you can imagine, following a team with such an off-field reputation has led to some interesting sights, but ones that I have never felt compelled to join in with. The idea of hanging round street corners on match days phoning people from the 6:57 Crew because they know how Manchester United are travelling and where we can meet them holds little, if any, attraction for me.

I do, however, dress in what you could classify as Casual gear: Lacoste, Burberry, Paul & Shark etc., but more because I like it and can afford it rather than what it symbolises. And I do know lots of people who could be termed 'lads' and I'm well aware of what goes on, which I suppose means that I can best be described as being ITK or 'In The Know'.

Anyway, enough about me, this is what happened on that fateful night. However, I must point out that all the names mentioned here, with the exception of the two already mentioned [and, obviously, those of the players], have been changed to protect their identities.

Leeds United had been going through a revival under the management of David O'Leary and the chairmanship of the charismatic Peter Ridsdale. Players such as Michael Bridges, Lucas Radebe, Alan Smith and Harry Kewell were taking the Premiership and Europe by storm and the vibes around the city reached fever pitch as we found ourselves in the semi-finals of the UEFA Cup.

When the draw was made and we found ourselves pitted against the Turkish side Galatasaray, the first thing I did was phone one of the lads to make sure I was down for the trip. The next thing to do was discuss it with my girlfriend who, for the purpose of this article, we'll call Susie. She's also a big football fan and we'd been to all the previous European away games mostly with the kids, spending family time in beautiful places such as Rome. However, this one was going to be very different.

Having seen enough film of the treatment handed out to Manchester United and Chelsea players, officials and supporters during their well-publicised excursions there, it was obvious that this trip had the potential to be nasty. Understandably, Susie wasn't keen on going and we never even discussed taking the kids. However, I was well up for going. Leeds United were in a major cup semi-final and there was no way I was going to miss out.

What I decided to do next was undoubtedly one of the worst family decisions I've ever made. I promised Susie that everything would be fine and that what we'd seen and heard about Galatasaray and their supporters was all just media hype. I assured her that nothing could or would go wrong and that we'd have a great time spending a couple of days exploring a new city. She took my word for it and the booking was made.

I still feel guilty for the broken promises I made and have apologised many times since, because she should never have had to go through what she did that night. But we're two of the lucky ones. What happened affected more people's lives more deeply than we could ever begin to imagine.

The game was on a Thursday night and so we booked to travel out to Istanbul on the Wednesday with an independent company who specialise in sports travel. We don't like to go through official Leeds United packages because they can be such a regimented pain in the arse. You pay through the nose, don't get any free time to yourself and always seem to be delayed flying out. All the match tickets, however, were official and were supplied directly from Leeds United.

It was an early morning flight from Manchester so it was with tired eyes that we set out to drive along the M62, but one part of that journey will live with me forever. About halfway across the Pennines, Susie said to me that she had a bad feeling about the trip and was seriously contemplating going back home. She also said that she knew she wouldn't be coming back home over the motorway.

Now she's no psychic and in the ten years I've been with her she'd never said anything like it before, so I still can't explain it. But what was my response? Well, being a bloke I just laughed and carried on. I can be so sensitive. Anyway, before we knew it and without any further discussions we were on the plane.

It was a specially chartered flight and was pretty much full with about 150 or so passengers. Everyone seemed genuinely excited because it had been such a long time since Leeds United had reached such heights and the mood as we got on the plane was buoyant. I can still remember to this day a lad with a white T-shirt, bleached blond hair and baseball cap, sitting a few rows in front of me, who was having a right laugh with one of the Flight Attendants; I'll tell you more about him later.

Now I'm not a good flyer at the best of times but this one was a shocker. At one point we hit some clear-air turbulence and it was more like being on a roller coaster than a plane. To make matters worse, as we approached Istanbul airport the captain came on to inform us we were in for a rough landing due to the high winds buffeting the Bosphorus. I was certainly a relieved man when I walked down the steps and into the arrivals lounge.

For those who don't know, it's a strange set-up at Turkish airports. You have to pay them £10 to enter the country and they then stamp your passport and allow you to move on to Passport Control. It's an odd sight seeing a pile of tenners on a big desk while in a foreign country and, if you've ever been on a football trip before, I'm sure you can imagine how difficult it was for some of the lads to understand that you had to queue up twice and hand over some cash before you were even allowed to leave the arrivals lounge!

By strange coincidence, the Leeds United team plane carrying the players and officials had landed at the same time and we ended up in baggage control together. Most of us thought it was great. We all made a beeline for them and spent what seemed like ages shaking hands and wishing them all the best. One thing that's stuck in my mind is the sight of the bloke with the bleached hair shaking Alan Smith's hand. I don't know why, but it has.

Later on that day, somebody told me that they had overheard a conversation between coach Roy Aitken and assistant manager Eddie Gray in which Eddie said 'I didn't think any fans were coming out until tomorrow.' Roy's reply was simply 'These are the lads Eddie, these are the lads.' As you can imagine, that made everyone feel good.

As the time came to leave the airport, I have to admit that I felt a little bit apprehensive. When you see the television pictures of English teams and fans arriving in Istanbul you always see what appears to be a mixture of jeering and sneering fans and journalists who appear to be on speed. You're also shown the mass of people holding up the 'Welcome to Hell' banner that has become synonymous with Galatasaray Football Club. The reality was that leaving the airport was a piece of piss. There were a few journalists there who tried to hassle the players by sticking cameras, flash bulbs and lights in their faces but nothing like I was expecting. Then, to my amazement – as anyone who's been on these kinds of trips before will testify – there was a whole row of coaches ready and waiting to take us to our hotels.

Although we were delayed on the buses for a while as one of the lads struggled to get through Customs, the trip to the hotel was pretty uneventful. The hotel was lovely, with a large, open, marbled reception area, a couple of bars and a restaurant, while the rooms were comfortable and clean.

Once we'd unpacked, as it was still early afternoon, Susie and I decided we'd go and look round the city. I spoke to a couple of the lads and told them what we were doing and said that we'd probably phone them later in the evening to see where they were so that we could try and meet up with them. Now for those of you who don't know Istanbul, the city is split in two by the Bosphorus. To one side is the Asian quarter (containing places such as the Blue Mosque and the famous indoor market), and to the other is the Western quarter where all the shops, bars, food halls and so on can be found. Our hotel was in the Asian quarter around three miles away from the Bosphorus. The tram ran right past the hotel so it wasn't long before we were taking in the sights.

My first impressions were that it was a nice city, but I took an instant dislike to the people, especially the men. Their manners were shocking and the way they treated the women with them was appalling. More importantly, the looks Susie was receiving from some of them were disgusting – the type of thing you'd never put up with at home. Despite that, we found a nice bustling place to eat in the Western quarter and it wasn't long before I was making the phone call to one of the lads to see where they were.

He told me that they'd just moved bars because things had started to get a bit out of hand at the Irish bar they'd been in. A few of the local 'lads' had discovered where they were drinking and there'd been a bit of a fight outside. He said it hadn't escalated into much but nobody wanted to hang around, just in case, because all they wanted were a few more pints and a good time. They gave me directions to where they were – it turned out to be the Han Bar – which was about a 20-minute walk from where we'd been eating so we set off.

On the way we passed a group of young Turks singing and chanting. A few of them had Galatasaray shirts and scarves on while others were just dressed casually, and I guessed from the look of them that they were the lads who'd tried to kick it all off at the Irish bar. You get a sixth sense about stuff like that.

Anyway, we left them behind and then had to walk through the main area of Taksim Square. The one thing that really struck me here was the number of police who were hanging around. They were more like soldiers than police, each one of them carrying a weapon. But they didn't seem too fussed about anything and were just hanging around chatting and smoking.

Once we were across the square, it took us about a minute to walk down to the Han Bar, but about another 20 minutes to find it. It's a really small place sandwiched between a Pizza Hut and some local shops and didn't stand out at all. We found it only because of the extra-ordinary number of shoeshine boys who were waiting around outside. It was an unusual sight seeing all these young boys there and, looking back on it now, I'm sure that they played some kind of scouting role for the people who were to attack us later.

When we walked into the bar, we found it to be a really narrow place with just a few chairs and tables at each side. There were only around 30 people in there (all Leeds fans) and, although it was still only around 6 p.m. local time, a fair few of them had been drinking for most of the day, which was beginning to show its effects. But everything was friendly and once we'd battled our way through to the bar and ordered some drinks, it was clear that the bar staff seemed genuinely pleased to have us in there.

As is usual when you're away from home, lads that we knew kept on coming up to talk to us to share experiences of the day so far and talk with increased fervour about the following day and the match ahead. We even had a chat with one lad who told us that he'd seen our Football Liaison Officer [from West Yorkshire Police] in Taksim Square and that he'd told him he was happy with everything and was now going off for a meal. Subsequently, when asked for his version of events, he said that he witnessed the trouble from opposite the Han Bar but was unable to intervene as he wasn't in uniform.

After only half an hour or so word went round that it was time to move on because the Han Bar had no television and the majority of people in there wanted to watch the Chelsea v Barcelona Champions League game that was taking place that night. Some were talking about finding another bar, but others were planning to go back to the hotel and watch the game there. As I was feeling a bit tired, we decided that after we'd finished our drinks that's what we were going to do. However, while we were still discussing this, some of the others had begun to drift out of the bar in dribs and drabs and were waiting for everyone else outside. There was certainly no mass exodus and if you had been a casual bystander outside then you would never have known that it was a group of English football supporters leaving the bar.

Around a couple of minutes after the first lot of people had left, a noise went up outside. If you've ever witnessed a fight at football you'll know exactly the type of noise I mean – a kind of a roar mixed with excitement and bravado – but it's the sound of trouble.

I was still at the bar with Susie and a guy called Brian, and we really didn't know what to do next. But Brian got up and walked over to the door so I followed him to see what was happening. It was kicking off right outside. Things were flying through the air: metal chairs, lumps of wood and signs that should be directing people to various shops and bars. The Leeds lads from the bar appeared to be on the back foot but seemed to be regrouping to try to fight back. The old motto of 'sticking together' seemed to be the only way out of this situation and that's exactly what they were doing. Within a minute or so, they'd got it together and were having a go back at the Turks, but all of them seemed to be completely unaware of the seriousness of the situation.

By now, I was outside on the pavement but my mind was racing – what do I do? I was torn between making sure the lads were OK and sticking with Susie. I knew that she was OK because she was still in the relative safety of the bar but out on the road there were already people on the ground injured. That's when the police started to arrive but they didn't seem to have a clue what was happening. They just stood there and watched as these 40-year-old Turkish blokes dressed in business suits kept running at the Leeds fans and lashing at them with what appeared to be long metal poles. There were also loads of local lads in their teens and twenties attacking people with anything and everything they could get their hands on. Basically, it was just mayhem.

Then, unbelievably, in the middle of all this appears a camera crew. Not some bloke with a little video camera but a proper crew: shoulder-mounted camera, big furry microphone, the lot. Then we started to see knives. They were not the sort of knives that they stock down the local craft shops either. These things were more like swords – certainly not something that anyone in their right mind would carry if they were just out for an evening stroll or quiet drink.

Suddenly my mind was made up for me and I knew what I had to do. But as I started to move back towards the bar to get to Susie, one of the lads, Tim, fell into my arms and I could see immediately that he'd been stabbed. At this point, Susie appeared in the door and screamed at us all to get back inside the bar, but just as we got through the door, Tim collapsed on the floor. That was when we really saw how bad he was. He'd been stabbed several times in the backs of both his legs and had deep slashes to his hands where he'd used them to defend his face.

At this point, someone started screaming at the owner of the bar to call an ambulance, but it was obvious that all he wanted was us out of there. Of course, everyone freaked out at him and he quickly got the message that we weren't going anywhere.

We managed to clean Tim up a bit and tried to stop some of the bleeding while Susie made him more comfortable by getting hold of a couple of chair cushions to use as pillows. By this time, the noise outside had subsided and all of us were just hoping that everyone was OK and that an ambulance would turn up. Then another one of ours, John, appeared at the door with blood pouring out of his mouth. A Turk wielding a metal chair had hit him in the face but as he'd tried to get back into the relative safety of the bar, one of the local coppers had given him an almighty smack across his head with his truncheon. Fuck knows why, I guess they'd just lost it completely.

After what seemed an age, the police finally came into the bar to see what was going on. Seeing Tim, they got a bit panicky, but there was still no sign of any medical help, so they eventually told us that they were going to take him to hospital in the back of one of their vehicles. On hearing this, Tim told Susie and me that he didn't want to go anywhere near a hospital, all he wanted was to go home, back to the safety of his own family and his own house. Of course the coppers weren't having that and so we all helped to lift him carefully and carried him outside to the waiting van.

Just as we'd got him inside, I noticed that John was already in there on his way to what he'd been promised was the local hospital but suddenly, one of the coppers grabbed my arm and threw it up my back as if he was arresting me. He then tried to force me into the van with the others.

Luckily for me, at precisely that moment it all kicked off again somewhere behind me and as the copper let go of me to see what was going on, I made a bolt for the bar. There was no way I was ending up in some Turkish nick for the crime of trying to help a friend.

Thankfully, I made it to the bar but, inside, I found Susie had been really panicked by the whole situation and so the barman who'd been serving us earlier took us through to a back room where we waited for ten minutes or so until things had calmed down outside.

At this time we didn't know the full extent of what had happened. Our only thoughts were of survival and getting back to the hotel. But by now I was so paranoid that I didn't even trust flagging down a taxi to take us there so, after a quick look around outside, we decided to make a bolt for a tram stop we'd seen about two miles away on the other side of the Bosphorus.

As you can imagine, we were walking pretty quickly, especially across Taksim Square, but we suddenly realised that we were both covered in blood. It was everywhere: on our trainers, trousers, tops and even under our fingernails. It was obvious that there was no way we would make it all the way back to the hotel like that, especially as we were hoping to catch a tram with other people on board. Luckily, we found a McDonald's and spent the next ten minutes locked in the toilets trying our best to clean ourselves up before continuing our journey back to the hotel.

Next came one of the scariest and strangest bits of the night for Susie and me. We'd been walking for nearly half an hour and were just about to cross the long bridge that separates the Western Quarter from the Asian Quarter when two men in jeans and leather jackets approached us. My initial thoughts were of more trouble, perhaps a mugging, because we obviously stuck out like sore thumbs in a foreign city with such a different culture. But I was actually relieved when they pulled out their warrant cards and introduced themselves as police.

It turned out that they'd followed us all the way from the Han Bar and now they wanted an explanation as to why we'd been there and what our role in everything had been. But before I could say much, they told me in no uncertain terms that what had gone on earlier that evening was very serious indeed and that they knew I'd been part of it. Then they called me an English hooligan and wanted to see my passport so that they'd have my details for later. There was no good cop, bad cop here; it was fucking bad cop, really fucking bad cop.

Thankfully, that was when Susie took control of the situation and she played a blinder. She told them that we were just tourists who'd stumbled into the Han Bar at the wrong time and that it wasn't the English way to carry round passports or identification papers. Each time I tried to add my bit she just told me to shut the fuck up as I was making matters worse. Then she said that we had to get back to the hotel quickly as we'd left our children there with a babysitter while we'd gone out for a meal and that's when they let us get on our way. I couldn't believe it. God knows what would have happened to me if she'd not been there to help.

After what seemed like a lifetime, we caught a tram and made it back to the relative safety of the hotel. There were a fair few people hanging round the lobby but the strange thing was that none of them were ones I'd been talking to a couple of hours earlier in the Han Bar, the ones who'd been on the receiving end of the ambush.

A couple of lads I knew, including MJ, came over and asked me if I knew anything about what had happened. They'd been in the Irish bar earlier on when the first incident had taken place and had decided after that to come back to the hotel. They'd heard second-hand rumours about the fighting and told us that at least one person was dead and another was in a critical condition.

We were stunned, and I mean stunned. But for some strange reason I felt incredibly vulnerable talking about it all in the hotel lobby so we took the lift up a few floors and found a couple of settees to sit on while we discussed these increasingly surreal goings on. My first question was why nobody from earlier was around and MJ told me that most of them were either at the local police station or down at the hospital. He then told us that he'd taken a call earlier from one of the lads down at the hospital who'd given him some information about the state some people were in. When he told me, well, I couldn't believe what I heard. It just didn't make any sense at all.

After an hour or so of talking, we decided to head for bed but, when we got in the rooms and switched on the TV, we just couldn't take in what we were seeing. Footage of the violence was already being shown on the local news channels and although we'd both been close to the incident it was only when we saw it on television that we realised what had been going on and how extremely violent it had been. But with all the commentary being in Turkish we couldn't work out if the stories about someone being killed were true or not. And to be honest, at that point we still genuinely found it difficult to believe because things that bad don't happen at football.

Then our thoughts turned to home. My dad was up from London spending a couple of days looking after the kids so we called to let him know that there'd been serious trouble and he might soon be seeing something on the news back home. However, he hadn't heard anything so far and didn't really seem that concerned, which was strangely comforting.

Somehow, we managed to get a bit of sleep but were up early with the television on. The news was showing more footage from the previous night and a lot of it was new stuff but some of it was horrific. It was far too sick to be shown on British television and the type of thing that should really only be seen by the people designated to investigate what actually happened. One of the clips clearly showed a motionless body lying in the middle of the road being repeatedly stabbed – to the best of my knowledge this footage has never been shown on English TV – while another was of the police blatantly hitting out at anything English while the Turks ran amok.

One of the other bits of film that sticks in many people's minds from that night is that of a lad with long, scruffy, mousy hair, SR, holding the lifeless body of Chris Loftus as he tries to get him into the back of a taxi and to hospital. This has been shown many times on the news but what no one ever sees is the film of SR trying to give Chris mouth-to-mouth resuscitation while being repeatedly truncheoned by police and kicked and hit by Turks. The guy was trying to save his friend's life and they were beating the shit out of him, but he didn't flinch once. He just wanted to do what he thought was right – as would any normal person with any respect or feeling for human life. Later that day I saw SR's wounds and they weren't nice at all, but he was one of the lucky ones.

The sad thing is, SR loved his football and he loved Leeds United. But since that day he's never been to see a game. I saw him in Leeds a while ago, just before the England v Italy friendly at Elland Road, and he was still deeply affected by what had happened that night. He was also still taking medication for the injuries the police had inflicted on him and, despite being only in his mid 30s, is now medically retired from work. Tragic. Just another forgotten victim of a brutal crime.

Anyway, back to the morning after. As soon as we were up we both threw on some clothes and went downstairs to find that, despite it still being early, there were a lot of people up and around. That's when we found out that two lads, Chris Loftus and Kevin Speight, had been murdered.

It's impossible to describe how we both felt. I suppose the best way to describe it is that we just felt sick and angry because we just couldn't work out why it had happened. Neither Susie nor myself knew Chris or Kevin very well but many people there did. Brownie, who had helped to organise the whole trip, was shell-shocked. He'd known Kevin since they'd met on a coach going to the 1975 European Cup final in Paris and he'd been mates with the Loftus brothers for over 20 years.

The rest of the morning was spent hanging around the lobby trying to take the news in, but we couldn't have left even if we'd have wanted to. The police had turned up and placed everybody under 'hotel arrest' for our own safety. There were also British Embassy officials milling around as well as a few journalists from the UK.

Tim was also there. He'd finally been taken to hospital and they'd managed to stitch his wounds but his arms, hands and legs were hardly visible through the tangle of bandages. Incredibly, he told us that despite obviously needing hospital treatment, the police had taken him directly to the police station after I'd managed to get away.

According to Tim and a few of the other lads, it had been pandemonium at the hospital because the staff there had made it clear that they wouldn't treat anyone until they had been paid in advance. They wouldn't even give anyone any blood until someone had handed over the money for it. As you can imagine, hardly anyone had been carrying a credit card or enough cash to cover what they'd wanted but that had been when Peter Ridsdale had turned up. He'd been having the traditional dignitaries' get-together with his Turkish hosts when his phone had rung to tell him that some Leeds fans had been badly injured and were in hospital. He'd left his meal immediately and gone down there to see if he could help, so as soon as he realised the seriousness of what had happened, and what was going on, he'd handed over his credit card to ensure there were no more hold-ups.

I know for a fact he doesn't want any praise for what he did, because he claims that anyone in his position would have done the same, but that was an amazing gesture and I would like to use this opportunity to say thank you to Peter Ridsdale for everything he did that night and subsequently. Have no doubt, that comes from everyone who was involved that night.

Another lad who was in the lobby had a wound across his face that had narrowly missed his eye. Again the hospital had refused to treat him until Brownie had come to his rescue and paid up front for the 100-odd stitches it had taken to sew his face back together. That guy must be reminded just how lucky he is to be alive every time he looks in a mirror.

Another very lucky lad was a very good friend of mine, TF. He'd been at the Han Bar and had come straight back to the hotel where he'd crashed out in the foyer, so he was still wearing the same clothes when we met him in the morning. What he hadn't realised was that he had a ten-inch gash right down the back of his thick, expensive jumper. When I pointed it out to him, he took it off to have a look only to discover that it had also gone right through his shirt but, somehow, he only had a few small cuts and grazes on his skin. None of us could believe it.

Others with various cuts, lumps and bruises were sitting around in obvious pain and shock, but there is one particular image that will live with Susie and me forever. Around mid morning, we watched two brothers, accompanied by British Embassy officials, check out of the hotel for an early flight home. Between them they were carrying three holdalls. One each for themselves and a third that belonged to their other brother. He wasn't with them because he'd been murdered the previous evening by a group of cowardly Turks armed with knives. Life can be cruel at times but nobody deserves to have to live through what they and their family have had to live through.

By lunchtime the pressure of the situation coupled with being cooped up in the hotel was beginning to get to Brownie. As I've mentioned earlier, out of everyone on the trip, Brownie was one of the closest to the lads who had died and, having organised the trip, he was obviously starting to feel guilty. Both Susie and I realised that we needed to get him out of there for some fresh air and the sake of his sanity.

The trouble was, the hotel was heavily guarded especially to the left of the entrance and that was the way into town. However, we figured that with Susie with us we could maybe pass as tourists. So, bold as brass and with sunglasses and hats on, we went for the exit and, having got out of the door, turned right and walked away from the city. After 50 yards or so a police officer shouted after us but we ignored him and kept going. Luckily, they didn't come after us and, a minute or so later, we were in a taxi and heading for the city. The next few hours were spent wandering around and talking. We found a lovely restaurant and had a late lunch and talked some more. Our aim was simply to do what we could to try and occupy Brownie's mind for a while and I think we did that. If nothing else, it got him, and us, away from the pressure-cooker situation back at the hotel.

We went back late in the afternoon but, as soon as we walked into the foyer, we could tell that the mood in there had changed. The reality of the situation had obviously begun to hit home and, since most of the people in there had been drinking the bars dry all day, a lot of them were starting to get a bit hate-filled.

What made it worse was that we didn't know if the game was going to go ahead or not. We certainly didn't want it to because we just wanted to go home. However, UEFA eventually took the decision that the game should be played. It's hard to say now whether that was the right decision or not but I'm pretty confident that not one ounce of compassion came into play when they made up their minds.

Once the decision had been made, however, our thoughts turned to what was going to happen. We'd already been told that, for security reasons, Leeds United had cancelled all of the official flights that had been due to come out so we knew that only those of us who were already in Istanbul would be there to support the team.

Then lads who had been staying in other parts of the city began turning up at our hotel. They'd been told that the only safe route to the ground was via the transport that would leave from the front of our building. That was when we found out that we would have to book out of our hotel and take our luggage with us to the game because we'd be going straight home after the final whistle. I can't say too many people were unhappy about that.

Once we had all packed and checked out, a row of coaches arrived to take us to the stadium, but the journey was horrendous. Even though we were under a heavy police escort that included armoured vehicles at the front and rear of the convoy, the streets near the ground were lined with Galatasaray fans who were hell-bent on causing more trouble. Not only did they throw stuff at the coaches but loads of them just stood there laughing as they pulled fingers across their throats. As you can imagine, this didn't go down too well and a lot of lads tried to open the emergency exits to get at the bastards. Luckily the police restrained them or the situation would have got even worse.

But if the journey was bad, getting into the ground was terrifying. It was around a 100-yard walk from our coach to the turnstile and, despite a line of police trying to make a safe corridor for us to pass through, the Turks were still trying to get at us and we were subjected to a barrage of missiles. There was also a mass of camera crews and photographers hassling and jostling us and at least one took a smack in the mouth for pushing one of the lads that bit too far. The police were also being handy with their sticks and were lashing out at anyone and everyone.

By the time we were through the turnstile Susie was in tears and, seeing this, I guess I didn't just feel helpless, I began to feel guilty. I'd brought her into this situation and there was nothing I could do to make it right.

As for the game itself, well I have mixed feelings. We were really pissed off that the Galatasaray players refused to wear black armbands or show any form of respect and the same thing goes for UEFA who refused to hold a minute's silence before the game. We also took a massive amount of abuse from the Turks and were subjected to constant throat-cutting gestures from their so-called fans. I also lost my rag with some twat who was having a go at people for not singing but, to their credit, when the game kicked off, all the Leeds fans turned their backs on the action for a minute to show what they thought of the match going ahead. I'm glad we did that.

After the game, coaches took us straight to the airport and out onto the runway where we walked straight on to the plane. Then we were forced to wait there for nearly three hours while government officials from Turkey and the UK came on and off, and on again. They talked to people, checked passports and even took people off the flight who had boarded without tickets. It was a bloody shambles, but eventually the flight was under-way and at last we were heading back to the safety of home. However, one person not on the flight was the blond-haired bloke I mentioned earlier. His name was Kevin Speight.

On the way home the captain made an unscheduled stop at Leeds/Bradford airport to let off those who desperately wanted to get home, and also avoid a potential media scrum at Manchester Airport. Susie was one of those who got off and she took a taxi home to see the kids, but I stayed on board, as did a few others, as our cars were at Manchester. She never did make that trip back over the M62. Next time I might just listen to her.

By 8 a.m. on the Friday morning, I was in my car and heading back towards Leeds. I'd seen some of the papers in the airport and, not surprisingly, they had been full of what had happened. Then I turned on Radio 5 and Nicky Campbell was opening the airwaves to let the great unwashed air their views on something that they knew nothing about. Almost immediately, I turned it off as first I became angry and then I became upset. Then I guess things just finally hit me and I burst into tears. All I wanted at that moment was to be safely at home with my family.

Well, that's it really. That's what happened in the Han Bar, Taksim Square, Istanbul, on 5 April 2000. It's different from the newspaper and television versions, isn't it? There's nothing about Leeds fans burning Turkish flags, nothing about us abusing women in the street and no mention of lads urinating openly in front of shoppers. Nor is there anything about us attacking some men in a van or about a lad who tore up some Turkish money. And d'you know why? Because none of it happened. None of it.

All that stuff they claimed we did which meant that they had to defend the honour of their country and their women is a lie. I swear to whatever God you believe in. What did happen is that people who have no honour or respect for human life murdered two innocent lads. And they weren't just murdered by one man but by several. This point was proved by the fact that both victims were stabbed not once, but repeatedly and with different weapons.

The one person convicted of the murders, well I hope he rots in hell for what he did. But that is not enough. There are still questions that have to be answered.

For example, if the ambush on 30 innocent Leeds fans wasn't planned in advance as has been claimed, how did they know where we were and how come so many Turks were out on the streets, mobbed up at 6.30 p.m. on the night before the game was due to take place? More importantly, how come a full-blown camera crew just happened to be there to capture it all on film?

Equally, why didn't anyone see what was happening outside the bar and come across to warn us to stay inside? And when it kicked off, why didn't they do anything to help us?

These questions are fundamental to the events of that night but they remain unanswered and I fear they will remain that way forever. That is an outrage, pure and simple.

In memory of Chris Loftus and Kevin Speight. May you both rest in peace.

Part Seven

CONCLUSION

There are some who will have read this book and think that, in many respects, it has been written almost to excuse the behaviour of English fans who leave these shores and cause trouble. It has not. Nor should it be considered as such.

For decades, the hooligans who have followed English football around the globe have been a source of frustration and irritation to both the game and the country, and their behaviour has often been inexcusable.

However, what I have tried to show is that not everything surrounding this issue is black and white. It is an inescapable fact that the kind of incidents we have seen far too often in the papers and on television will often have been preceded by hours if not days of provocation and abuse. Sometimes this violence will be from the hands of the very people who one would hope had been charged to protect rather than antagonise or abuse. Similarly, the lack of support from the authorities for English fans abroad is often nothing less than shameful. Can you imagine, for example, two Formula 1 fans being hacked to death at the Nurburgring simply because they supported Williams rather than Ferrari and next to nothing being said by our government? Or a group of rugby fans being baton-charged by the Italian police and our sports minister not condemning it?

Of course, one could argue that the baggage of history

provides some degree of understanding as to why both rival fans and police forces across Europe behave like that, but it does not excuse why they are allowed to. After all, as the authorities in this country never tire of telling us, the hooligans are a minority.

More importantly, that minority is actually shrinking, particularly with the national side. This is primarily because the police are finally making inroads into removing the hardcore – as they should be with the amount of legislation and resources at their disposal – but also because more and more non-violent football fans are seeking to follow England abroad. Indeed, if Japan proved one thing it was that if even the violent minority of English fans are given a bit of space and not confronted with either aggressive policing or locals intent on provoking a row, they can not only behave, they can be a positive boon. Equally, it showed that there is an increasing desire among the nation's football supporters to create a positive mood around the international side and this has to be regarded as a huge step forward. Yet as events in Bratislava showed only too graphically, it is a step that is not being universally recognised.

The other thing I have tried to show in this book is that the problems we have surrounding the English game are nothing compared to what is going on in other countries. This is especially true of the racism issue which, thanks to the efforts of the 'Kick Racism' movement, we have largely, but not entirely, driven out of our game.

As Bratislava proved, many countries in Europe have not been as successful as we have and, indeed, in many instances the move to drive out the racists has barely begun. However, that is no excuse, and this is one area of the game that UEFA really need to act on – and fast. Both nationalism and fascism are increasing problems on the terraces of Europe, and the game's governing bodies could strike a significant blow by highlighting the disgust felt by the vast majority of right-minded football fans.

But if UEFA are going to punish a club or a nation then it must be done properly and not with the kind of derisory fines we saw handed down to Feyenoord and Hajduk Split following their fans' racist abuse of Arsenal and Fulham players respectively. Better still, hit them where it really hurts by making them forfeit the points gained at games where such abuse is encountered. This would be a far more powerful and meaningful step and would certainly focus attention on the problem. But I doubt UEFA would ever take it.

However, hooliganism and racism, despite what many people believe, are two separate issues and, while moves are afoot to deal with the racists, the same cannot be said of the hooligans.

The problem with hooliganism is that the whole culture of football is changing almost by the week. One reason for this has been the growth in Internet use which now provides almost instant contact between rival firms. Whereas in the past, news of hooligan activity only filtered through the terrace grapevine in the following weeks or months, these days it can be online within minutes and post-violence debates can rage for days and even weeks. Indeed, for months after the tragic events of Istanbul one particular Galatasaray message-board was bombarded with anti-Turkish abuse.

Conversely, relationships between groups have been forged which has seen information exchanged and hooligans crossing borders to visit and even fight alongside their new-found allies. In Slovakia, for example, England fans were accompanied by lads from Austria Vienna, Rapid Vienna and CSKA Sofia – all of whom were bedecked in the traditional hooligan's uniform of Stone Island and Burberry.

This constant development is an obvious source of problems for the various European police forces who increasingly seem unable to do anything but react to problems. In cases where cross-border cooperation is involved, often they simply do not seem to bother.

The reality of course is that no matter what the security forces do, you will never solve this problem. All you can do long-term is to try to reduce it and that can only be done by persuading the individuals concerned to give up by choice. In many countries across Europe where hooliganism and the Ultra scene are integral elements of the supporting culture, that would be an impossible task, as we have seen.

Quite where we go from here is unclear, but what is certain is that something has to be done. With Euro 2004 being held in Portugal, the 2006 World Cup in Germany and now Euro 2008 in Austria and Switzerland – two countries whose fans are rapidly making a name for themselves in hooligan circles – the potential for a fresh explosion of hooliganism in Europe is a very real one. Indeed, given recent history and the natural desire for revenge, there are very real concerns that serious trouble at either of the Euro 2004 qualifiers between England and Turkey, particularly the game in Istanbul in November, could finally turn out to be the straw that breaks UEFA's back.

That would be nothing less than catastrophic for the future of the European game and especially the millions of non-violent fans across the continent who follow it.

This book would not have been possible
without the help of football supporters
from across Europe.

If you have any views on the content of this or any
of my other books, please do not hesitate to
contact me via the address below.

All correspondence will be treated with the
utmost confidentiality.

Dougie Brimson
PO Box 766
Hemel Hempstead
Herts
HP1 2TU

www.brimson.net

If you are a student requiring information on issues
relating to hooliganism, please do NOT write to
me. I've had enough!

More Sports Writing from Headline

BARMY ARMY

DOUGIE BRIMSON

'Brimson knows what it's all about' *The Times*

The hooligans are on the march again, with arrests for violent disorder and affray showing a steady increase each season. And yet although it has become one of the most talked-about issues in recent years, attracting more attention than almost any other aspect of football, the whole concept of hooliganism is still hugely misunderstood by most people and remains shrouded in mystery.

In *Barmy Army*, Dougie Brimson, one of the most authoritative and controversial voices on the subject, looks at why hooliganism continues to pose a major threat to the modern game and reveals how football violence has evolved from the terrace conflict of the 1970s into the Internet-led designer combat of the millennium.

Barmy Army is a hard-hitting examination of an extraordinary problem.

Reviews of Dougie Brimson's previous bestselling books:

'Probably the best book ever written on football violence'
Daily Mail

'Offers a grim insight into the mind of the football thug'
Daily Mirror

'A fantastic book' *Total Football*

'Horribly readable' *Time Out*

NON-FICTION / SPORT 0 7472 6305 1

More Sports Writing from Headline

ARMED FOR THE MATCH

COLIN WARD and
STEVE 'HICKEY' HICKMOTT

From the early 1970s and well into the 1980s, English football hooligans wreaked havoc throughout England and Europe, even if the lads participating saw it only as 'a bit of a laugh'. Then, in the aftermath of the Heysel disaster in 1985, Margaret Thatcher personally declared war on the whole football hooligan culture.

The Chelsea Headhunters were viewed as being among the worst offenders in the country, and within that group one man was deemed to be public enemy number one: Steve 'Hickey' Hickmott. One March morning in 1986 his front door was kicked in at 6 a.m. by the police and the full power of the British state was unleashed against him and eight other Chelsea fans. Hundreds more arrests were to follow. Whatever pain and savagery these lads had experienced in fifteen years on the terrace front line, nothing had prepared them for the judicial battle they were about to undergo.

An explosive true story, told in Steve's own words, this is an unflinching look at life on the terraces and one man's battle to clear his name, told with Colin Ward's characteristic black humour and honesty.

NON-FICTION / SPORT 0 7472 6292 6

More Non-fiction from Headline

PSYCHO
The Autobiography

STUART PEARCE

The bestselling football autobiography of the year

With the whole nation willing him on, Stuart
Pearce took two famous penalties – and no one
can forget what happened next. But what was it
like for the man in the middle of it all? In *Psycho*,
Pearce reveals all. Not just about those penalties,
but about life at the top over the past two decades.
This is a remarkable story from one of the most
popular and charismatic footballers of our time.
Packed with brilliant anecdotes, this updated
edition will fascinate and inspire all who read it.

'Unputdownable . . . Pearce's honesty shines
through' Sarah Edworthy, *Daily Telegraph*

NON-FICTION / AUTOBIOGRAPHY 0 7472 6482 1

Now you can buy any of these other bestselling non-fiction titles from your bookshop or *direct from the publisher*.

FREE P&P AND UK DELIVERY
(Overseas and Ireland £3.50 per book)

Manchester United   Colin Shindler   £6.99
    Ruined My Life
A wonderfully evocative, bestselling account of a childhood spent in sixties Manchester as a City fan when all were turning to United.

A Lot of Hard Yakka   Simon Hughes   £6.99
The William Hill prize-winning insider's account of the ups and downs, the lifestyle, practical jokes and sheer hard yakka of county cricket.

Midnight Rugby   Stephen Jones   £7.99
An award-winning writer provides the inside story of the rugby revolution since the arrival of professionalism in 1995.

The Wildest Dream   Peter and Leni Gillman £7.99
A powerful and affecting portrait of doomed hero George Mallory, assessing the motives and goals of this inspirational yet complex figure and including previously unpublished family papers.

TO ORDER SIMPLY CALL THIS NUMBER
AND QUOTE REF *50 SPORT*

01235 400 414

or visit our website: www.madaboutbooks.com

Prices and availability subject to change without notice.